Including the Gifted and Talented

Making inclusion work for more gifted and able learners

Edited by Chris M. M. Smith

Routledge
Taylor & Francis Group

LONDON AND NEW YORK

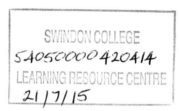
First published 2006 by Routledge
2 Park Square, Milton Park, Abingdon, Oxon, OX14 4RN

Simultaneously published in the USA and Canada
by Routledge
270 Madison Ave, New York, NY 10016

Routledge is an imprint of the Taylor & Francis Group

Transferred to Digital Printing 2009

Typeset in Goudy by
GreenGate Publishing Services, Tonbridge, Kent

British Library Cataloguing in Publication Data
A catalogue record for this book is available from the British Library

Library of Congress Cataloging in Publication Data
A catalog record has been requested for this book

ISBN10: 0-415-36109-5 (hbk)
ISBN10: 0-415-36110-9 (pbk)

ISBN13: 9-78-0-415-36109-5 (hbk)
ISBN13: 9-78-0-415-36110-1 (pbk)

Contents

Illustrations

Figures

Tables

Contributors

Chris Smith is a lecturer in the Department of Educational Studies at the University of Glasgow. Chris taught in schools for fifteen years, initially as a teacher of geography and then as a learning support teacher in both primary and secondary schools. Since moving from school into higher education Chris has been heavily involved with the Scottish Network for Able Pupils and is currently Project Leader of this national initiative. Chris's current research interests are related to more able learners, inclusion and motivation.

Carrie Winstanley is a Senior Lecturer at University of Surrey Roehampton, working with education students with a particular interest in Special Educational Needs. She taught in schools for a decade, and has higher degrees in psychology and history of education. She continues to run workshops in museums and galleries, as well as for GIFT, an organisation providing for more able pupils. Her current PhD studies (Institute of Education, London University) consider the notion of high ability from a philosophical perspective.

Roger Moltzen is Chair of the Department of Human Development and Counselling and Director of Special Education Programmes at the University of Waikato, New Zealand. A former teacher and principal, Roger has been involved in the education of gifted and talented students for many years. Currently, he is director of a national programme of teacher support in the area of giftedness and talent. His research interests include programme differentiation for gifted and talented learners, and the life stories of gifted adults. He recently chaired a Ministerial Working Party on Gifted Education, which resulted in a comprehensive set of new initiatives being introduced in New Zealand.

Margaret Sutherland qualified as a primary teacher and now works in the Department of Educational Studies, University of Glasgow, where she lectures on inclusion. She also works for the Scottish Network for Able Pupils, where she is responsible for organising national events to highlight issues surrounding the education of more able pupils. Margaret has published in teacher education magazines as well as journals on gifted and talented education, with particular reference to the education of young able learners.

Lynne McClure Now living in Scotland, Lynne was until recently Principal Lecturer in the Research Centre for Able Pupils at Oxford Brookes University, where she developed and delivered the national training programme for 'gifted and talented' coordinators in primary and secondary schools in Excellence in Cities areas all over England. Working within the Excellence in Cities initiative, she is Principal Examiner for the international World Class Tests for able pupils, and sits on the national steering group for the Xcalibre cross-curricular G and T website. Since leaving Oxford, Lynne has begun working with several LEAs in developing policy and strategy for able pupil provision, and has lectured on the subject in the UK and abroad. Lynne also edits the Mathematical Association's primary mathematics journal, chairs the Mathematically Promising Network and combines that with writing, lecturing and designing teaching and learning materials in mathematics. Her research interest concerns mathematically able students and the provision of an appropriate curriculum for them. She is co-editor of and contributor to *Gifted and Talented Provision in the Primary Curriculum*, recently published by David Fulton, and has contributed chapters to various other edited collections on mathematics, thinking skills and able pupils.

Valsa Koshy is a Reader in Education and Co-director of the Brunel Able Children's Education (BACE) centre at Brunel University. She has worked as a class teacher and advisory teacher for mathematics prior to joining the university, where she is also the Director of Academic and Professional Development programmes. Her research interests include the identification of gifted mathematicians, mathematics education, assessment and the development of gifts and talents in children aged four to seven.

Ron Casey is a Senior Research Fellow and Co-director of the BACE centre at Brunel University. His theoretical models of intervention for gifted pupils inform the projects undertaken by the centre. His research interests include the conceptualisation of ability, creativity and the search for submerged talent in areas of relative deprivation.

Colm O'Reilly is the Director of the Irish Centre for Talented Youth (CTYI) at Dublin City University. CTYI provides fast-paced classes for academically talented students aged six to sixteen years from all over Ireland and overseas. Currently the Centre caters for over 3,000 students per annum and it is the only recognised teaching centre for gifted children in the Republic of Ireland. CTYI runs over 100 academic courses annually for gifted students. Colm has worked in the area of gifted and talented education for the past eleven years and has presented papers at numerous conferences around

Europe. He has experience in teacher training for gifted students around Ireland and is responsible for the implementation of many classes and initiatives for gifted children in the Republic of Ireland.

Miraca Gross is Director of the Gifted Education Research, Resource and Information Centre (GERRIC) at the University of New South Wales in Sydney, Australia. The first half of her career was spent as a teacher and school administrator and her research interests focus on how curriculum and school programmes can best be developed to respond to the individual characteristics and needs of children. Her research on the education of gifted and talented children is internationally recognised.

Lynn Bosetti is Professor of Educational Policy Studies at the University of Calgary, Canada, and formerly Director of the Centre for Gifted Education. She has held numerous administrative positions at the University of Calgary including Special Assistant to the Provost and Vice President, Academic, Vice Dean of the Faculty of Education, and Associate Dean of the Graduate Division of Educational Research. She has recently completed a national study on the first charter schools in Canada, and is currently conducting research on school choice in Alberta, with funding from the Social Science and Humanities Research Council of Canada.

Michael Pyryt is an Associate Professor of Applied Psychology and Director of the Centre for Gifted Education at the University of Calgary. Dr Pyryt has 20 years' experience as a university-based teacher, educator and researcher in gifted education. He has presented numerous papers at national and international conferences in North America, Europe and Australia, and has published papers on a variety of topics related to gifted individuals and gifted education. He is currently an Associate Editor of the *Journal for the Education of the Gifted* and a member of the Editorial Advisory Board of *The Gifted Child Quarterly* and *The Journal for Secondary Gifted Education*.

Deborah Eyre is Director of the Academy for Gifted and Talented Youth at the University of Warwick. She has had a long-standing interest in the education of able/gifted pupils and has worked in this field for over twenty years. After a career in teaching and LEA advisory work Deborah moved into the university sector to teach and research. Deborah is an active researcher and a leading expert in the education of able pupils in England. She advises the Department for Education and Skills (DfES), the Qualifications and Curriculum Authority (QCA), and the Teacher Training Agency (TTA) and is a specialist advisor to the House of Commons Education Select Committee. She has written extensively on the subject of able/gifted children and her book *Able Children in Ordinary Schools* (David Fulton Publishers) is considered a seminal text.

Diane Montgomery is a qualified teacher, chartered psychologist and Emeritus Professor of Education at Middlesex University, London, where she was Dean of Faculty and Head of the School of Teacher Education. She is Director of the Learning Difficulties Research Project in Maldon and Programme Leader and author of distance-learning programmes for Middlesex: MA SEN, MA SpLD and MA Gifted Education. Her books are on Gifted and Talented Children with SEN; Improving Teaching through Classroom Observation; Able Underachievers; Educating the Able; Reversing Lower Attainment; Spelling and Dyslexia; Appraisal; Learning Difficulties; Managing Behaviour Problems; Teaching and Learning, and Reading Skills. She is Editor-in-Chief of the NACE journal *Educating Able Children*, in-service trainer and speaker at many national and international conferences.

Belle Wallace has worked in an advisory capacity (Essex LEA) with the brief for the education of gifted and talented children across all phases; she was Co-director of the Curriculum Development Unit (University of Natal, South Africa) with the double brief for developing assessment strategies and curriculum extension for very able, disadvantaged learners, and training curriculum planners; she designed and was senior author of a series of language and thinking-skills texts to redress cognitive underdevelopment in pupils from six to seventeen years; she now works as a consultant on the education of gifted and talented pupils both nationally and internationally. Belle has been a delegate to the World Council and has also served on the Executive Committee of the World Council for Gifted and Talented Children; she has been a radio presenter dealing with questions on gifted education; and an international consultant. She has been Editor of *Gifted Education International* (AB Academic Publishers) since 1981; and is currently President of NACE (National Association for Able Children in Education). Her most recent publications includes a series of edited books for David Fulton Publishers on Teaching Thinking Skills.

Acknowledgements

The editor and publishers wish to thank the following for permission to use copyright material: David Fulton Publishers, on behalf of the author, for material from Wallace, Belle (2000) *Teaching the Very Able Child: Developing a Policy and Adopting Strategies for Provision* (A NACE/Fulton Publication); Wallace, Belle (2001) *Teaching Thinking Skills Across the Primary Curriculum: A practical approach for all abilities* (A NACE/Fulton Publication); Wallace, Belle; Maker, June *et al.* (2004) *Thinking and Problem-Solving: An Inclusive Approach* (A NACE/Fulton Publication).

Introduction

This book emerges from a seminar series organised by the Scottish Network for Able Pupils (SNAP). SNAP is located in the Faculty of Education within the University of Glasgow and is supported by the Scottish Executive Education Department (SEED). The background of the lecturers involved with SNAP is, first and foremost, as teachers with experience in support for learning for children with special educational needs. The Scottish Office Education Department (now SEED) deliberately chose to establish a support network for teachers of able pupils within this wider context of support for learning. Therefore, since 1995, when SNAP was established, the education of able pupils in Scotland has been inextricably linked to the concept of inclusion.

Alongside the developments in inclusive education within Scotland its nearest neighbour, England, seemed to be taking a very different approach. The Excellence in Cities initiative was launched in 1999 and the terms 'gifted' and 'talented' were adopted. Schools in England are now required to identify 5 to 10 per cent of their population as being gifted and/or talented. In tandem with the Excellence in Cities initiative there is also a commitment to inclusive education (DfES, QCA 1999). Looking further afield it became increasingly apparent that Scotland was adopting a position which seemed to be at odds with established practices in the field of gifted education. However, while practices differed, the United Nations Declaration on the Rights of the Child (UN 1989) meant that these same countries were also trying to find ways of reconciling a commitment to inclusion while at the same time addressing the needs of able learners. Given, then, that there seemed to be many countries firth of Scotland facing the same challenge. and a paucity of material addressing the issues that this challenge raised, we felt that the time was ripe for a focussed discussion.

As a means of exploring the relationship between inclusion and the education of able pupils SNAP initiated a seminar series to be held in the University of Glasgow. We were fortunate in securing a commitment to take part from a range of respected experts in the field of gifted education from a variety of countries. There was no hard and fast remit for the series, no specific question to answer and no particular viewpoint sought. Contributors were simply asked to offer their own perspectives on how, or indeed if, the two areas of education were compatible so that we might consider further the relationship between them. The result was a fascinating series of insights which, in the end, illustrated a good deal of consensus.

The education of able pupils and an inclusive education system are not necessarily contradictory but much depends on the interpretation and resolution of two key issues. The first relates to the definition of inclusion. Although it is clear that a universally agreed definition does not yet exist, some principles that might underpin an inclusive system can be identified. The second relates to the degree of flexibility that might exist for selecting and grouping children for appropriately challenging provision within an inclusive educational system. If inclusion is interpreted narrowly as all children being educated with their age-appropriate peers in a mainstream classroom, then appropriate provision for able children is very difficult, if not impossible. If, on the other hand, inclusion is interpreted widely, as a means of achieving social inclusion beyond school, then the flexibility to select, group and regroup children within school for different provisions becomes possible. Under this wider interpretation inclusive provision for able children becomes not only possible but desirable.

From the discussions on the seminar series it seemed to us that the issues debated would be worthy of a much wider audience and so the idea of an edited book was raised. We hope that this resultant publication helps others as much as it has helped us in considering how we might best support able learners in the context of an international drive towards inclusion.

The contents of this book

Including the Gifted and Talented is about the place of gifted and talented children in increasingly inclusive education systems. The chapters have been grouped into three sections which address particular questions related to the inclusion of gifted and talented learners. The book is not intended to cover old ground such as the meanings of particular terminology or to be a 'how to' book for teachers. Rather this book is aimed at the reflective professional who wishes to think through some of the difficult issues that inclusion has raised for those interested in the education of gifted and talented learners. In the course of addressing these issues many practical ideas are provided for professionals interested in promoting a classroom environment that seeks to ensure that gifted and talented learners are fully included.

Part I deals with the concept of inclusion. The chapters all address in some way the same question: *What does inclusion mean for the gifted and talented?* Chapter 1, for example, offers an overview of how it is that inclusion differs from what has gone before by identifying key principles that underpin the two paradigms. It then locates different approaches to gifted education within these two paradigms. Chapter 2 addresses some of the vexing and difficult questions with which advocates of gifted education are often faced. Issues of equality, rights and excellence are used to attack provision for gifted pupils yet, as is argued in Chapter 2, to deny appropriate educational experiences to some pupils is in itself exclusive. Chapter 3 argues that mainstream classes should be the primary way of dealing with appropriate education for gifted children. Chapter 4 suggests that early years settings are inherently inclusive and that it is important that we build on these early experiences. Finally in this section, Chapter 5 critiques the inclusive nature of the approaches adopted in England and identifies crucial tensions that emerge when trying to marry effective provision for gifted and talented learners with inclusive education policies.

Part II, *Can selective interventions be inclusive?*, examines the ways in which provision, targeted towards particular groups of selected pupils, might still be interpreted as being part of an inclusive system. In Chapter 6, for example, inclusion is viewed as being much wider than school education and its author posits that through selective school provision we can increase equality of opportunities beyond school for disadvantaged young people. In other words, some forms of selective educational provision can enhance social inclusion more widely within society.

Part III asks *What can ordinary schools do to promote inclusion for gifted and talented learners?* Each of the chapters in this section offers ways of working that can enhance the experiences of gifted and talented pupils within mainstream schools.

Part I

What does inclusion mean for the gifted and talented?

Chapter 1

Principles of inclusion

Implications for able learners

Chris M. M. Smith

Inclusion has dominated the educational agenda of the United Nations since 1989 (UNESCO 1989; 1990; 1994; 1996; 2001). It has been the focus of increasing attention in educational literature and has influenced heavily policy and legislative developments in many countries. However, there has been a major difficulty from the point of view of able learners. The inclusive movement emerged primarily from a concern that the rights of disabled and maginalised individuals were being denied and as such have been part of an evolving terminology associated with special education and social exclusion. It has been used to support moral, economic and political arguments for educational and social reform directly aimed at the integration and reintegration of these disabled and marginalised individuals. Hegarty (1993), for example, sees inclusion as a means to reforming the special school system while Percy-Smith (2000) sees it as a way of achieving social equity. In this sense the inclusive movement has been interpreted as a reaction against existing exclusionary circumstances and related only to specific marginalised groups such as those who attend special schools. With the focus on special education and disability it has been assumed, logically in my opinion, that able pupils have no place in the inclusion agenda. But is this the only interpretation of inclusion?

In this chapter I will explore the concept of inclusion and argue that, despite its origins in special education, a parallel history of evolution from segregation to inclusion is evident in the education of able pupils. In addition I shall suggest that, because of its special educational roots, a narrow interpretation of inclusion restricted to location has been adopted but a much wider interpretation is possible. It is this wider interpretation which is highly relevant and applicable to the education of able pupils. Finally, using Scotland as an example, I will argue that moving towards inclusion involves a paradigmatic shift in principles, attitudes and practices and that this shift, despite changes in terminology, has not yet taken place.

THE ORIGINS OF INCLUSION

Dyson (2001) suggests that the history of special education has been a history of 'contradictory tendencies within the education system's responses to diversity and of resolutions of the "dilemmas of difference" to which these tendencies give rise' (2001: 25). Certainly, in Scotland, the dominant response to diversity has been based on a model of diagnosis and treatment which seeks to identify difference and to eliminate or, at the very least, reduce it. Special education, in particular, has been heavily criticised for being dominated by a medical model which has the aim of identifying who is normal and who is abnormal in order to treat identified groups differently. The 1945 Education (Scotland) Act, for example, stated nine official categories to aid the identification of disabled children.[1] In addition to the early segregation of children on the basis of disability the qualifying examination sifted and sorted the remainder on entry to secondary school. On the basis of so-called scientific measures of intelligence the most able children were selected for education in senior secondary high schools while the remainder were educated in junior high schools. The qualifying examination (the selection instrument) was essentially an IQ test that young people sat at the end of primary school (usually around the age of eleven) and was popularly known as the 'eleven plus'. These processes of segregation took place on the basis of two related assumptions: that some children were inherently and manifestly different from the 'norm' and that, as a result, they required different educational 'treatments'.

There was, however, growing disquiet about how well the selective system was working. First, research evidence cast 'doubt on the fairness and reliability of the qualifying examination' (Bryce and Humes 1999: 39) and second, there was found to be a strong social class bias in terms of who was allocated to the different educational provisions. The concerns about inequity, therefore, extended beyond the school gates and into fundamental questions about the nature of Scottish society. Senior secondary schools were accused of perpetuating the class system because the selection procedures and tests favoured white, middle-class children at the expense of other groups. It was felt that many who would have benefited from a senior secondary education were being denied the opportunity. The growing criticism eventually resulted in the introduction of the comprehensive system as a means of achieving social equity.

> Instead of early labelling, it was argued, a system which offered opportunity to as many young people as possible would reap benefits not only in terms of individual achievement but also in terms of wider social unity.
>
> (Bryce and Humes 1999: 39)

The abolition, however, of the junior and senior secondary education system did not affect the selection procedures for placement in special educational establishments. Children and young people continued to be diagnosed and labelled using IQ tests, the results of which were used to segregate them from the mainstream of education. As a result, special education, based on an identified and individual deficit, flourished. Indeed it was not until 1974 and the introduction of the Education (Mentally Handicapped Children) Act that all children were deemed educable in law. Yet as Dumbleton (1990) points out: 'education is a specifically human activity which is usually seen as a means of promoting those aspects of humanity that are most highly valued. To question a person's educability is to question an aspect of their humanity' (1990: 16).

The watershed in terms of special education came in 1978 with the publication of the Warnock Report (DES 1978). This report recommended, among other things: the increased integration of children from special educational settings into mainstream; that the categorisation of disability be abolished and replaced with the concept of a special educational needs continuum; and that a system of recording children's needs be introduced.[2] At the time, the report was seen as a major step forward in reforming the special school system.

While Warnock abolished the categories established by the 1945 Act, new categories soon emerged. Social and emotional behavioural difficulties (SEBD), moderate learning difficulties (MLD), hearing and visual impairment (HI and VI respectively), autism, Asperger's syndrome, all the 'dys' (e.g. dyslexia, dyspraxia, dysphasia), language and communication difficulties, Down's syndrome, physical disability and many more came into common usage in Scottish schools, along with English as an additional language (EAL). Gifted and/or talented were not among the new labels although there was some use of the term 'able' in national documentation (SOED 1993).

In addition, the Warnock Report encouraged the movement of children from special educational settings into mainstream. The procedures for transfer drew heavily on the medical model of disability and involved only those children deemed 'capable of transfer' by the gatekeepers in the system (Tomlinson 1982). The child being moved was expected to fit in with the mainstream class and little, if any, adjustment was made to 'normal' classroom teaching methods to account for the 'incomer'. Some children experienced a miserable time in mainstream schools as a result. Of course, if it all became too much for the school to cope with then, more often than not, the child was removed once again to specialist support settings. Like oil and water it was generally accepted that the 'integrated child' and the mainstream class could not mix successfully and as a result the separation remained visible.

The response to the needs of able pupils, in the meantime, was primarily through ability grouping within and across classes. Scottish secondary schools have, over the years, variously experimented with streaming, setting and mixed ability teaching. However, in recent years there has been increasing national pressure placed on schools to expand their use of setting (SOEID 1996) as a means of raising attainment and meeting the needs of able pupils. Even the First Minister of the Scottish Parliament[3] has urged that Scottish schools should 'make more use of setting' (McConnell 2002). Given that research has indicated a link between setting and social disadvantage (Hallam and Toutounji 1996;

Suknandan and Lee 1999) it seems incongruous that a First Minister so concerned with social exclusion should encourage such a move.

Much evidence exists of the disadvantages to those assigned to lower sets. A study by Suknandan and Lee (1999) concluded that grouping pupils by ability has no influence on their performance but can have a negative effect on the attitudes, motivation and self-esteem of pupils in lower sets. In addition, the work of Boaler (1997a, b, c) highlights that ability grouping serves to disadvantage those in top sets as much as those in low sets. The conclusion from a three-year study of the teaching of mathematics in schools was that a 'range of evidence ... linked setting to under-achievement, both for students in low and high sets, despite the widely held public, media and government perception that setting increases attainment' (Boaler *et al.* 1998: 3). All pupils – both girls and boys – characterised their experiences as

> fast, pressured and procedural ... Top-set children, it seems, do not need detailed help, time to think, or the space to make mistakes. Rather they can be taught quickly and procedurally because they are clever enough to draw their own meaning from the procedures they are given.
>
> (Boaler *et al.* 1998: 5)

When students were asked whether they enjoyed mathematics it was invariably the top set students who were most negative. In Scotland, a small-scale study into pupils' views of setting and mixed ability teaching (Smith and Sutherland 2003) confirmed some of the findings from previous research with pupils identifying difficulties with set arrangements that existed in their schools.

Thus, the education system in Scotland, like others in the UK and the rest of the world, has struggled over how difference should be taken into account:

> whether to recognize differences as relevant to individual needs by offering different provision, but that doing so could reinforce unjustified inequalities and is associated with devaluation; or, whether to offer a common and valued provision for all but with the risk of not providing what is relevant to individual needs.
>
> (Norwich 1994: 293)

While Scotland has wrestled with this dilemma, the response that has dominated has been the identification and treatment of difference at the expense of more inclusive practices. Shortcomings of the comprehensive system have been an over-reliance on responses that attempt ever more effectively and accurately to sift and sort individuals for different educational treatments. Poplin (1988a) identified commonalities among the various theories and models that seemed most influential in shaping practice in special education. An examination of the medical model, the psychological process model, behaviourist theories and the cognitive or learning strategies view elicited a list of common characteristics which, she concluded, represented a reductionist paradigm.[4] It is this paradigm, she suggests, that dominates in education, thus undermining any moves to change or reform systems. Thus, while more recent talk, both national and international, has been of inclusion the concept has been introduced, in Scotland at least, in the face of a very dominant and powerful reductionist paradigm.

HOW DOES INCLUSION DIFFER FROM WHAT HAS GONE BEFORE?

Since 1989 and the UN Convention on the Rights of the Child (UNESCO 1989) the discourse has been increasingly about inclusion rather than integration. Yet until recently there has been a lack of clarity about what inclusion actually is and it is often mistakenly assumed to be little more than the integration of children from special schools into mainstream settings. UNESCO (2004) has reinforced this view by stating that regular schools with an inclusive orientation are the most effective means of achieving education for all (para. 2). This link between inclusion and mainstream location is also made throughout the literature. For example, Takala and Aunio (2005) suggest that inclusion is 'a flexible educational approach in which all kinds of children have the opportunity to participate in general education programmes' (2005: 39). In Scotland, the evolution of the education system has revolved around where rather than how children should be educated, so the movement of children from special educational settings into mainstream provision is not a new phenomenon.

Unlike integration with its medical model approach, inclusion draws heavily on the social model of disability and requires systemic change. It is a political matter that aims to remove economic, environmental and cultural barriers (Takala and Aunio 2005). The mainstream class is expected to change to accommodate diversity and the responsibility for making sure that all children, irrespective of their differences, are regarded as full and active members of the class lies with the classroom teacher. Like mixing food colouring into water the colour of the whole changes. The water takes on a different hue and the single drop has changed, forever, the whole.

A change in terminology from integration to inclusion on its own, however, does not necessarily mean that inclusive practices are in place. The inability of practice to keep pace with the changing terminology has much to do with the lack of clarity that the concept has had. There was, initially, a lack of theorisation available to underpin the concept of inclusion and a lack of research to back up its claims. As such the concept has been variously interpreted. Dyson and Milward (2000), for example, illustrated this variety of interpretation by offering six, very different, ways of defining inclusion:

1 an inclusive national system where all learners are offered a comparable education, albeit in different types of schools;

2   an inclusive locality, in which a particular community (e.g. a local educa-
    tion authority) educates all its own children, though it may do so in
    different types of schools;
3   an inclusive classroom, in which all learners are educated together,
    regardless of characteristics and 'needs';
4   an inclusive curriculum, whereby all learners follow the same broad pro-
    gramme, though they may do so in different classrooms or schools;
5   inclusive learning experiences, in which learners with different charac-
    teristics work collaboratively and learn together;
6   inclusive outcomes, whereby all students achieve high outcome levels, or
    have enhanced life chances, or are enabled to participate in an inclusive
    society once their formal education is complete.
                        (Dyson and Milward 2000: 15–16 with minor adaptions)

The difficulty in being able to interpret the concept so widely is that it becomes all
things to all people and almost any country in the world could claim that it is inclusive by manipulating the definition that it uses. This concentration on the issue of
location has served to confirm the idea in the minds of many that inclusion is about
a particular group of children – those with special educational needs. As such inclusion has little relevance for able pupils. So, as Wedell suggests, the practical
implication of inclusion must include the 'decoupling of stigma from diversity'
(1995: 6) and this will take a major shift in attitudes.

At present, there is no agreed definition of inclusion. There is, however, a growing body of work that has moved away from the issue of location and concentrated
instead on the characteristics of inclusive practice. In other words, what is it that
schools who are successful in changing their hue to accommodate a diversity of
learners actually do? Thomas *et al.* (1998) suggest that an inclusive school:

- is community based and non selective;
- is barrier free in terms of accessibility, curricula, support systems and methods of communication;
- promotes collaboration as opposed to competition;
- promotes equality through democracy.

More recently, in a systematic review of research on the effectiveness of school-
level actions for promoting the participation by all students, Dyson *et al.* (2002)
suggest that inclusive education is about the participation of children and young
people in key aspects of their schools: their cultures, their curricula and their
communities. Three key themes were identified that seemed to characterise
inclusive schools:

1   The importance of cultural factors – the 'norms, values and accepted ways of
    doing things' (Dyson *et al.* 2002: 45) that reflect the values and attitudes

held by school staff and where a culture of collaboration that includes all participants is valued and promoted.

2　The importance of structures and practices that could be regarded as participatory. These include a tangible movement from segregating to integrating structures and constructivist approaches to teaching and learning. Such schools have good links with parents and the community.

3　The presence of leaders who are committed to inclusive values and who share these with the school community whilst encouraging distributed leadership and participative decision-making; a shared vision is a prerequisite to an inclusive school.

For Dyson *et al.* inclusion is a process that can be shaped by school-level action and is:

> not so much concerned with provision for one or other group of students as for student diversity per se. The issue for schools is not that they have to accommodate a small number of atypical students into their standard practices, but that they have to respond simultaneously to students who all differ from each other in important ways – some of which pose particular challenges to the school [and is] not simply about maintaining the presence of students in schools but about maximizing their participation in specified aspects of the school.
>
> (Dyson *et al.* 2002: 7)

Even in theory there has been a shift away from the attempt to describe inclusion by means of an all-encompassing and agreed definition. Lewis (1998), for example, suggests indicative principles that might characterise inclusive practice. Building on the work of Poplin (1988b) Lewis argues that there are systemic connections underpinning certain models and theories associated with inclusion.[5]

Inclusion, then, has not yet been defined. However, we can identify some of its principles and characteristics. It is, for example, about valuing and celebrating difference, and its beliefs and values must be applied equally to all learners, not just marginalised minorities. It is built on a particular view of learning and teaching which might be described as socially constructivist and holistic. It is a means of educational reform, but not merely the reform of special schools or services for the purpose of integration or reintegration of specific marginalised groups. Rather, it applies to the reform of education more generally so that it accommodates, addresses and celebrates difference. Inclusion, then, applies to able pupils just as much as any other group of individuals and it relates to the ways in which educational systems are conceived, constructed and delivered.

INCLUSION AND ABLE PUPILS

The literature on able pupils demonstrates that it has a parallel history to that of special education. Its origins lie in narrow definitions and identification techniques which sought to identify and label children as different from the 'norm' and if provision was made it was segregated and 'special'. Within this literature we can identify evidence that a similar reductionist paradigm has dominated educational responses. Building on the work of Lowe (2002), ten commonalities can be identified:

1   The focus is on the individual rather than the culture or context in which they find themselves.
2   A narrow view of what intelligence is exists and relates to the notion of 'g' (general ability).
3   Gifts and talents are seen as phenomena in themselves.
4   Theories and models are based on identification, the goal of which is to document innate abilities.
5   Identification can be made using scientific methods based on medical knowledge. IQ tests are legitimate as the sole or major method of identification and cut-off scores can be drawn. The bell curve is used to explain the distribution of 'g' within and across given populations.
6   Children are identified as more able or less able. At an early age children can be placed on a normative curve using a one-off test score. Their position on this curve in relation to others will remain stable throughout their lives.
7   Identification forms the basis of intervention. In other words only once a child or group is identified is a response or intervention devised.
8   The development of ability is the responsibility of the learner (individuals can be accused of wasting or throwing away their gift or talent).
9   Children identified as able are assumed to be manifestly different from their peers and therefore require special programmes and specially trained teachers to teach them. There are special methods and techniques that only apply to able children and are unsuitable for others.
10 Categorisation and segregation are supported.

These principles underpin and drive educational responses that rely on identification and segregation. They are often the principles relied on in arguing for segregated provision for able pupils, especially in the face of inadequate or inappropriate provision being available. It has been through similar debates to those held in the literature on special education about fairness, equality and rights, that changes in how intelligence is viewed and understood has become evident. 'Together with the theorisation of the holistic and contextually specific nature of ability, there has been recognition of the developing nature of achievement and its inherent modifiability' (Bonshek 2002). If we are to see able pupils within an inclusive system then there needs to be a fundamentally different set of principles emerging from this theorisation to guide practice.

The work of Renzulli and Purcell (1996), Gallagher (2000), Lowe (2002) and Brown *et al*. (2005) suggests that the principles underpinning an emerging, more inclusive approach towards the education of able pupils would dovetail well with the social constructivist and holistic approach underpinning the inclusivity that has evolved from special education. Ten such principles of an inclusive approach to the education of able pupils might be identified:

1   'Giftedness' is not a one-off and fixed state of existence – abilities emerge, develop and show themselves in different settings and at different times. In other words, the demonstration of ability is believed to be context specific.
2   In this paradigm there are expanding sources of evidence. Assessment procedures seek to develop authentic tools that can accurately profile the strengths and development needs of individuals. Assessment is ongoing, wide ranging and flexible.
3   Abilities are seen to 'emerge in the way that students engage and re-engage themselves with escalated learning opportunities' (Lowe 2002: 89). This requires a variety of opportunities and contexts to be available to all children and the recognition of the multiple manifestations of giftedness.
4   A wide view of what 'able' means is important since ability can be demonstrated either in a specific area of endeavour or across several areas. Giftedness, therefore, is recognised as multi-faceted.
5   It is recognised that able pupils, like all learners, have a desire to learn and be intellectually stimulated. However, the need to self-regulate and self-preserve within the culture and context in which they find themselves dominates. In a reductionist climate this can lead to the suppression of this desire.
6   Able pupils learn best from experiences about which they are passionately interested and involved. Emotions are central to learning and feed motivation and commitment to a task.
7   As with other learners able pupils learn in social situations and learn best from people that they trust. To benefit most from these socially constructed learning situations able pupils need interaction with intellectual as well as age- and stage-appropriate peers. Schools that offer such opportunities are characterised by collaborative efforts and a philosophy of inclusiveness. The fact that inclusive schools identify all members of the community as learners offers opportunities for young able learners to find their intellectual peers from the adult community.
8   Learning experiences that are connected to present interests, knowledge and experience are learned best and errors are critical to learning.
9   Learning is an interaction between the whole and the parts of a learning experience. The whole experience is of more importance than the individual parts.
10 Schools that cater well for able pupils are characterised by a climate of ongoing innovation, reflection and evaluation.

In this paradigm the fluidity of the concept of 'giftedness' and the flexibility required to deal with it would suggest that the only way to handle such differences effectively would be within the context of mainstream schooling. All children need appropriate challenges and appropriate support and all teachers can develop expertise to cater for this.

Given that the origins of inclusion lie in special education, this has resulted in the language and terminology obstructing 'an analysis of more deep seated problems in respect of both funding and policy for improving the quality of education for all children' (Armstrong et al. 2005: 74). In particular it has excluded the educational needs of able pupils from any debate. If able pupils are recognised as having 'needs' at all, these needs are seldom, if ever, regarded as 'special educational needs'. It is perfectly logical, then, to assume that able pupils have no place within an inclusive system because the evolution of the concept has been, almost exclusively, dominated by issues related to special education and social exclusion.

It was a concern with human rights – more specifically the rights of children with disabilities – together with moral arguments about the kind of society we might wish to see evolve and ethical arguments about how individuals are treated that led to the international demand for inclusive schools (UNESCO 1989). The Salamanca Statement (UNESCO 1994) recognised both the uniqueness of individuals and their fundamental right to education. Inclusion and participation, it asserts, are essential to human dignity and to the exercise and enjoyment of human rights. The *Star Trek* type society where difference and diversity are not just tolerated but celebrated seems to be envisaged. This utopian dream can be achieved, it is argued, through children experiencing and participating in such a society while at school. The key to whether or not children experience inclusion is dependent on the school's and community's understanding of what inclusion is, how far they believe in it as an educational principle and how far they are willing to change their practices. However, a clear understanding of inclusion is not universal and there is evidence (Brown et al. 2005) that even if educators claim to believe in the principle, practice proves difficult to change.

Asking educators if they think that the principles outlined for an inclusive approach for able pupils are useful and valid is a bit like asking whether they approve of motherhood or apple pie. Despite this, the reductionist principles continue to dominate in practice. Brown et al. (2005) investigated this notion of beliefs and its impact on practice and found that, while educators seemed to believe in an approach oriented towards developing 'gifted' behaviours, their practice was dominated by an absolutist view of 'the gifted'. Gruppetta (2005) also reports on research which found that teacher beliefs about able learners are generally stereotypical and reductionist and suggested that it is this deficit viewpoint that 'shapes the lens with which they view the parents in the area, and the students within the schools' (2005: 138).

In essence it is the ways in which we treat difference that are the key to the dilemma in which we find ourselves. As Artiles (1998) points out, we tend to deal with difference by treating certain groups of students either differently or the

same. Both approaches, he suggests, have the same end result: they affirm difference. In this way it would appear that to acknowledge difference in any way poses
difficulties in terms of how we provide appropriately. Do we provide similar or
preferential treatment, neutrality or accommodation, integration or segregation?
Thus, as Dyson (2001) identifies, there is a contradiction within the educational
systems[6] between equality of treatment and opportunity and the celebration and
valuing of difference.

> The more ... educational responses emphasise what learners have in com-
> mon, the more they tend to overlook what separates them; and the more
> they emphasise what separates and distinguishes each individual learner, the
> more they tend to overlook what learners have in common.
>
> (Dyson 2001: 25)

The difficulty has been that the commonalities of the reductionist paradigm
have emphasised what separates and distinguishes learners one from another and
'it is, of course, special education that has tended to face these dilemmas in their
most acute form' (Dyson 2001: 25).

Inclusion has much to offer and it applies to able pupils just as much as to any
other group. In fact, it cannot be inclusion if able pupils are not an integral part.
Inclusion is, however, unfairly criticised on the basis that certain children are currently being educated within mainstream classrooms but are, to all intent and
purpose, excluded from them. This is certainly true for some able pupils in
Scottish schools. However, it is not fair to say that inclusion does not work, only
that these Scottish schools are not yet inclusive enough. If a child is excluded
from a school's cultures, curricula and/or communities, then that school cannot
yet be described as inclusive. If a school is not at least committed to the journey of
inclusion, then placing children in its classrooms will not result in them being
included. At best we will be back at integration. The call for special provision for
such groups, therefore, tends to be a reaction against the inadequacies of current
practice rather than the inadequacies of inclusion as an ideal. Let's be careful
therefore not to judge inclusion on the basis of current systems and conclude that
it does not work for able pupils. These systems are not yet inclusive.

> Yet inclusive education is not an end in itself, but a means to an end, that of
> the realisation of an inclusive society.
>
> (Barton 2001, cited by Armstrong *et al.* 2005)

INCLUSION IN SCOTLAND: IS THE GRIP OF REDUCTIONISM WANING?

In Scotland there is stated commitment to inclusive education at a national level.
It is one of the five national priorities for education and a plethora of legislation

designed to promote an inclusive system has been introduced. Legislation specifically related to the education and care of young people has been heavily
influenced by UNESCO (1989; 1990; 1994; 1996; 2001) directives.[7] It is designed
to take forward the national agenda of social inclusion and support a policy framework within which inclusive schools can, supposedly, flourish. In essence
inclusion is high on the political agenda.

In line with thinking about the characteristics of inclusion outlined by Dyson
et al. (2002), national documentation stresses cultural factors along with structures and practices. Her Majesty's Inspectors of Education (HMIE 2002), for
example, suggest that an inclusive approach to education involves the creation
of a particular ethos (in this case it is described as an ethos of achievement)
within which diversity is valued in 'a broad range of talents, abilities and
achievements' (HMIE 2002: 4) and where participation and a sense of belonging
are increased. The Beattie Report (SEED 1999) similarly suggested that inclusion is about a particular culture where diversity is recognised and supported, that
the institution should be learner centred, that staff values are important and that
collaborative practices are key. A plethora of legislation has also been introduced
in recent years all aimed at reflecting 'the development of social policy and concepts of social justice throughout the United Kingdom' (HMIE 2002: 6), thus
confirming Percy-Smith's (2000) view that inclusion is a vehicle for social
reform and achieving social equity.

The most recent development at national level is the Education (Additional
Support for Learning) (Scotland) Act 2004. This Act explicitly ties the education of able pupils into the special education arena. The Act replaces the term
special educational needs (SEN) with the new term additional support needs
(ASN) because it was felt that SEN had become too firmly associated with pupils
with disabilities or difficulties. This new term is accompanied by a redefinition of
what it means to have educational 'needs'. This is an attempt, yet again, to
reduce our dependency on categorisation and to remove the stigma of deficit
from the concept of inclusion. The Act states that:

> A child or young person has additional support needs for the purposes of this
> Act where, for whatever reasons, the child or young person is, or is likely to
> be, unable, without the provision of additional support, to benefit from
> school education provided or to be provided for the child or young person.
>
> (Section 1)

The Draft Code of Practice (SE 2005) which accompanies the Act clarifies this
wider concept of ASN:

> All children and young people need support to help them learn. The main
> sources of support… are the staff who, through their normal practice, are
> able to meet a diverse range of needs. With good quality teaching and
> learning and an appropriate curriculum most children and young people are

able to benefit appropriately from education without the need for additional support. Some children and young people require support which is additional to, or otherwise different from, the educational provision that is generally provided to their peers in order to help them benefit from school education.

(SE 2005: 16)

The Draft Code offers examples of the kinds of ASN that might be identified and lists: have motor or sensory impairment, are being bullied, are particularly able or talented, have experienced a bereavement, are looked after, are living with parents who are abusing substances, are living with parents who have mental health problems, have English as a second language, are not attending school regularly, have emotional or social difficulties, are on the child protection register or are young carers (SE 2005: 11). It, helpfully adds that:

A need for additional support should not imply that a child or young person lacks ability or skills. For example, bi-lingual children or young people, whose first language is not English, may already have a fully developed home language and a wide range of achievements, skills and attributes. Any lack of English should be addressed within a learning and teaching programme which takes full account of the individual's abilities and learning needs. Similarly, more able children or young people may require a more challenging educational provision than that of their peers.

(SE 2005: 20)

So does this new Act reflect a move towards the systemic connections of the inclusive paradigm? In many ways it is a good example of the tensions that exist between the paradigms.

The Act changes the terminology to signal a shift in concept. It reduces the emphasis on deficit by extending the range of pupils who might be considered to have ASN to include able children along with bilingual and multilingual children. However, the very idea of extra or additional support carries with it the idea that a 'norm' exists. The danger is that the new terminology does not develop the concept in the way that is intended. So strong are the reductionist tendencies of the system that ASN could be interpreted as existing only on the extremities of the normative curve. The only difference will be that ASN recognises both 'ends' whereas SEN only recognised one. The idea of the bell curve itself is not challenged and yet this needs to happen if a paradigm shift is to take place.

The draft code of practice also shifts the focus very clearly away from the individual to the wide range of 'factors' which give rise to additional support needs and so, unlike SEN which placed the deficit within the individual, ASN places the 'needs' within the environment in which that individual finds themselves. Additional support needs, in this sense, are context specific and place the need for change on to the classroom and school. Thus the Act is aimed at systemic change within the system and is in line with an inclusive paradigm. However, the Act builds on existing planning documents such as personal learning plans (PLPs) and individualised education programmes (IEPs) and introduces coordinated support plans (CSPs) for children requiring the support of more than one service. The aim of all these plans is to profile children's abilities by documenting and tracking the development of their strengths and development needs. But it is this very identification of individual difference that has driven intervention in the past. In addition there is no guarantee that strengths will be given equal status with deficits and it is possible that these documents will continue to form the basis of a medical approach based on diagnosis and cure. Existing IEPs, for example, require learning targets, both short and long term, to be identified. Such targets, especially SMART targets (Specific, Measurable, Achievable, Realistic and Timed), are likely to encourage the segmentation of learning into steps and sequences – a singularly reductionist tendency.

While insisting that additional support needs arise not from within the individual but from contextual factors, the draft code also illustrates who is to be included by using familiar terminology such as social and emotional behavioural difficulties and learning difficulties – thus confirming old ideas about SEN rather than new ideas about ASN. 'It seems that despite a long-standing dissatisfaction with a category-based system for describing different types of special educational need, we find it difficult to dispense with them' (Farrell 2001: 4).

Finally, the Act itself fails to address some of the important aspects of the reductionist legacy. In particular it does nothing to address learning and teaching or attitudes and beliefs. Able pupils, in a consultation about their views of the new Act, gave the Scottish Network for Able Pupils (SNAP) a very clear message that teachers do not adequately understand their needs and that, in practice, a deficit system of support is being experienced: learning support, for example, is only available if you have a 'problem'. In addition, early anecdotal evidence from teachers on the Support for Learning diploma programme at the University of Glasgow suggests that the change in terminology is having little impact. Few people are aware of the implications that the Act has for able pupils and many are already reinterpreting additional support needs as simply special educational needs revisited. Unless the Act is accompanied by systemic changes in the system there is a real danger that it will serve to undermine the inclusive movement that it purports to promote.

Inclusion, therefore, is not yet with us in Scotland. We have a commitment to it. We have a range of legislation and policy that attempts to promote it. But we are caught in a reductionist set of beliefs that mean contradictions and tensions appear in the system. This makes practice very difficult to change. It also means that currently we have able pupils who are not being dealt with appropriately. We are betwixt and between paradigms and that is unsatisfactory for everyone and individual children are suffering. This is not a reason, however, for abandoning the inclusive ideal.

CONCLUSION

Seldom is there a clearly identifiable path from barbarism to enlightenment. Similarly, there has been no simplistic evolution from reductionism to holistic constructivism. Rather, both paradigms have always been with us. A holistic constructivist approach to the education of all pupils has been advocated for some time (for example, Dewey 1933 and 1956; Piaget 1950; Vygotsky 1962; Freire 1970; Bruner 1996). Likewise, there has, for some time, been a multi-faceted and pliable view of intelligence (for example, Guilford 1967; Gardner 1983; Sternberg 1985). And, from the inception of what was arguably the first national education system in the world in 1872, there have been Scottish teachers who have embraced the principles underpinning inclusion in their classrooms. What I have argued here is that one paradigm has dominated: reductionism.

Inclusion offers an opportunity to shift the balance in favour of holistic constructivism but we need to be aware of the reductionist trap. For the wider interpretation of inclusion described in this chapter to take hold changes are required: attitudinal, structural and methodological. Schön's (1983) belief, that while individual schools and teachers are becoming more inclusive the system remains firmly rooted in its reductionist history, is as true today as it was in 1983. We are still, therefore, facing the same question that he posed so many years ago. Is it possible to establish inclusion in a system that has been conceived and developed according to reductionist beliefs or are the changes required just too great? In the case of Scotland it is too early to tell. There is evidence that reductionist tendencies are still exerting a powerful influence but we shall have to give the new legislation and policies time to be enacted. I remain optimistic.

Notes

1 The nine categories were: deafness, partial deafness, blindness, partial sightedness, mental handicap, epilepsy, speech defects, maladjustment and physical handicap. England and Wales (the 1944 Education Act) had two additional categories: delicate and educationally subnormal.

2 In Scotland this was introduced by the 1980 Education (Scotland) Act and was known as a Record of Needs. In England this was introduced by the 1981 Education Act and was known as a Statement of Needs.

3 The First Minister at this time was the Right Honorable Jack McConnell MSP (Member of the Scottish Parliament). At time of printing this is still the case.

4 A paradigm is described by Lewis (1998) as an interconnecting set of assumptions, values and methodologies that are accepted as self-evident. In the reductionist paradigm learning difficulties are seen as phenomena in themselves. They exist as tangible entities within the individual. Theories and models assume a right and wrong posture about the teaching and learning process and are based on the principle of diagnosis – the goal of which is to document defects – and cure. Thus, categorisation and segregation are supported within the education system. However, while this diagnosis forms the basis for intervention, responsibility for the 'cure' is placed on the learner. Learning in the reductionist paradigm is an individual endeavour. It is related to what

occurs within the individual's mind and has little relationship with social situations or contexts. The 'big picture' is less important that the individual parts of the learning process and therefore teaching concentrates on small incremental movements that build one on another. Thus learning is segmented into parts, with steps and sequences being highly valued within the delivery system. Teaching in the reductionist paradigm is deficit driven. The instructional imperative is to eliminate deficits. Teaching and learning are viewed as unidirectional and so teaching is believed to be most effective when tightly controlled and the learner is predominantly passive. School goals supersede life goals in terms of importance.

5   These systemic connections include the idea that learning is more than simply a cognitive activity. It involves passion and emotions and is a community activity rather than an isolated one. As such, learners learn, primarily, through social situations and learn best from those that they trust. The belief that all people are learners and that classrooms should seek to create a community of learners is central. Learning is lifelong and so teachers become part of, rather then creators of, this learning community. Learning should connect to and build on present knowledge and experience and should be based on a reciprocal interaction between the whole and the constituent parts. This interaction transforms the individual's spiral of learning (the whole) and the single experience (the part), thus the whole experience becomes much greater than the sum of its parts. Finally, there is an unquestioned acceptance that integrity is a primary characteristic of the human mind and that we each actively seek learning experiences that help us to preserve our sense of self and our integrity. Of course we will all make mistakes along the way but this is also a critical aspect of Poplin's (1988b) connections. In this paradigm, errors are essential learning experiences.

6   Alan Dyson refers here to UK-wide educational systems.

7   This legislation includes: the Children (Scotland) Act 1995; the Human Rights Act 1998; the Standards in Scotland's Schools etc. Act 2000; the Race Relations (Amendment) Act 2000; the Special Educational Needs and Disability Act 2001; the Education (Disability Strategies and Pupils' Educational Records) (Scotland) Act 2002 and the Education (Additional Support for Learning) (Scotland) Act 2004.

References

Armstrong, A. C., Armstrong, D., Lynch, C. and Severin, S. (2005) 'Special and inclusive education in the eastern Caribbean: policy, practice and provision'. *International Journal of Inclusive Education*, 9 (1), Jan–March, pp. 39–54.

Artiles, A. J. (1998) 'The dilemma of difference: enriching the disproportionality discourse with theory and context'. *Journal of Special Education*, 32 (1), pp. 32–6.

Boaler, J. (1997a) 'Setting, social class and survival of the quickest'. *British Educational Research Journal*, 23 (5), pp. 575–95.

Boaler, J. (1997b) 'When even the winners are losers: evaluating the experiences of "top set" students'. *Journal of Curriculum Studies*, 29 (2), pp. 165–82.

Boaler, J. (1997c) *Experiencing School Mathematics: Teaching Styles, Sex and Setting.* Buckingham: Open University Press.

Boaler, J., Dylan, W. and Brown, M. (1998) 'Students' experiences of ability grouping–disaffection, polarization and the construction of failure'. Paper presented at the British Educational Research Association Annual Conference, Queen's University of Belfast, Northern Ireland, 27–30 August.

Bonshek, J. (2002) 'Postcode provision: a case study of provision for able socially deprived primary school pupils in greater Manchester'. *Support for Learning*, 17 (2), pp. 80–7.

Brown, S. W., Renzulli, J. S., Gubbins, E. J., Seigle, D., Zhang, W. and Chen, C. H. (2005) 'Assumptions underlying the identification of gifted and talented students'. *Gifted Child Quarterly*, 49 (1), pp. 68–79.

Bruner, J. (1996) *The Culture of Education*. Cambridge, MA: Harvard University Press.

Bryce, T. and Humes, W. (1999) *Scottish Education*. Edinburgh: Edinburgh University Press.

DES (1978) 'Special Educational Needs: Report of the committee of inquiry into education of handicapped children and young people' (The Warnock Report). London: HMSO.

Dewey, J. (1933) *How We Think: A Restatement of the Relation of Reflective Thinking to the Educative Process*. Chicago: Henry Regnery.

Dewey, J. (1956) *The Child and the Curriculum: The School and Society*. Chicago: University of Chicago Press.

Dumbleton, P. (1990) 'A philosophy of education for all?' *The British Journal of Special Education*, 17 (1), pp. 16–18.

Dyson, A. (2001) 'Special needs in the twenty-first century: where we've been and where we're going'. *Support for Learning*, 28 (1), pp. 24–9.

Dyson, A. and Milward, A. (2000) *Schools and Special Needs: Issues of Innovation and Inclusion*. London: Paul Chapman.

Dyson A., Howes, A. and Roberts, B. (2002) 'A systematic review of the effectiveness of school-level actions for promoting participation by all students' (EPPI-Centre Review). In *Research Evidence in Education Library*. London: EPPI-Centre, Social Science Research Unit, Institute of Education.

Farrell, P. (2001) 'Special education in the last twenty years: have things really got better?' *Support for Learning*, 28 (1) pp. 3–9.

Freire, P. (1970) *The Pedagogy of the Oppressed*. London: Penguin.

Gallagher, J. J. (2000) 'Changing paradigms for gifted education in the United States'. In Heller, K. A., Monks, F. J., Sternberg, R. J. and Subotnik, R. F. (eds) *International Handbook of Giftedness and Talent*. Oxford: Elsevier.

Gardner, H. (1983) *Frames of Mind*. New York: Basic Books.

Gruppetta, M. (2005) 'Investigating the role and experiences of gifted and talented coordinators'. *Gifted Educational International*, 19 (2) pp. 132–41.

Guilford, J. P. (1967) *The Nature of Human Intelligence*. New York: McGraw-Hill.

Hallam, S. and Toutounji, I. (1996) *What Do We Know About the Grouping of Pupils by Ability?* London: Institute of Education.

Hegarty, S. (1993) (2nd edn) *Meeting Special Needs in Ordinary Schools: An Overview*. London: Cassell.

HMIE (2002) *Count Us In*. Edinburgh: HMSO.

Lewis, J. (1998) 'Embracing the holistic/constructivist paradigm and sidestepping the post-modern challenge'. In Clark, C., Dyson, A. and Milward, A. *Theorising Special Education*. London: Routledge.

Lowe, H. (2002) 'Excellence for all: able pupils in urban secondary schools'. *Support for Learning*, 17 (2), pp. 88–94.

McConnell, J. (2002) Speech on the future of education, given by the First Minister of the Scottish Parliament to an audience of headteachers in Glasgow, 5 November.

Norwich, B. (1994) 'Differentiation: from the perspective of resolving tensions between basic social values and assumptions about individual differences'. *Curriculum Studies*, 2 (3), pp. 289–308.

Percy-Smith, J. (ed.) (2000) *Policy Responses to Social Exclusion: Towards Inclusion?* Buckingham: Open University Press.

Piaget, J. (1950) *The Psychology of Intelligence*. London: Kegan Paul.

Poplin, M. (1988a) 'The reductionistic fallacy in learning disabilities: replicating the past by reducing the present'. *Journal of Learning Disabilities*, 21 (7), Aug–Sept, pp. 389–400.

Poplin, M. (1988b) 'Holistic/constructivist principles of the teaching/learning process. Implications for the field of learning disabilities', *Journal of Learning Disabilities*, 21 (7), pp. 401–16.

Renzulli, J. S. and Purcell, J. H. (1996) 'Gifted education: a look around and a look ahead'. *Roeper Review*, 173, Feb–March.

Schön, D. A. (1983) *The Reflective Practitioner: How Professionals Think in Action*. London: Temple Smith.

Scottish Executive (SE) (2005) *Supporting Children's Learning: Draft Code of Practice*. Edinburgh: HMSO.

Scottish Executive Education Department (SEED) (1999) 'Implementing Inclusiveness: Realising Potential'. (The Beattie Committee Report). Edinburgh: HMSO.

Scottish Office Education and Industry Department (SOEID) (1996) 'Achievement for All'. HMSO: Edinburgh.

Smith, C. M. M. and Sutherland, M. (2003) 'Setting or mixed ability? Pupils' views of the organisational arrangement in their school'. Paper presented at the annual Scottish Educational Research Association (SERA) Conference, Dundee.

SOED (1993) *The Education for Able Pupils P6–S2*. Edinburgh: HMSO.

Sternberg, R. J. (1985) *Beyond IQ: A Triarchic Theory of Human Intelligence*. New York: Cambridge University Press.

Suknandan, L. and Lee, B. (1999) *Streaming, Setting and Grouping by Ability*. Slough, Berks: NFER.

Takala, M. and Aunio, P. (2005) 'Exploring a new inclusive model in Finnish early childhood special education: a three-year follow-up study'. *International Journal of Inclusive Education*, 9 (1), Jan–March, pp. 39–54.

The Education (Scotland) Act 1945.

The Education (Mentally Handicapped Children) Act 1974.

The Children (Scotland) Act 1995.

The Human Rights Act 1998.

The Race Relations (Amendment) Act 2000.

The Standards in Scotland's Schools etc. Act 2000.

The Special Educational Needs and Disability Act 2001.

The Education (Disability Strategies and Pupils' Educational Records) (Scotland) Act 2002.

The Education (Additional Support for Learning) (Scotland) Act 2004.

Thomas, G., Walker, D. and Webb, J. (1998) *The Making of the Inclusive School*. London: Routledge.

Tomlinson, S. (1982) *The Sociology of Special Education*. London: Routledge.

UNESCO (1989) The United Nations Convention on the Rights of the Child. Paris: UNESCO.

UNESCO (1990) World Conference on Education for All. Jomtein, Thailand, 5–9 March.

UNESCO (1994) The Salamanca Statement and Framework for Action on Special Needs Education. World Conference on Special Needs Education, Access and Quality. Paris: UNESCO. http://www.unesco.org/education/educpro/sne/salamanc/index.htm.

UNESCO (1996) Mid-decade Review of Progress Towards Education for All. Paris: UNESCO.

UNESCO (2001) Education for All – Background Documents: Information kit on Education for All. Available online at http://www.unesco.org/education/efa/ ed_for_all/background/background_kit_achieve_goal.shtml.

UNESCO (2004) The Right to Education for Persons with Disabilities: Towards Inclusion. http://unesdoc.unesco.org/images/0013/001378/137873e.pdf (Accessed 12.10.05)

Vygotsky, L. (1962) Thought and Language. London: Harvard University Press.

Wedell, K. (1995) 'Making inclusive education ordinary'. British Journal of Special Education, 22 (3), pp. 100–104.

Chapter 2

Inequity in equity

Tackling the excellence–equality conundrum

Carrie Winstanley

This chapter considers the age-old conundrum of how we should best allocate resources in education to ensure both excellence and equity. Here, the complexity is increased by considering how we should ensure that highly able children are fully included in schools and provided with challenge appropriate to their abilities. There is an undeniable tension in striving for both equality and excellence in education. When it comes to the limited pot of education budgets and resources, who has priority? Those advocating for more able pupils are often met with criticism and sometimes even disapproval, accused of elitism and inegalitarianism. We cannot afford to ignore the comments and views of our detractors, and need to construct coherent, well-supported arguments against their charges. This chapter tackles this contentious issue head on, exploring the issues raised by inclusion of the able, and reviewing and refreshing some of the more common arguments used in discussing provision.

The following is a summary of some of the difficulties faced when catering for the able in the Brazilian education system, which serves as a useful introduction to the issues raised in this chapter. The problems are:

> tension between the goals of equity and excellence manifested in attitudes toward the gifted such as expectations of perfection, over-identification of already privileged students from upper and middle classes, assumptions that giftedness is rare and that the gifted are a homogeneous population with many common traits.
>
> (Alencar 1994, cited in Rudnitski 2000: 676)

Before considering policy issues, however, it is necessary to clarify something about the population of children in question.

WHO COUNTS AS ABLE? AN INCLUSIVE MODEL

Able children constitute a heterogeneous group of people with wide-ranging needs. It is often assumed that provision for them is unnecessary as highly able children are assured success. This is a falsehood. It is not true that high ability equals success, evidenced by the underachieving able. Neither is it true that all able children come from privileged backgrounds. It is a fact, though, that children from privileged homes do indeed demonstrate advanced knowledge of academic conventions and have familiarity with the atmosphere and attitudes of school, unfairly allowing for success in selection tests. Some will have been prepared for the examinations, conducted invariably in their first language and in a recognisable format. This suggests it would be fairer to change entry criteria rather than disallow the disadvantaged able pupil from partaking in provision. To help refute the argument that the able need no support, it is useful to summarise potential variations amongst pupils, despite this analysis being rather simplistic.

1   Average or low level of aptitudes and unfavourable home environment
2   Average or low level of aptitudes and favourable home environment
3   High level of aptitudes and favourable home environment
4   High level of aptitudes and unfavourable home environment

Children in the first category have some programmes to help them and no teachers would wish to deny them this help and support. Similarly the second group have a certain advantage, this time stemming from their background. It is often assumed that all able children fit the third group, but this is not the case, as shown by the fourth group. Pupils in this last group are likely to exhibit unconventional behaviour or disaffection, as their home background is more likely to be in conflict with the values of the school, and because of their high ability, they may be acutely aware of this fact. Of course pupils from a favourable environment can also fall victim to disaffection, but this is less likely.

Children who could most benefit from provision are sometimes denied these opportunities because where activities are seen as fun rewards, able children with poor behaviour are excluded on the grounds that they do not fit the conventional image of 'good behaviour' (which usually means unquestioning compliance). Teachers' concern is often for rewarding conventional behaviour and task completion rather than encouraging less obviously talented pupils.[1] This is disappointing, as enrichment could provide these pupils with the chance to explore unusual ideas, unlocking motivation, or just the freedom to explore their own strengths in a non-judgmental environment, free from the pressures of peers who think their abilities are 'uncool'.

Other children who do not fit the stereotype of the able child are those with learning difficulties and disabilities. They are generally described as having 'double or multiple exceptionalities' and the common response of hard-pressed schools is to focus on remedying children's problems, rather than tackling their high ability with further challenge. Though entirely well-meaning, this tactic is often counter-productive. Since the concept and understanding of high ability is such a troublesome area, it is unsurprising to learn that research into the nature and needs of children with multiple exceptionalities is rather rare.

Those who have tried to bridge the gifted/special gap over the years have had difficulty obtaining resources or research funding because the topic falls between two stools and could be regarded as too small a population to merit concern. Equally, from the intervention point of view, the most obvious sign of difficulty is the special need; the other, the giftedness, is regarded as a bonus but they can cancel each other out.

(Montgomery 2003: 5)

The able population must be inclusive. Children with learning problems and dis-abilities must be allowed the opportunity to benefit from provision, as must children from disadvantaged backgrounds.

THE GLOBAL CONTEXT

It is certainly worth considering the international context of this issue to demon-strate its complexity and importance as well as showing how concepts of ability, elitism and fairness impact on provision for the able. In examining the policies and attitudes to education of the highly able in different countries, it quickly becomes clear that there are common problems in all countries. These usually include a very limited budget and many competing requirements as well as changing social situations and the commensurate difficulties in adapting the edu-cation system to meet rapidly changing needs. Most countries acknowledge that highly able children should be nurtured in order to ensure that their considerable potential is translated into achievement.

However, different social and education concerns impact on how concepts of potential and achievement are perceived and how success can be achieved. The notion of fairness is cited in some cases where egalitarian models deny able chil-dren any specific provision. It seems that there is no country for which the dual complexities of identifying the able and funding their activities remain unprob-lematic.

Clearly policies in different countries vary, reflecting a range of cultures with different values and social histories. Reviewing some of these differences can be illuminating. Before considering how policy for the able can be designed to ensure a fair deal for all, it is vital to understand how the educators and policy makers of the country in question conceptualise the origins and nature of gifted-ness.

Cultural influences on gifted and talented programmes are often quite marked (Robinson 1992). These influences stem from beliefs and values. Many cultures have deeply ingrained beliefs about concepts such as the nature of giftedness and the purpose of education.

(Moon and Rosselli 2000: 501)

A familiar notion found particularly in Britain, Australia and North America is that high ability has genetic origins and that the environment can be favourable or unfavourable, contributing to the realisation or otherwise of the potential high abilities. In contrast, in many Asian countries the notion prevails that effort is the key to variations in achievements and abilities. It is impossible to overstate how deeply such beliefs affect policy.

> For example, Norwicka (1995) cites denial of the existence of genetic differences during the communist period as a historical barrier to the development of gifted education in Poland.
>
> (Moon and Rosselli 2000: 501)

Similar deeply held notions are found concerning attitudes to the success of high achievers. Feather (1989) noted that in countries where individualistic achievement is favoured, rewards are directed at able high achievers. In communities with different outlooks, however, 'research (Feather and McKee 1993) had indicated that in collectivist cultures people showed a tendency to want to see high achievers fail' (Hernandez de Hahn 2000: 556). Although this individualist–collectivist dichotomy may be rather simplistic, the point is made that cultural attitudes affect the way that able children are treated. Similarly, how able children are taught reflects the values of the society in question:

> Curriculum for the gifted, its goals and purposes, as well as its delivery systems speaks loudly as to how talent and its development is honoured and nurtured in a society.
>
> (Van Tassel-Baska 2000: 360)

A case study for this concept is the approach adopted in the 1980s and 1990s in Australasia, where egalitarian concerns have overridden the needs of the able for some years.[2] As a result of reviewing the poor performance of minority groups, schools tried to redress the balance, particularly from the 1950s to the 1980s.

> In its starkest form, the issue was seen in terms of alternatives: education could concentrate on those with special needs (the disadvantaged) or those with special abilities [...] the New Zealand Education Act of 1989 decreed that 'equity objectives shall underpin all activities within the school'. There were moves to downplay the concept of *giftedness* as such and use different terminology [...] *highly able*, or children with *special abilities*.
>
> (Van Tassel-Baska 2000: 780–1)

This falsely dichotomises high ability with disadvantage and it is now widely accepted that children with special educational needs or cultural disadvantage can also be highly able. In Australia and New Zealand, some states have found their drive for equity incompatible with the success of programmes for the previously disadvantaged able pupil. Teachers report that they are unable to continue programmes as inequality is being created by allowing the more able to succeed (Benbow and Stanley 1997).

Policies for educational provision are rarely coherently stated with a public justification for their specific goals and strategies. This lack of transparency and clarity can result in understandable suspicion, particularly when some abilities are considered as fair opportunities for investment, while others are viewed as elitist.

> Democratic societies, whether long established or newly forming, often have reservations about special programmes that meet the needs of only a few – particularly when those programmes expand the gifts of the already talented individuals.
>
> (Wollam 1992: 67)

Students from difficult backgrounds with less obvious opportunities should be targeted, but even when this happens, it is frequently reported that 'poor and minority students are disproportionately excluded from programs for the gifted' (Kornhaber 1999, research from the USA). Similar negativity is found when reviewing the range of talents that society is prepared to support. Gross here compares how extra funding for sporting prowess is often considered more acceptable than extra funding for academic areas:

> Both nations (USA and Australia) abhor racial, social, and religious bias. [...] yet we do hold a pervasive, insidious bias when it comes to talent development. All gifts are equal, we seem to say, but some gifts are more equal than others. [...] Our bias becomes apparent, however, when the children's precocity is sited in the cognitive domain.
>
> (Gross 1999: 3)

Many Asian societies account for individual differences and high ability through effort, with an emphasis on 'teacher skill and pupil diligence'. These countries tend to develop programmes with aims of economic development and of maximising the nation's human resources. Underlying principles suggest the populace is governed 'on the basis of employing the talented' and a 'societal tendency to value intellectuals and the wise' (Wu et al. 2000: 775).

> Therefore, they believe that the government should not enhance individual differences by intentionally providing special programs for those who are already doing well.
>
> (Wu et al. 2000: 769)

The Scandinavian ideal is of inter-dependence and 'reluctance to reward or pro-mote policies or actions that would cause some individuals to excel more than others' (Persson *et al.* 2000: 718). Nordic provision is exceptionally egalitarian and it is even considered improper to exhibit pride of self. Schooling and society reinforce the sense that no one is 'special'.

> exclusiveness and out-of-the-ordinary achievements often give rise to envy and therefore to malicious pleasure when the stars 'fall'. The high value awarded to *sameness* makes all personal success problematic.
>
> (Daun 1994 cited in Persson *et al.* 2000: 719)

In China, psychologists use the term 'supernormal' to describe the able (since 1978). It conflates two key concepts in gifted education in China: the statistical meaning of being 'relatively superior to most normal children' and the role of God-given talent. 'Gifted' in Chinese, 'tian cai', means 'the gods' bestowal upon man' (Shi and Zha 2000: 758).

Historical inequity, colonial rules, political struggles, civil unrest and lack of funding have dominated educational development in Africa and Latin America over the last century and the notion of singling out a small group for special treatment is reminiscent of elitist practices of the past (Taylor and Kokot 2000: 803).

Misconceptions about the able are rife in Central and South America, apart from Cuba, where differentiated curricula have been in place since 1991. For the most part, however:

> a strong prejudice is firmly rooted in popular and teachers' thinking that any differentiated practice with the gifted threatens equity and democratic prin-ciples of education.
>
> (Soriano de Alencar *et al.* 2000: 823)

It is commonly considered that able pupils need no instruction as high ability will be clearly evident in every sphere. High ability is equated with high accom-plishment and it is thought that social and emotional troubles are inevitable (Soriano de Alencar *et al.* 2000: 823–4).

Fairness is controversial in all countries with policies for the able. The exam-ples demonstrate that the issue cannot be overstated and that cultural factors are vital. In sum (and rather baldly dichotomised):

> On the one side, it seems, stand critics who equal talent-selection to creat-ing a socially privileged societal stratum potentially beyond democratic principles. On the other side stand proponents arguing the democratic rights of children to develop to their full potential.
>
> (Persson *et al.* 2000: 703)

High ability is not recognised in special needs legislation in England, and only recently in Scotland (2004), and the most vociferous campaigners for education for gifted education have been parents' groups.

In the UK, there are various options within education (comprehensive, selective, independent, public), where competing systems and schools vie for the most able children. Despite this range of provision, it is still a battle to create provision specifically for the able.

> Due to the dominance of political egalitarian conviction, as in the Scandinavian countries and former Communist Europe, resistance to focus on gifted education as a separate issue in the English school system – irrespective of the existence of traditional elite schools – has been formidable.
>
> (Rudnitski 2000: 723)

Most of the countries considered above are struggling to tackle the question of elitism and so it needs to be unpacked if we are to find ways of demonstrating how provision for the able can be inclusive rather than exclusive.

ELITISM, EXCLUSIVITY AND MERITOCRACY

Teachers and policy makers understandably balk at accusations of unfairness, but programmes for the able often attract such accusations, and are more readily criticised than programmes for children with more obvious difficulties that arouse greater sympathy. Those who consider programmes for the able to be unfair commonly describe them as elitist, a word loaded with negative connotations in everyday usage. There is confusion about the term elitism and its true meaning.

Ordinary dictionary usage is represented by the following:[3]

1. The belief that certain persons or members of certain classes or groups deserve favoured treatment by virtue of their perceived superiority, as in intellect, social status, or financial resources.
   a. The sense of entitlement enjoyed by such a group or class.
   b. Control, rule, or domination by such a group or class.

This is the understanding most people are invoking when they accuse people running programmes for the able of being elitist. Of course 'favoured treatment' should not result from 'perceived superiority' and the entitlement and rule expressed in parts (a) and (b) of the definition are patently wrong, deriving as they do from an unfair principle. People are quite right to reject such a system.

As well as the 'superiority' of 'intellect, social status, or financial resources', other aspects exist such as race, gender and certain abilities/disabilities.

Throughout history and in different cultures, women, people with disabilities, ethnic minorities, homosexuals, people of certain religions and of lower socio-economic status have been variously excluded from a variety of activities and institutions. The excluding institutions have been dubbed elitist and it is undeniable that disallowing people access to resources and opportunities on the basis of irrelevant criteria is abhorrent and intolerable. Such attitudes amount to prejudice and bigotry.

Elitism can, though, have a different interpretation. Back to the dictionaries...

> 2. (adj) Selected as the best; 'an elect circle of artists'; 'elite colleges' (n) group or class of persons enjoying superior intellectual or social or economic status.

This definition is rather muddled, but helps to show that elite can sometimes be synonymous with 'best'. Above, the adjective refers to people who actually are the best at something, whilst the noun is used for status that need not have been earned. 'Elect' implies chosen, and the selection criteria and the fairness or otherwise of such criteria would determine the validity of the group in terms of its egalitarian nature.

If someone is disallowed membership to a group through their lack of ability to benefit from a specific activity this is a different matter to someone excluded for irrelevant criteria. There would be little point applying to become an engineer without any background in mathematics, or trying to become a chef without any knowledge or experience of cookery.

Despite being anti-elitism, most people would agree that society should nurture elite performances and abilities. This kind of elite that is acceptable concerns, for example, our acceptance and encouragement of highly trained surgeons, praise and rewards for our best musical performers and adoration for our superlative sportspeople.

For an example of the complexity of the concept of elitism, note here the Royal Society grappling with this difficult idea when reviewing its funding and membership policies:

> The Royal Society, by its very nature, is an elitist organisation. What else can a national academy of science be? Its whole *raison d'être* is to represent the best of science in this country. [...] The word elitist means different things to different people [...] elitism has (also) become an all-purpose boo word for condemning any kind of exclusivity, justifiable or not. One doesn't want to be elitist in the sense of saying 'we're only going to have white men' or 'we're only going to have people who went to Oxford', [...] the society has an historic problem.

(Watts 2002: 18)

Governments are exercised by the way that people immediately react with negativity to any policy that can be construed as elitist. The following quotation from then Secretary of State for Education Estelle Morris in 2002 shows a rare apology on behalf of earlier Labour Party policy, admitting to some confusion with elitism and excellence:

> We have always wanted to make opportunity open to all, to allow people to progress and improve themselves by merit and hard work, and to tear down the barriers that prevented the disadvantaged from making a better life for themselves. But we made a mistake. In our determination to open up opportunity to the whole of society, we confused elitism with excellence. [...] We were embarrassed to celebrate excellence, for fear we would be taken for celebrating the elite. It went further. There were those who thought that the highest achievers could take care of themselves and our efforts should be put into those who were under-performing. We thought there was a trade-off between tackling underachievement and promoting excellence – we created our own set of illusionary taboos. It is time to break them.[4]

There are other forms of elitism which we all tend to live with and accept as they are very much part of the fabric of society. For example, religions are often based on hierarchies of power and only certain members are able to perform specific roles and make key decisions. This notion of divine elitism is difficult to refute, as it would entail proof, or not, of a divine being or beings. As with royal families, an historic tradition has built up over centuries, ingraining these ideas, and individual or group claims to favoured treatment are infrequently questioned.

Birthright elitism concerns parents giving advantage to their children and is acceptable to many people. Passing on the benefits of hard-earned wealth and life experience to one's own children is considered tolerable despite its advocates simultaneously being in favour of equality. Some educational advantage is bound to result from such sharing, perhaps increasing societal inequality. This is a common contradiction, identified by Swift who notes that '... many people say they want "equality of opportunity" when what they really want [...] is actually just less inequality of opportunity' (2001: 101).

In the fight against old-school elitism a popular system to invoke is that of meritocracy. This would allow the able to achieve highly and ensure that nothing acts as a barrier to these accomplishments. In fulfilling criteria for such an approach, it is necessary to increase access to educational opportunities to all. In so doing, the exclusivity of certain fields is questioned, often resulting in the criticism that excellence has been abandoned in favour of open access: the accusation of 'dumbing down' education. Note here, for example, Tony Blair on the defensive:

'There are some traditionalists who believe that more means worse – that only a minority have the brains to go on to university […] It is a cosy elitism that has bedevilled and weakened our education system for more than a century.'

(Blair, quoted by Goddard 2002: 3)[5]

There is no reason why providing for the able should be elitist in the negative sense of the word, if suitable criteria are applied. There is little point designing activities of no value to potential participants. Restricting them to people who have the requisite skills, experience or interest is acceptable. It would be less contentious, however, to describe this tactic as 'appropriate provision', rather than 'elitist provision'. Reactions against elitism often hinge on notions of fairness and desert. We tend to feel that privilege should be earned, and where it seems that people are awarded extra entitlements for no good reason we quite rightly consider this to be elitist and unfair. People should be awarded privileges in keeping with their effort and achievements; they should be given advantage through merit.

Merit can be described as 'talent times effort', defined as the principle that: 'each person's chance to acquire positions of advantage and the rewards that go with them will depend entirely on his or her talent and effort' (Miller p. 177, cited in Brighouse 2002). In Western societies, this concept is broadly agreed by the majority of governments, with the proviso that people must be allowed equality of opportunity to demonstrate their talents and their efforts through a range of experiences in schooling. Miller goes on to note:

In such a society inequalities in different people's life chances will remain, but social institutions will be designed to ensure that favoured positions are assigned on the basis of individual merit (talent times effort) and not allocated randomly, or by ascriptive characteristics such as race or gender, or by the machinations of the already powerful.

(Miller p. 177, cited in Brighouse 2002)

Problems with Miller's notions arise, however, when we consider that people cannot be held accountable for their degree of talent and that very often difficult backgrounds preclude them demonstrating effort through lack of opportunity. For example, how can a potentially gifted pianist show their talent and effort if they have no access to music lessons or a piano? It is difficult here to separate issues of merit from those of need. A talented musician may 'need' facilities for their musical development as part of their healthy growth, but if their talent comes from their privileged background, or their natural ability, what have they done to 'deserve' or 'merit' such extra resources? Brighouse notes:

natural ability, like social class background, is something we cannot reasonably be held responsible for, […this] suggests a strongly compensatory principle, that significantly more educational resources should be spent on the less able than the more able.

(2002: 40)

This would be true if merit outweighed all other factors such as personal need and the development of talent for societal improvement. It seems that popular opinion endorses the concept of desert, whereby people are entitled to earn more than one another even when this is for reasons beyond their control. Different conceptions of desert exist and these have been summarised by Swift who contrasts the 'conventional', 'extreme' and 'mixed' views. The 'conventional' view of desert already mentioned allows for inequality in earnings and reward despite advantage deriving from luck. The 'extreme' view disallows reward for effort as well as talent because it is considered that how hard someone works is out of their control. It is irrelevant whether a strong work ethic is inborn or instilled at an early age; it should not be an incentive for higher pay. The 'mixed' view allows for rewarding aspects that people can control and choices they have made. Some political philosophers (e.g. Rawls) reject the mixed view as it is impossible to discern which aspects of someone's performance can be derived from their own efforts.

Teachers tend to hold the mixed view, which can result in children being prevented from participating in enrichment programmes where these are perceived as fun rewards. Children are expected to demonstrate both parts of the merit equation (talent and effort) and are disqualified if they are considered lazy, sometimes even when there are extenuating reasons for underachievement, such as learning problems. The Western attitude is that a work ethic is well within an individual's control and any given talent should be properly utilised. A poor attitude to work is sometimes wrongly dismissed as laziness. This notion contrasts with Asian and Pacific Rim cultures in which talent is viewed exclusively as the reward of effort. University places and other such educational privileges are distributed entirely on the basis of a concept of talent as success earned through endeavour.

Using desert as a basis for provision for the able at first sight seems reasonable: reward for hard work, not unfair advantage. However, if hard work is as much a result of background influence as other aspects of talent, pupils who are able but have not been encouraged are likely to be excluded from such schemes. High achievers are favoured again and some pupils with potential to benefit from unusual activities can be passed over in favour of those who are less able but more conformist.

Some children have less talent and work hard and others can achieve the same results with abundant talent and less work. If merit is to be used as a basis for reward, there must be a way of ensuring that every child has a fair opportunity to demonstrate both effort and ability. Underachievers can fail to apply themselves for a range of reasons, or can present a false image of exertion. This makes it difficult to assess ability accurately or to know how much effort they are making and consequently what they merit. Astute underachievers can convince teachers and parents that they do not need the extra work bound to follow from a true assessment of their ability. Some do not exert effort as they see little purpose in a set task, and some are so lacking in confidence that they cannot engage with the task at all.

EQUALITY AND FAIRNESS

In order to be fully and fairly inclusive, a school policy must be grounded on a discussion and agreed understanding of what the teachers define as high ability and what counts as reasonable effort. Teachers mostly strive for equality, but it is not always clear what they understand by the term, particularly when this concerns the fair distribution of resources. On the face of it, providing for the less able seems to be a reasonable way to move towards equality. However, there is no good reason why everything should be equalised. It may well be that the distribution of resources and provision for pupils is unequal as this ultimately allows for greater fairness. Despite being an unpopular statement to make, it is acceptable to pursue a non-egalitarian distribution of goods in order to achieve fairness.

> It is perfectly coherent to reject equality at the philosophical level, as a fundamental ideal, while arguing that, for other reasons, resources should be more equally distributed – perhaps *much* more equally distributed – than they are at present.
>
> (Swift 2001: 92)

It seems counter-intuitive to want to be both fair and inegalitarian, but if teachers have a genuine commitment to meeting everyone's educational needs, they are likely to have to adopt an anti-egalitarian stance (White 1994: 180). A more hard-line egalitarian would call for the principle of equality of treatment to be upheld and this:

> requires that goods and outcomes be allocated equally to all, regardless of factors of entitlement, need or desert.
>
> (Winch 1996: 115)

Few teachers would ignore entitlement, need and desert when deciding how to allocate resources. As Swift summarises:

> What matters is not that people have equal shares of good things. Nor is it even that people have equal opportunity (or access) to good things. What matters, if we think about it, is that everybody has enough, or that those who have least have as much as possible, or that people who most need things take priority.
>
> (2001: 92)[6]

Meeting needs should be separated from valuing equality, and equal access to leading a flourishing life need not mean equal distribution of goods (White 1994: 174). There are different understandings of equality, and it would be useful to clarify these concepts. The literature tends to focus on three areas: equality of resources; equality of opportunity; and equality of outcome.

Equality of resources is inappropriate as people have widely differing needs and subjects have different costs. In educational philosophy, the rather woolly notion is suggested that resources should be awarded to those who can 'profit from them most' (Wilson, cited by Brighouse 2002). This is criticised (e.g. by Brighouse) as it is far clearer to apportion resources to children based on needs.

Swift maintains that:

> Equality of opportunity can range from a minimal view suggesting people's gender, religion or race, etc, must not prevent them from opportunities in areas such as education and employment to more radical interpretations where untalented children – whether rich or poor – should have the same opportunities as talented children.
>
> (Swift 2000: 102)

The first view is rather thin and does not offer much in terms of actively improving fairness. The second would oblige the state to rethink some of its fundamental values. An initially attractive middle ground is the 'conventional' which suggests that not only should people's competences be considered above their race, etc., but that they should have had an equal chance to acquire the competences in the first place. (This echoes the meritocratic principle of rewards for talent times effort, with the added dimension of aiming to assure a level playing field as a backdrop.) Many people like this idea but balk at some of the measures that would have to be taken to ensure its realisation, for instance restricting or demanding certain practices in the home, such as supporting children with homework. Without equalising parental support, 'conventional' equality of opportunity cannot be assured. In sum, equality of opportunity is only a desirable ideal if qualified by other principles to stop it undermining more important values (Brighouse 2002).

Equality can also be concerned with outcome:

> Equality of outcome is a principle of equality that asserts that the endpoint of a process ought to be the same for everyone who goes through it.
>
> (Winch 1996: 115)

A generous interpretation of this egalitarian principle requires nothing more than a nationally agreed curriculum with a fairly rich minimum of educational experience, covering general subjects and equipping children with a reasonable set of life skills. This is the conception commonly found in school systems in which highly able children without problems often complete requirements earlier than their peers, but are still expected to stay in school. A much stronger interpretation would require specificity about the school experience, or process, implying less diversity in schooling. Such programmes have resulted in children being held back: the 'tall poppy syndrome' (in Sweden and Australia, for example).

EQUALITY OF CHALLENGE

A useful notion of equality would focus on the experience of being educated meaning more than leaving school with a good clutch of examination results. Educational experience should involve positive social interaction, learning about one's strengths and weaknesses, and feeling part of a community, among other personal and social factors.

The quality of schooling or learning experience is linked to the potential–achievement gap in a way that is particularly pertinent for the highly able. In this model, pupils are not measured by their success, but by the relationship of this success to their potential achievement. There are difficulties associated with measuring potential, but it is sometimes clear that students are failing to be appropriately challenged by their schoolwork. It may be that Astrid is achieving higher grades than Carlos and the obvious response is to try and help raise Carlos' results. However, if Astrid is working well below her potential level of success, she may be bored and develop the associated problems of disaffection and frustration. In terms of flourishing, and closing the potential–achievement gap, resources and/or effort should also be directed towards helping Astrid to improve her performance. Of course, no one would want to take away from Carlos to ensure Astrid's flourishing, but the resource pot is unlikely to be big enough to cope with both children's needs. Decisions need to be made about how best to apportion resources, especially when Carlos may never reach Astrid's level in terms of grades. It is perhaps possible that he is able to flourish fully at his current level of achievement.

Providing equality of challenge, or equality of quality of learning, should therefore be a key factor in schooling and able pupils are likely to need provision beyond established curricula, in order to ensure such stimulation. While there is a statutory requirement to attend school, there is a moral obligation for schools to ensure that pupils are not wasting their time. Pupils need to be engaged in their learning and this can truly only happen when tasks are challenging. Even the most determined of us can only sustain a certain amount of motivation for simple tasks that lack any intrinsic value.

INGREDIENTS OF CHALLENGE

In designing tasks that truly challenge, the aim is to allow pupils to move at their own intellectual pace, or as near to this as is practically possible, regardless of whether that pace is 'normal' for their age. Challenge is intimately bound up with motivation and when this is intrinsic to the task it can be very powerful.

It is helpful to establish that the subject area is stimulating or potentially stimulating, and vital to consider previous knowledge and experience in order to match tasks to existing levels of ability. Pitching tasks is an important skill: too easy and children are bored; too hard and they are frustrated. Cognitive challenge was well described by Vygotsky, in terms of the zone of proximal development, where challenge is defined by what can currently be achieved with support, moving toward what can be accomplished without help. The support recommended by Vygotsky was that of an adult or more capable peer, but support can be provided through written or recorded instruction. Many able pupils find computer technology ideal in terms of being able to control the amount of support they require. Piaget and other developmentalists use the term 'cognitive dissonance' to describe the sense of sufficient challenge to ensure optimum learning.

Both risk of failure and potential for success should be part of the task. Highly able achievers sometimes slip into a 'comfort zone' of easy work and become coasters, used to continual success. Underachievers become habituated to their constant failure and success can be met as a welcome surprise. It is also helpful to try and incorporate some kind of novelty or difference into some tasks, but only when these complement rather than distract the learner. The (non-exhaustive) list of ingredients can be summarised:

- Subject area of potential or actual interest
- Use made of children's prior knowledge
- Use made of children's existing skills
- Cognitive dissonance/zone of proximal development
- Risk of failure
- Chance of success
- Novelty/difference.

Of course practical constraints make it difficult to deliver such challenge, but the dangers of a lack of challenge are palpable:

> boredom and lack of cognitive challenge in the daily curriculum is playing a more significant role in causing pupils across the ability range to become disaffected than was originally suspected. […] more pupils, including the highly able and the more creative, are rejecting such 'schooling' and are switching off.
>
> (Montgomery 2000: 130–1)

More pervasive problems can result from the able being habitually bored. Children can also become disruptive:

> when lessons are too easy, they lose the satisfaction of tackling and resolving problems. To compensate, they may deliberately provoke disturbance, either in their own minds or among others in the classroom, just to taste the spice of stimulation.
>
> (Freeman 1997: 488)

Often, we are able to find our own level of challenge and the able child in the classroom is capable of this if the available materials match their needs. I am doubtful that any research could find the perfect formula for creating challenge, as it will, of course, vary across individuals.

In sum, all children should be provided with an enabling education with sufficient resources to allow the development of their talents to a high level, particularly when there is a significant discrepancy between their potential and their performance. This is true even where potential achievement exceeds expected requirements. A clear way of considering what it is fair to do for the able is to aim for some kind of equality of quality of learning, or equality of challenge.

SUMMARY AND CONCLUSION

Coping with the contradictory dual aims of excellence and equity is a significant problem in all countries that provide for the highly able. Pacific Rim countries, with their notion of talent as the reward of effort, have less trouble with the issue of equity, and talent comes from merit through effort. The concept of wasting 'natural talent' is therefore irrelevant, yet other serious difficulties arise such as extreme pressure on students to achieve consistently. In recent decades, understandable and generally admirable aims of political correctness have resulted in unfortunate policies in which some children are denied provision in the name of equality.

In other countries then, egalitarian aims have resulted in policy makers and teachers worrying about highly able children outstripping their peers, increasing social imbalance. These fears are associated with unfair access to enrichment activities. It is important, therefore, to secure fair access to activities for all who would benefit from them, rather than cancelling provision. This raises the issue of concepts of equality and demonstrates that inegalitarianism can sometimes be the best way to meet people's needs.

The role of schooling cannot be to level the playing field of society's inequalities, but to help pupils achieve to the best of their ability. It is a fact that some provision for the highly able may result in a broader gap between the less and more privileged. Whilst this is not a desired outcome, it would be unethical to hold children back through denying them access to appropriate provision.

At the end of the chapter, I propose a type of equality that should be in place regardless of a child's background, disabilities, or personal difficulties. This is equality of challenge. Whilst difficult to implement, the basic notion of challenging all children is a useful tenet for considering how best to provide for the able.

Notes

1 I am not suggesting that teachers only 'like' conventional pupils, but that school structures work in favour of these pupils. Teachers sometimes emphasise behaviour and self-control as key factors for choice of provision and this may be practical, but lacks pedagogical validity.

2 Despite Australian states having different policies from one another and New Zealand having its own education system, Braggett and Moltzen discuss the Australasian issues together (2000: 779–97). They note the following:

> During the 1980s and 1990s there were three major influences that were common to both countries and which influenced educational provision for gifted students. The first was an egalitarian outlook that sought to promote social justice, to remove handicaps, and to develop welfare systems for those in need [...] it is felt to be elitist to identify gifted students and to provide for them in a differential manner [...] it is difficult to convey the egalitarian sense that permeated Australasian society during the 1980s and 1990s. [...] those who succeed are likely to receive genuine approbation, particularly when they overcome obstacles on the way to their success. On the other hand, too much success may engender resentment and lead to the *tall poppy syndrome*: very tall poppies should be cut down (except where sport is involved).
> (pp. 780–1)

3 Taken from Collins and Oxford English dictionaries.

4 Estelle Morris, Secretary of State for Education, speaking at the Institute for Mechanical Engineering on 16 May 2002. The whole speech can be accessed at http://www.dfes.gov.uk/speeches. The speech is a little confusing concerning underperforming pupils. Surely the Labour Party is not suggesting that effort should no longer be put into helping these people?

5 However, Blair has been attacked for 'the rise of the parentocracy, and [...] the fall of the meritocracy rather than its ascendancy' (Hellawell 2002).

6 Differentiating again between social and school policy, while most teachers would agree with Swift about what matters, they would also want to take into account Kymlicka's notion of an 'egalitarian plateau'; the principle that 'members of a political community should be treated as equals, that the state should treat its citizens with equal concern and respect', cited in Swift (2001: 93).

References

Benbow, C. P. and Stanley, J. C. (1997) 'Inequity in equity: how equity can lead to inequity for high-potential students' in *Roeper Review*, 2 (2), pp. 249–92.

Braggett, E. J. and Moltzen, R. I. (2000) 'Identifying and nurturing giftedness and talent in Australia and New Zealand'. In Heller *et al.* (eds) *International Handbook of Research and Development of Giftedness and Talent*. Oxford: Elsevier Science, pp. 779–97.

Brighouse, H. (2002) 'Meritocracy and educational equality'. Seminar on 'Social mobility and meritocracy: Interdisciplinary perspectives on current issues', Nuffield College, Oxford University, 16 February.

Feather, N. T. (1989) 'Attitudes towards the high achiever: the fall of the tall poppy'. *Australian Journal of Psychology*, 41(3), pp. 239–67.

Freeman, J. (1997) 'The emotional development of the highly able'. *European Journal of Psychology of Education*, 12(4), pp. 479–93.

Goddard, A. (2002) 'Blair attacks "cosy elitism of opponents of access targets"'. *Times Higher Education Supplement*, 20 March, p. 3.

Gross, M. U. M. (1999) 'Small poppies: highly gifted children in the early years'. *Roeper Review*, 20 (3).

Hellawell, D. (2002) 'The fall of the meritocracy: a response to Roy Hattersley.' *Education and Social Justice*, 4(2), pp. 33–26.

Hernandez de Hahn, E. L. (2000) 'Cross cultural studies on gifted education'. In Heller *et al.* (eds) *International Handbook of Research and Development of Giftedness and Talent*. Oxford: Elsevier Science, pp. 549–63.

Kornhaber, M. (1999) 'Enhancing equity in gifted education: a framework for examining assessments drawing on the theory of multiple intelligence'. *High Ability Studies*, 10 (2), pp. 143–61.

Montgomery, D. (2000) *Able Underachievers*. London: Whurr Publishers.

Montgomery, D. (ed.) (2003) *Gifted and Talented Children with Special Educational Needs*. London: NACE/Fulton.

Moon, S. M. and Rosselli, H. C. (2000) 'Developing gifted programs'. In Heller *et al.* (eds) *International Handbook of Research and Development of Giftedness and Talent*. Oxford: Elsevier Science, pp. 499–521.

Persson, R. S., Joswig, H. and Balogh, L. (2000) 'Europe: programs, practices, and current research'. In Heller *et al.* (eds) *International Handbook of Research and Development of Giftedness and Talent*. Oxford: Elsevier Science, pp. 703–34.

Rudnitski, R.A. (2000) 'National/provincial gifted education policies: present state, future possibilities'. In Heller *et al.* (eds) *International Handbook of Research and Development of Giftedness and Talent*. Oxford: Elsevier Science, pp. 673–79.

Shi, J. and Zha, Z. (2000) 'Psychological research on and education of gifted and talented children in China'. In Heller *et al.* (eds) *International Handbook of Research and Development of Giftedness and Talent*. Oxford: Elsevier Science, pp. 757–63.

Soriano de Alencar, E. M. L., Blumen-Pardo, S. and Castellanos-Simons, D. (2000) 'Programs and practices for identifying and nurturing giftedness and talent in Latin American countries'. In Heller *et al.* (eds) *International Handbook of Research and Development of Giftedness and Talent*. Oxford: Elsevier Science, pp. 817–29.

Swift, A. (2001) *Political Philosophy: A Beginners' Guide for Students and Politicians*. Cambridge, UK: Polity.

Taylor, C. and Kokot, S. (2000) 'The status of gifted child education in Africa'. In Heller *et al.* (eds) *International Handbook of Research and Development of Giftedness and Talent*. Oxford: Elsevier Science, pp. 799–815.

Van Tassel-Baska, J. (2000) 'Theory and research on curriculum development for the gifted' in Heller *et al.* (eds) *International Handbook of Research and Development of Giftedness and Talent*. Oxford: Elsevier Science, pp. 345–66.

Watts, G. (2002) 'A bunch of jolly good fellows or old cronies who don't deserve £25m a year?' *Times Higher Education Supplement*, 1532, 5 April, pp. 18–19.

White, J. P. (1994) 'The Dishwasher's Child: education and the end of egalitarianism'. *Journal of the Philosophy of Education*, 28 (2), pp. 170–92.

Winch, C. (1996) 'Equality, quality and diversity' *Journal of Philosophy of Education* 30 (1) special edn, pp. 113–28 (ch. 10).

Wollam, J. (1992) 'Equality versus excellence – the South Korean dilemma in gifted education'. *Roeper Review* 14 (4), pp. 37–43.

Wu, W. T., Cho, S. and Munandar, U. (2000) 'Programs and practices for identifying and nurturing giftedness and talent in Asia (outside mainland China)'. In Heller *et al.* (eds) *International Handbook of Research and Development of Giftedness and Talent*. Oxford: Elsevier Science, pp. 765–78.

Chapter 3

Can 'inclusion' work for the gifted and talented?

Roger Moltzen

Ask any group of people, professional or lay, what they consider the most appropriate context for educating the gifted and talented and you will almost certainly encounter a dramatic division of opinion. Those who have witnessed or participated in such debates can also attest to how adamantly positions are held and how vehemently these can be expressed. Few issues in education seem to elicit such strongly held opinions. Debate about whether gifted and talented students should be educated with their age peers or their intellectual peers usually touches on much broader philosophical, political, social and even religious beliefs. The various perspectives espoused, even in professional circles, are usually done so without reference to research, or else to a very limited number of very context-specific studies. This is not altogether surprising, as the research base here is limited, both in number and nature. This means that those endorsing one approach over another usually draw on their own values and experiences in defending their stance. In addition, much of the research (and opinion) in this area comes out of the United States, and informs and is informed by approaches to learning and teaching that frequently have limited applicability beyond that context.

The wide range of educational alternatives available for gifted and talented students can be reduced to three primary approaches: segregation, acceleration and inclusion. Many schools and teachers combine approaches. For example, those advocating for an inclusive approach would generally maintain that within this context, gifted and talented students should be permitted to work at an accelerated pace. Many supporters of segregation maintain that the gifted and talented should have exposure to more inclusive situations from time to time. Those arguing for the advanced placement of gifted and talented students will concede that this context may not be appropriate for every area of every accelerated student's education. However, in most schools there is a 'primary' approach to providing for gifted and talented students and, although a raft of secondary programmes and/or provisions may be included, these tend to be more supplementary in nature.

In this chapter, a case is made for the inclusive classroom as an effective 'primary' environment for gifted and talented students. Frequently, and especially by experts in the gifted and talented field, the inclusive or regular classroom is viewed as the default option: the option that is not really an option because it represents the status quo. In fact, there are those who would maintain that, while the inclusive classroom may be the *'least* restrictive environment' for students with special needs, it is the *'most* restrictive environment' for students with special abilities. In advocating for the inclusion of gifted and talented students in regular classrooms, this writer is not simply trying to make a silk purse out of a sow's ear, or advance a 'politically correct' agenda, but is suggesting this as a 'preferred' choice that can be defended pedagogically and practically.

POSITIONING GIFTED AND TALENTED EDUCATION

The concepts of integration, mainstreaming, and latterly inclusion, reflect shifts in the discourses associated with disability. Inclusion represents a move from medical, charity and lay discourses of disability, to a rights discourse (Neilson 2005). The term inclusion is often seen as simply referring to learners with special needs, where it is interpreted as the 'complete acceptance of a student with a disability in a regular classroom' (Elkins 2002: 77). However, the notion can also be viewed much more broadly. Mitchell (1999), for example, says that internationally, inclusive education is taken to mean that schools:

- respect the rights of all children to enrol and receive education in state schools, to be treated with respect, to have dignity and independence, to have access to a fair share of available special education resources, and not to be directly or indirectly discriminated against;
- reduce barriers to learning;
- have a philosophy of providing for all children, including children with special needs;
- recognise and respond to the diversity of their populations;
- accommodate children's different styles and rates of learning;
- ensure equality of educational opportunity through appropriate curriculum, school organisation, use of resources and partnerships with their communities.

(Mitchell 1999: v)

While the narrower definitions of inclusion may be considered of limited relevance to gifted and talented students, this broader definition certainly is relevant. As Andrews and Lupart (2000) point out, classrooms today are viewed much more as communities where all children have the right to belong. Teachers, they observe, are now expected to provide differentiation to meet the wide range of learning needs in their classrooms, and many teachers have readily accepted this role. In numerous countries, the one-size-fits-all and lock-step approaches to teaching and learning are a legacy of a quite distant past, and teachers nowadays accept and employ much more learner-centred pedagogies.

Interestingly, amongst the many discussions and debates that centre on inclusion, the implications for the education of the gifted and talented usually pass unmentioned. In the absence of any concerted criticism of inclusion for learners with special needs from the gifted and talented community, one can only assume that most of this group support the notion, both philosophically and practically. Yet many of those who advocate on behalf of gifted and talented students maintain that it is unrealistic to expect the regular classroom teacher to accommodate this group's special needs. It seems rather perverse that teachers are considered capable of acquiring the knowledge and skills to provide for special needs, but not for special abilities.

At the heart of this issue seems to be where gifted and talented education is positioned both philosophically and politically. In some countries and educational jurisdictions, the gifted and talented are considered a group with special educational needs, and as such, are viewed as part of special or inclusive education. However, in many other places this issue seems to remain unaddressed or unresolved and the education of the gifted and talented is sometimes placed within special education, and on other occasions positioned outside of it. New Zealand is a good example of this dichotomy, where attitudes and approaches generally reflect an acceptance of special abilities as a subset of special needs but officially, the messages are mixed. For example the *National Educational Guidelines*, which mandate services for the gifted and talented, refer to 'Groups of students ... who have special education needs (including gifted and talented students)' (Ministry of Education 2004: 1). Yet the same Ministry of Education's special education unit, the agency that provides national special education support to teachers and schools, does not work with the gifted and talented. This illustrates the tension that exists between the two areas in many countries and is part of the reason the education of the gifted and talented often 'falls between the cracks' at a national, regional and school level. The reason why the gifted and talented remain outside special education is not just resistance to their inclusion from those seeking a better deal for these students. Some of those in special education are also vehemently opposed to this union or amalgamation, albeit for different reasons.

Those who embrace the term inclusion and what it represents celebrate the discarding of the term 'special'. In reality, arguments about whether or not gifted and talented education should be part of special education are probably rather dated. If conceptually, the aims and approaches of special, and gifted and talented education seemed antagonistic, the issues associated with this debate have little relevance to the ideals of inclusion. While some fear that inclusion of the gifted and talented will result in this group being relegated to an educational wasteland, a much more optimistic view is that the broad pedagogical principles and practices that are critical to ensuring inclusion is a success for students with special educational needs are the same principles and practices that underpin effective educational provisions for the gifted and talented.

WHY 'INCLUDE' THE GIFTED AND TALENTED?

While there are some very good reasons why inclusion should be considered a viable option for the gifted and talented, many cynics would contend that is an unrealistic expectation to place on regular class teachers. Yet, if we accept that it is possible for teachers to meet the needs of students, for example with physical, intellectual and sensory disabilities and from diverse ethnic, cultural, national and socioeconomic backgrounds, then surely it must be within their capabilities to provide for 'most' of the needs of 'most' gifted and talented students. In spite of the ever-increasing diversity that characterises the inclusive classroom, the pressures associated with an overcrowded curriculum, and an increased emphasis on assessment and standards, many teachers provide brilliantly for their most able students. In addition, an in-depth examination of the vast array of literature providing guidance on working with gifted and talented students clearly shows that there are almost no recommended models, methods or approaches that cannot be applied to the inclusive classroom. Thus, the pertinent question is not, 'Can teachers do it?' rather it is, 'How can teachers do it?'

The most commonly espoused arguments for the gifted and talented to be educated in regular schools and regular classrooms centre on the perceived discriminatory, undemocratic and elitist nature of the alternatives (e.g. Oakes 1985; Sapon-Shevin 1994). These criticisms do not constitute a credible rationale for 'supporting' the inclusive classroom as an appropriate placement option but rather a rationale against homogeneous grouping on the basis of ability. One does not have to resort to these negative discourses to promote inclusion for the gifted and talented; there are some very persuasive pedagogical arguments that can be used. That is not to say, however, that there are no 'social' benefits that accrue when the gifted and talented are taught in mixed-ability classes (just as there are some potential disadvantages). However, this should not be considered a primary justification in choosing this option.

A logical reason for arguing for the inclusive classroom for the gifted and talented is purely and simply because that is where the majority of this group spend the most of their time at school. On its own, this would hardly represent a primary reason to support this placement option, but considered alongside some identified strengths of this approach, and alongside some of the shortcomings of the alternatives, it is a significant issue. From the time of Lewis Terman and Leta Hollingworth, the case for segregating and/or accelerating gifted and talented students has been repeatedly voiced. In spite of this, all but a few of these students spend most of their time in regular classrooms, and will almost certainly continue to do so in the future.

A major advantage of the inclusive classroom over other approaches is that schools and teachers do not have to make definitive decisions about who is, and who is not, gifted and talented. It is generally accepted that gifts and talents emerge at different times and under different conditions. Some other placement options require decisions to be made about who will be included in, and of course who will be excluded from, a class or programme. When this occurs, issues of definition and selection become paramount. Many schools now take a much more liberal approach to defining giftedness and talent, at least in their documentation, but of course encounter problems with this when making decisions on the establishment of a special class or group. Typically, these schools revert to a much more conservative concept for selection of students for these accelerated or gifted classes, to avoid them becoming much like any other mixed-ability class.

Every teacher has been taken aback when a student, whose abilities had never previously been considered exceptional, offers a brilliant response to a particular problem, activity or question. In the inclusive classroom, where there is a very blurred line between those considered gifted and talented and those not, activities designed with more able students in mind can be accessed by any student in the classroom. Such an invitational environment means that a much greater number of students have the opportunity to demonstrate their abilities. There is always a danger that when some students are identified as 'the' gifted and talented group, the remainder are never considered as potentially gifted and talented. This can mean that the classroom programmes for the perceived 'non-gifted' become less conducive to the emergence and demonstration of exceptional abilities. This should not be such a concern in the inclusive setting, where every teacher in the school is considered a teacher of the gifted and talented. In this context, the students' regular class teacher has the primary responsibility for the gifted and talented students in his or her class. Other programmes emerge from or feed into this environment, rather than operating independently of it.

The separate class approach, part- or full-time, tends to see primacy given to the more traditional talent areas and in particular those associated with academic abilities. The inclusive classroom environment, especially at the primary school level, can accommodate a wide range of special abilities, and also provide equitable support for all of these. In addition, the inclusive classroom can better accommodate the jagged profile of abilities that is characteristic of most gifted and talented students. Few gifted and talented students are outstanding across the board, and the ability of many is much less spectacular in some areas than in others. In the case of gifted and talented students with learning difficulties, specific support in some subjects may be required. The greater flexibility of the inclusive classroom over the segregated or accelerated context means that students with diverse ability levels can be more easily and naturally provided for. In other words, the inclusive classroom has the potential to offer much more holistic support, not just in intellectual and academic areas, but also in the affective and social.

In a similar manner, the inclusive classroom environment, particularly at primary school level, but not exclusively so, lends itself to curriculum integration, an approach advocated by many curriculum experts (e.g. Beane 1997) and one also considered consistent with the strengths and learning styles of gifted and talented students. Van Tassel-Baska (2003) believes that this integrated approach to the curriculum works well in heterogeneous classes, claiming that it can address 'all salient characteristics of the gifted learner simultaneously, attending to precocity, intensity, and complexity as integrated characteristics that represent cognitive and affective dimensions of the learner' (2003: 175).

The regular classroom can allow for much greater flexibility of time than some other options. When a gifted and talented student achieves mastery in one curriculum area quicker than his or her peers, it is a simple task to allow this time in credit to be used to pursue special interests or topics. The facility to work on a topic for a sustained period of time appeals to many gifted and talented students, who sometimes feel so frustrated when the discontinuation of an activity is determined by the attention span of their less able peers that they avoid immersing themselves in a topic to avoid the frustration of premature closure.

An approach that is very popular with schools is withdrawal (pullout) programmes, where students spend a small part of their time with others of like ability and/or interest. This can be an effective approach when combined with the inclusive classroom. However, the motivation for this option is sometimes less defensible. The popularity of withdrawal programmes is often associated with the fact that the approach has the flexibility to be all things to all people. First, it can be seen to appease those advocating for dedicated provisions for the gifted and talented. Second, by offering opportunities across a diverse range of abilities, the withdrawal approach is unlikely to offend egalitarians. As a consequence, withdrawal programmes are often stand-alone provisions that do not articulate with the regular classroom programme. Cox et al. (1985: 44) refer to withdrawal programmes as 'patchwork' and 'fragmented' and contend that it is a model whose time has come. When withdrawal programmes 'are' the gifted and talented programme, they will always be inadequate. After all, the gifted and talented are gifted and talented all day, every day, and not just on Tuesday afternoons. When they are part of and articulate with the inclusive classroom, they can be extremely effective.

To many children, being selected for special classes or programmes on the basis of their ability is validating and rewarding. For others, such attention and recognition is unwelcome and even culturally inappropriate. In fact, there is evidence that some students will deliberately underachieve to avoid being selected for programmes or provisions that will isolate them from their peers (Moltzen 2004). For some cultural groups, the discomfort with separation from their peer group is closely related to how giftedness and talent is defined within their culture. For example, how the New Zealand Maori view giftedness and talent is quite different to how it is conceptualised by many other groups. 'There is an inherent expectation that a person's gifts and talents will be used to benefit others' (Bevan-Brown 2004: 179). In researching Maori perceptions of giftedness and talent, Bevan-Brown reports strong pleas from Maori adults against programmes that isolate talented children from their peers. She encountered stories of gifted and talented children who 'failed, misbehaved or opted out of programmes in which they felt isolated, uncomfortable and unfamiliar' (2004: 179). The Maori share this aversion to be being separated from their peers with many other groups.

HOW TO 'INCLUDE' GIFTED AND TALENTED STUDENTS

It would be erroneous to suggest that all, or maybe even the majority of class-rooms are ideal learning, social and emotional environments for gifted and talented students. In reality, many do represent the most restrictive environ-ments for this group. However, the notion that grouping the gifted and talented together or placing them at a higher class level equates with improved learning opportunities is equally erroneous. The context does not determine the quality of teaching and learning experiences. The gifted and talented can receive an inap-propriate curriculum and learning experiences in the inclusive, separate or accelerated classroom. As so much recent research has demonstrated, the key to an effective learning environment is the teacher. In their *International Handbook of Teachers and Teaching*, Biddle *et al.* (1997) state, 'We have gained a good deal of convincing empirical evidence confirming large differences in the quality of instruction among teachers and classrooms and that these differences have sig-nificant impact on students' academic performance' (p. 673).

For many years, this writer has defended the efficacy of the inclusive class-room environment for gifted and talented students, and students with special needs. He has also assisted thousands of regular class teachers to include both groups in their classroom. The initial response from teachers to the suggestion that it is possible to meet such a diverse range of needs in their classrooms is always mixed. Some are clearly already competent at doing this. Others accept the concept but lack the knowledge and skills to accomplish it. A significant group dismiss the idea as unrealistic and may accuse the 'messenger' of ivory-tower thinking, or of advancing a politically correct agenda. Teachers' attitudes and dispositions towards the idea of inclusion are closely connected to their own teaching methods, which often reflect how they were taught as students and trained as teachers. Where teaching is very much underpinned by an age/stage approach, where curricula are rigidly prescribed for specific grade/year levels, where whole-class teaching is common, and where grade/year level text books form a large percentage of the curriculum content, teachers often find the idea of catering for individual differences an anathema. Where teacher training, teach-ing practice, curricula and resources embody a learner-centred educational philosophy, the attitudes towards meeting the needs of diverse groups in regular classrooms are usually much more positive. This is not to imply that amongst this second group these ideals always translate into effective practice. Nor is it to sug-gest that the task of moving from the philosophical to the practical is easy or straightforward. As Strang (2001) found out in an in-depth examination of this process, teachers find it much more difficult to differentiate their practice than most of those involved in delivering teacher professional development or train-ing assume.

An attitude that appears to pervade many schools and classrooms is that ded-icated provision for the gifted and talented is discretionary rather than mandatory. It seems that this view is associated with the notion that the gifted and talented will 'make it on their own' and that additional support, while desirable, is not critical. In spite of this, many regular class teachers provide outstanding programmes for their gifted and talented students. Sometimes these teachers work in relative isolation, and on occasions even in antagonistic school environments. However, whether or not a gifted and talented student encounters a teacher with the knowledge and skills to respond appropriately to their needs is often a matter of chance.

In many countries, the movement towards including learners with special needs in regular schools and classrooms has been accompanied by programmes of teacher professional development. It is naïve and unrealistic to expect the gifted and talented to be successfully included without a similar commitment to dedicated, intensive and ongoing support. Roberts and Roberts (1986: 108) suggest professional development needs to focus on:

- *Awareness* – arousing interest and providing information about how the gifted programme relates to other aspects of the school and curriculum.
- *Information* – providing general information about the gifted programme and what it provides for students.
- *Personal* – providing clarification of role expectations.
- *Management* – providing direction related to day-to-day demands, such as timetabling, funding and organisation.
- *Consequences* – providing opportunities to examine evaluation issues and refine teaching skills.
- *Collaboration* – providing time for working together, exchanging ideas and guiding one another.
- *Refocusing* – providing opportunities for new ideas to be piloted.

Sustainability of improvements in this area is dependent on changes to the school culture. This requires a shift from provision being viewed as an 'optional extra' to one where this becomes part and parcel of school's core business. This will only occur with a schoolwide commitment in this area, where senior management is totally involved in and supportive of developments, and where policy or other appropriate documentation is developed.

There are three important areas that must be addressed in preparing regular classroom teachers to meet the needs of their gifted and talented students: attitudes, knowledge and skills. There are many myths associated with the gifted and talented that impede their educational progress. Teachers need to be made aware of these and sometimes their existing attitudes and stereotypes need to be challenged before inclusion will ever be successful. As Dettmer and Landrum (1998: 1) point out, 'It has been recognised for more than two decades that teachers do adopt more accepting and facilitative attitudes toward gifted students after just one course in the education of the gifted.' However, one-off professional development sessions are of minimal value in effecting long-term and sustainable change. Altrichter *et al.* (1993) note, 'The introduction of new teaching strategies presupposes a change in the routine perceptions and actions of teachers and pupils. This is often a long-term process in which all the participants have to become conscious of the new roles, explore them, and test their reliability' (p. 46).

There are some key principles and practices that are critical to creating an inclusive classroom that is effective in meeting the needs of the gifted and talented. These include the following.

1   *Dedicated and planned approaches*   There is no question that in the busy classroom, where there is a very diverse range of needs – which is most of today's classrooms – the group that often falls to the bottom of the priority pile is the gifted and talented. Many of these students are not overtly demanding of teacher-time and have little difficulty mastering the work deemed relevant for their age group. Teachers do not overlook this group out of disinterest; it is simply that what are perceived as more pressing needs get first claim on their time. The solution is both attitudinal and organisational. First, teachers need to understand that there is a price to pay for neglecting the gifted and talented, and that it is also unethical and inequitable to 'leave them to their own devices'. Second, teachers must plan in advance how they are going to provide appropriately for the advanced abilities of this group. Arguably, the worst that happens for the gifted and talented comes from ad hoc, spur of the moment responses to the quick and accurate task completion rates, typical of more able students. This situation often results in teachers reaching for additional activities which, when examined critically, often constitute 'more of the same', with little increased challenge. This 'busy work' is often aimed at keeping the gifted and talented occupied until the other students catch up.

2   *Recognition of prior learning*   Although this principle would seem an obvious consideration in planning to meet the needs of gifted and talented students, the fact that many educational provisions for this group are less than thoroughly planned means that prior learning is often not taken into account. One can only speculate how often gifted and talented students are required to undertake activities that they have already achieved a high level of mastery in, sometimes years previously. Leta Hollingworth (1926) estimated that without attention to appropriately differentiating the curriculum, children with IQs above 140 waste about half their time in school classrooms, and children with IQs in advance of 170 spend most of their time in 'bizarre and wasteful' activities.

An important element of this practice is not only determining areas of strength, it is also about determining areas of weakness. Many gifted and talented students have areas where they need support because they lack some essential skills or understandings. Often their exceptional abilities in other areas can mask this need, and only focused formative assessment will reveal these.

The idea of ascertaining prior knowledge is often equated by teachers with testing, and conjures up images of pre-testing in every subject for every topic. Certainly, assessment of prior knowledge has to be an ongoing and focused activity, but there are multiple ways this can be accomplished. It may involve testing, but it could also be based on teacher observation, anecdotal records, portfolios of work, interest inventories, quizzes, informal interviews, etc. Those who have a high level of understanding will differ from one subject to another, and even from one topic to another. The teacher in the inclusive classroom can be extremely responsive to changing group profiles. In addition, every student in the inclusive classroom can be provided with the opportunity to demonstrate advanced ability and understanding in a specific topic, and then access activities at a higher level in that area.

3   *Qualitative and quantitative differentiation*   Here, qualitative differentiation refers to enrichment and quantitative differentiation to acceleration. According to Townsend (2004), 'Acceleration occurs when children are exposed to new content at an earlier age than other children or when they cover the same content in less time' (p. 290) and, 'Enrichment occurs whenever children are engaged in additional activities or more demanding activities than their classmates' (p. 291). Simply stated, acceleration is about 'pace' and enrichment is about 'depth and breadth'. As Townsend rightly points out, these two approaches, often presented in the literature as in competition with each other, should be seen as a 'union' not a 'choice'. In practice, many classrooms seem to emphasise one at the expense of the other. There can be a reluctance to expose students to content in advance of what is perceived as the relevant curriculum for their class level, for fear of encroaching on the material 'belonging' to the next level. This often results in an overemphasis on depth and breadth, which in reality can mean an overdose of more of the same. With advanced placement, students are introduced to work earlier, but frequently the pace of their learning remains the same at the higher class level, and there may be little attention to enrichment.

Differentiation for the gifted and talented should focus on three key areas: content, process and products. The content needs to be more abstract, integrated, advanced in complexity and sophistication, and inclusive of moral and ethical issues. The processes need to allow for independent inquiry, 'real' research of 'real' problems, higher order and creative thinking, and opportunities for students to reflect on their own learning. The products should allow for self-selection, be designed for and shared with an appropriate audience, and transform these students from consumers of knowledge to producers of knowledge.

4   *Real challenge*   It is widely claimed that gifted and talented students experience a high degree of boredom at school, primarily due to an unstimulating curriculum. Moltzen (2005) found that when gifted and talented students

were moved from mixed ability to high ability classes, some, after a short period of initial enthusiasm, complained about the change and requested a return to their former class. One of the main reasons these students found the new class unpleasant was the discomfort they experienced with increased expectations and challenge. It was clear that some of these students had been operating well within their 'comfort zones' and this sudden change of culture unsettled them. There is little doubt that in many inclusive classrooms, the level of expectation and demand placed on gifted and talented students is well below their capabilities. Unfortunately, while some students will protest this mismatch, occasionally in quite dramatic ways, others are content to simply 'cruise'. It is important that regular class teachers recognise their inability to adequately challenge some gifted and talented students in some areas and seek outside assistance to achieve this. This may mean exceptionally able students, for some of their school day, spend time outside the regular classroom. However, the key consideration is that the special programme or provision develops from and is linked to the inclusive classroom programme.

5   *Opportunities to develop persistence and perseverance*   This is an aspect of gifted and talented programmes that seems to attract little attention, yet almost every study of gifted adults gives primacy to these traits. Researchers from Galton (1869) to Bloom (1985) have demonstrated that motivation, persistence, perseverance and hard work characterise extraordinary achievers. Cox (1926) concluded that 'high but not the highest intelligence, combined with the greatest degree of persistence, will achieve greater eminence than the highest degree of intelligence with somewhat less persistence' (p. 187). This may help explain why some gifted and talented students fail to reach the heights expected of them and why those whose early abilities were more modest surprise many with what they achieve. What is much less clear from any of the studies in the field is first, the source of this tendency to strive, and second, how it might be encouraged and developed. A number of studies (e.g. Goertzel and Goertzel 1962; Streznewski 1999) report that outstanding achievers tend to be raised in homes where at least one parent exhibits high levels of drive. These parents not only espouse hard work, persistence and perseverance as virtues; even more importantly, they model these in their own attitudes and actions. There is also evidence that teachers who model these behaviours have a positive influence on achievement (e.g. Csikszentmilhalyi *et al.* 1993). The development of persistence and perseverance is very much contingent upon exposure to demanding levels of challenge.

6   *The reinforcement of intrinsic motivation*   From a very young age gifted and talented young people tend to be extremely intrinsically motivated. A number of writers see this as a primary trait of these children (e.g. Renzulli 1986; Winner 1996). There is little doubt that spending time with others who are equally 'driven' to learn enhances one's levels of intrinsic motivation. In

environments where there is a heavy emphasis on extrinsic rewards, levels of intrinsic motivation can diminish (Amabile 1983). This can be an issue in many inclusive classrooms, where reward and reinforcement are often considered core tactics in the busy teacher's repertoire of management options. However, the aim of teachers should be to develop intrinsic motivation in all children. While this ideal is not something that will occur overnights, strategies such as offering students a chance to be involved in planning, setting goals and deciding on how work will be evaluated, negotiating options, and generally encouraging them to take responsibility for their own learning, are beginning to be developed in inclusive schools. The modelling of a love of learning is also a critical part of the process of encouraging intrinsic motivation. In their study of adult luminaries, Goertzel and Goertzel (1962) reported that 'In almost all the homes there is a love of learning in one or both parents' (p. 272). Bloom (1985) said of the parents of his 120 outstanding achievers that they were, 'hardworking, active people ... [who] wanted to be involved in something, learning about something, working on something, as often as possible' (p. 440). According to Csikszentmilhalyi *et al.* (1993), teachers who model a love of learning can make an important contribution to the development of talent in young people.

7   *Assisting students with feelings of being different*   In the inclusive classroom, gifted and talented students will invariably be in a minority. The potential to feel different, odd, and out of place and out of step with their classmates is certainly greater than in homogeneous classes. Feelings of isolation and loneliness can have a greater impact on children who are more emotionally sensitive, as many gifted and talented children are. Adults play an important role in assisting gifted and talented students to understand how they are different and offering strategies for dealing with the associated pressures. A key aspect to this support is helping the gifted and talented to see their unique abilities, qualities and dispositions as strengths, and to explore with them ways of capitalising on these. Some, like Gardner (1997) and Simonton (1999), suggest that feeling totally comfortable, secure and part of the mainstream of society tends to constrain achievement and creative productivity. Gardner (1997) maintains that those who have been marginalised and who achieve great things have made the most of their differences. They have seen this as a strength and have exploited it.

SOME CAVEATS

There are some conditions attached to advancing inclusion for the gifted and talented. First, it can be said of teaching the gifted and talented in the regular class that 'it is easy to do badly and hard to do well'. To do it well does require effort, and especially for teachers who are at the early stages of differentiating their programmes to more effectively include this group. Gifted and talented students absorb ideas and finish tasks much more rapidly, and often have an insatiable appetite for learning, and to keep abreast of this can be demanding. The real benefit of a schoolwide approach is that teachers can support each other and their combined expertise and experience can be invaluable. Second, it is unlikely that the teacher in the inclusive classroom can provide for all the needs of all his or her gifted and talented students. It may be possible and appropriate to bring extra support into this environment but it may also mean some students have to move to work in another environment with other students for some subjects or topics. The case being made here is for the inclusive classroom as the primary setting for the gifted and talented, not the only setting. As noted above, this context will invariably be inadequate in providing opportunities for the gifted and talented to have contact with like-minded peers.

CONCLUSION

This title of this chapter posed the question, 'Can inclusion work for the gifted and talented?' In the considered view of this writer, with extensive experience as a teacher, principal, researcher and director of numerous teacher professional development projects, it *can* work, and can work very well. Evidence to support this claim can be found in thousands of classrooms around the world. Not only *can* inclusion work well for the gifted and talented, it *has to* work well for this group, because this is where most of them are located now and will continue to be in the future. Unfortunately, in many 'inclusive' classrooms, possibly the majority, the gifted and talented remain largely excluded. In the absence of a depth of understanding of the nature and needs of the gifted and talented, many of the teachers of these classes probably consider that these students *are* included. The key to changing this situation is knowledge. This should start when teachers are in training and any courses offered in inclusion or inclusive education must include the gifted and talented. There also needs to be a commitment to in-service professional development that is schoolwide, in-depth, and ongoing. At the school level, the professional development must be owned by the staff but also enjoy the active support of senior management.

The communities most people live in today are characterised by much greater diversity than at any time in the past. Until quite recently, initiatives that supported diversity were regarded with suspicion and sometimes even thought to be divisive. We are now much more aware of the potential of diversity to enrich our lives. The truly inclusive classroom is an environment where diversity is affirmed and accommodated, and where individuality is encouraged. It is a place where the gifted and talented feel a sense of belonging just as much as any other group. The challenge this holds for teachers should not be minimised and every effort should be made to support their efforts towards this end. Only with this support can inclusion work for the gifted and talented.

References

Altrichter, H., Posch, P. and Somekh, B. (1993) *Teachers Investigate their own Work: An Introduction to the Methods of Action Research*. New York: Routledge.

Amabile, T. M. (1983) *The Social Psychology of Creativity*. New York: Springer-Verlag.

Andrews, J. and Lupart, J. L. (2000) *The Inclusive Classroom: Educating Exceptional Children* (2nd edn). Scarborough, ON: Nelson.

Beane, J. (1997) *Curriculum Integration. Designing the Core of Democratic Education*. New York: Teachers College Press, Columbia University.

Bevan-Brown, J. (2004) 'Gifted and talented Maori learners'. In D. McAlpine and R. Moltzen (eds), *Gifted and Talented: New Zealand Perspectives* (2nd edn, pp. 171–97). Palmerston North, NZ: Kanuka Grove Press.

Biddle, B., Good, T. and Goodson, I. (eds) (1997). *International Handbook of Teachers and Teaching*, Vol. 2. Dordrecht: Kluwer Academic Publishers.

Bloom, B. S. (ed.) (1985) *Developing Talent in Young People*. New York: Ballantine.

Cox, C. (1926) *Genetic Studies of Genius: Volume II. The Early Mental Traits of Three-hundred Geniuses*. Stanford, CA: Stanford University Press.

Cox, J., Daniel, N. and Boston, B. (1985) *Educating Able Learners: Programs and Promising Practices*. Austin, TX: University of Texas Press.

Csikszentmilhalyi, M., Rathunde, K. and Whalen, S. (1993) *Talented Teenagers: The Roots of Success and Failure*. New York: Cambridge University Press.

Dettmer, P. and Landrum, M. (1998) *Staff Development: The Key to Effective Gifted Education Programs*. Waco, TX: Prufrock Press.

Elkins, J. (2002) 'The school context'. In A. Ashman and J. Elkins (eds) *Educating Children with Diverse Abilities*. Frenchs Forest, NSW: Prentice Hall, pp. 73–113.

Galton, F. (1869) *Hereditary Genius: An Inquiry into its Laws and Consequences*. London: Macmillan.

Gardner, H. (1997). *Extraordinary Minds: Portraits of Exceptional Individuals and an Examination of our Extraordinariness*. New York: Basic Books.

Goertzel, V. and Goertzel, M. G. (1962) *Cradles of Eminence*. Boston: Little, Brown.

Hollingworth, L. S. (1926). *Gifted Children: Their Nature and Nurture*. New York: Macmillan.

Ministry of Education (2004) *Sharpening the Focus*. Wellington, NZ: Ministry of Education.

Mitchell, D. (1999) *Creating Inclusive Schools*. Hamilton, NZ: University of Waikato.

Moltzen, R. (2004) 'Underachievement'. In D. McAlpine and R. Moltzen (eds) *Gifted and Talented: New Zealand Perspectives* (2nd edn). Palmerston North, NZ: Kanuka Grove Press, pp. 371–400.

Moltzen, R. (2005) 'Students with special abilities'. In D. Fraser, R. Moltzen and K. Ryba (eds) *Educating Learners with Special Needs in Aotearoa/New Zealand* (2nd edn). Palmerston North, NZ: Dunmore Press, pp. 333–76.

Neilson, W. (2005) 'Disability: attitudes, history and discourses'. In D. Fraser, R. Moltzen and K. Ryba (eds) *Educating Learners with Special Needs in Aotearoa/New Zealand* (2nd edn). Palmerston North, NZ: Dunmore Press, pp. 9–21.

Oakes, J. (1985) *Keeping Track*. New Haven, CT: Yale University Press.

Renzulli, J. S. (1986) 'The three-ring conception of giftedness: A developmental model for creative productivity'. In R. J. Sternberg and J. E. Davidson (eds) *Conceptions of Giftedness*. New York: Cambridge University Press, pp. 51–92.

Roberts, J. L. and Roberts, R. A. (1986) 'Differentiating inservice through teacher concerns about education for the gifted'. *Gifted Child Quarterly*, 30, pp. 107–9.

Sapon-Shevin, M. (1994) *Playing Favorites: Gifted Education and the Disruption of Community*. Albany, NY: State University of New York Press.

Simonton, D. K. (1999). *The Origins of Genius: Darwinian Perspectives on Creativity*. New York: Oxford University Press.

Strang, P. (2001) 'Balancing act: Catering for the gifted and talented in the regular classroom'. Unpublished Masters thesis. University of Waikato, Hamilton, NZ.

Streznewski, M. K. (1999) *Gifted Grownups: The Mixed Blessing of Extraordinary Potential*. New York: John Wiley & Sons.

Townsend, M. (2004) 'Acceleration and enrichment: A union rather than a choice'. In D. McAlpine and R. Moltzen (eds) *Gifted and Talented: New Zealand Perspectives* (2nd edn). Palmerston North, NZ: Kanuka Grove Press, pp. 289–308.

Van Tassel-Baska, J. (2003) 'What matters in curriculum for gifted learners: Reflections on theory, research and practice'. In N. Colangelo and G. A. Davis (eds) *Handbook of Gifted Education* (3rd edn). Boston: Allyn & Bacon, pp. 174–83.

Winner, E. (1996) *Gifted Children. Myths and Realities*. New York: Basic Books.

Chapter 4

The early years setting – an inclusive framework

Margaret J. Sutherland

Young children and their learning are at the heart of early years education. Understanding the child in terms of how they learn and their abilities is key to providing challenging opportunities for all. By their very nature early years settings are places where young children are encouraged to explore and grow in their understanding of the world around them. The child-centred, play-based approach to learning and teaching allows children to explore and develop ways of learning. Katz (1992) suggests that we need to develop 'learning dispositions' in all young children. These, she argues, are what should be uppermost in the early years educator's mind when planning learning opportunities. It is the development of these dispositions that will support learners as they engage with school-based activities in later life. Carr (2001) identified five learning dispositions for development with young children.

1   Being interested.
2   Being an active participator.
3   Persisting in the face of difficulty.
4   Interconnecting with those around.
5   Assuming ownership and accountability.

If we accept that we want learners to become active participants in the learning process, then it is the discovery and development of the other four dispositions that will allow this to become a reality.

THE EARLY YEARS SETTING

The introduction of documentation such as *A Curriculum Framework for Children 3 to 5* (SCCC 1999) in Scotland and the distinct *Foundation Stage* (DfES 2000) in England points to the recognition of the importance of good quality early education experiences and suggests they are crucial elements in the raising attainment agenda. In relation to children who are gifted and talented they offer opportunities for the educator to plan appropriately challenging activities in an inclusive setting.

Of fundamental importance in the early years setting is the central place of play. Far from being a frivolous pastime, play is essential to young children's development. When a three-year-old begins to engage independently in formal school-related activities such as maths and reading the temptation within the early years setting can be to focus on these abilities through formal learning opportunities. In other words we start three-year-olds on a formal 'reading book'. While we should not stop the child reading, we have to ensure that the reading experience incorporates all aspects of reading and not simply the decoding of text. Moyles (1989) points out that young children do much of their learning while playing and so to concentrate on formal activities with young gifted and talented learners may be denying them vital opportunities for learning. If we are truly trying to develop the dispositions outlined by Carr (2001) then young gifted and talented learners, like all learners, need to engage in play that allows them to experiment, be spontaneous and be in control of their own learning. Indeed they need to engage in meta-cognition – 'learning how to learn' or 'thinking about thinking'. Young children have to be involved in thinking processes which include planning the approach they will take towards a given task, scrutinising understanding during the task, and assessing how well they have completed the set task. Thus meta-cognition aids the development of successful learners.

Young gifted and talented learners may have different interests to their age peers but they need the opportunity to explore these interests in the same ways as other young children. These opportunities will enhance the learning of gifted and talented young children and, irrefutably, the learning of all young children.

The early years setting offers wonderful opportunities for the discovery and development of gifts and talents. The child-centred features of the early years, combined with the focus on the development of learning dispositions, will ensure that learning is embedded in meaningful contexts, thus leading to challenge and opportunities for all. It was widely accepted that there were 'critical periods for learning', in other words times when the brain was susceptible to learning certain things, and if this critical period was missed, then it was hard to catch up. There was a suggestion that it was 'learn it now or not at all'. Hall's (2005) study of the contribution of brain science to teaching and learning suggests that neuroscientists now consider there are certain types of learning that are subject to 'sensitive periods'. While they acknowledge that there are 'times when the brain appears to be particularly primed for certain types of input and ready to adapt itself to meet such demand' (Hall 2005: 16), they argue that 'sensitive periods' are not a case of 'learn now or not at all'. Thus early years education is highly significant but not the only 'sensitive period' in children's development.

IDENTITY AND YOUNG GIFTED AND TALENTED LEARNERS

Young children spend much of their time working out who they are and how they fit into the world. It is thought that young children don't really understand the concept of intelligence. If a young child 'fails' at a task it does not automatically lead to unconstructive feelings about herself and her abilities, as it seems to do in older children. Dweck (1999) proffers the view that while young children are not really interested in intelligence (this, she contends, develops as they become older), they are interested in ideas about 'goodness' and 'badness'. This can be seen in the early years setting and in life generally as young children scrutinise the world around them and often take issue with the rules and possibilities that are set before them. Family members, peers and adults in the early years setting will react and interact with young children thus helping the young child to begin to build up a picture of herself. Dweck makes a case that vulnerable young children 'feel they are bad when they encounter failure or criticism. And – just like older children with intelligence – they think that badness is a stable trait' (Dweck 1999: 97). When this happens, young children may well grow up presuming that mistakes and failure are 'bad'. It will therefore make them feel 'bad'. This in turn is likely to result in them spending much of their time avoiding situations where they may make mistakes. This is not advantageous if, as it seems, mistakes are a fundamental to the learning process. Consequently when these ideas of 'goodness' and 'badness' or 'failure' and 'success' are transferred into school and academic life it is perhaps predictable that we find children who are frantically trying to show you how clever or smart they are. They need you to know 'I'm not stupid'.

From an early age learners start to evaluate their own abilities and so build up a 'personal theory' relating to intelligence. McLean (2003) suggests that children use three sources of information as they build up this theory. He suggests they do it through:

1   comparison with others
2   the feedback from significant others, and
3   interactions within their own particular context.

The early years educator, as a significant other, can influence the context children find themselves in and so the early years setting offers adults a plethora of opportunities for potentially influencing how children view themselves and their abilities. It would appear that it should be possible, through provision and feedback, to impact on young children's views about learning and their views about themselves. Porter (2005) offers a word of caution. While we know much about school-age children in relation to self-image we have to be careful if we extrapolate the findings to young children as 'these children have received very little research focus' (Porter 2005: 66). However, she goes on to argue that 'people need to feel in command of themselves' (Porter 2005: 91). If we were to support young learners it would seem that we have to take cognisance of the development of identity and the contribution educators make to this through positive and carefully constructed learning experiences.

IDENTIFYING GIFTED AND TALENTED LEARNERS IN THE EARLY YEARS SETTING

If we are to cater for the needs of the young gifted and talented learner then we have to have some idea of whom we are talking about. The term 'gifted and talented' can often evoke images of a child with freckles and glasses. They are sometimes referred to as 'the little professor'. However, this kind of stereotyping, while common, is not helpful if we're considering the education of young gifted and talented children within an inclusive education framework, indeed this stereotyping is not helpful whatsoever. Perhaps of prime concern is the fact that subscribing to these orthodox views of who the gifted and talented are will go on to shape and influence what adults do with young children in their care. Identifying young gifted and talented learners is a complex and controversial business. Is it the child who is articulate and confident and reads well for their age? Is it the child who is 'mature' and vivacious and whose charismatic approach to life is evident? Is it the child who comes from a long line of 'bright' siblings? Is it the child who demonstrates a good general knowledge accompanied by well-developed fine and gross motor skills? Perhaps. Equally, it might be the child who is quiet and withdrawn and struggles with words. Conceivably it is the child whose fine and gross motor skills are poorly developed. It might be the child who presents as dishevelled and unappealing or the child for whom English is an additional language. It is perhaps this diversity that makes identification so difficult and the early years setting the ideal place to begin.

Tannenbaum (1992) proffers the view that 'despite a fast-growing stockpile of research on giftedness in children … little attention has been directed to the gifted among infants, toddlers, and preschoolers' (Tannenbaum 1992: 27). George (1997) argues that there is only the 'potential for giftedness' in young children and that in order for this to be developed an 'optimum environment' must be provided. Similarly, Tannenbaum (1992) states that 'what does emanate from the present available research documentation is knowledge about what constitutes an optimal environment for learning in the first years of life' (p. 27). Gross (1993) also supports the view that the search for exceptional ability in preschool children is, by its very nature, 'a search for potential' (p. 82). She goes on to argue that 'the precocious development of speech, movement and reading are extremely powerful indicators of possible giftedness' (p. 83). Gross does, however, acknowledge that not every child who displays these particular skills at an early age will go on to be *gifted*.

There is an anxiety on the part of educators and parents that labelling a child as gifted and talented at an early age may lead to them being isolated from their peers. Others (Mares 1991) fear that once labelled, 'hot-housing' may occur, during which time young children may 'switch off' their special talent or ability. Baker (2003) indicates that in a study of top-rated swimmers by Barynna and Vaitsekhovskii (1992), those who started training early spent less time on the national team and tended to retire earlier from their chosen sports career than those who started intensive training at a later stage. However, others (Porter 1999) argue that whilst 'hot-housing promotes adults' ambitions; gifted education seeks to foster the skills and interests of the children themselves' (p. 115). Whilst care must be taken to avoid such scenarios in terms of 'hot-housing' it should not be at the expense of providing appropriate and challenging activities for young children. Concern of this nature can lead to passive inactivity. However, perhaps before launching into identification, educators have to understand and have considered what they believe about intelligence. It is, perhaps, the educators' beliefs about intelligence that will most heavily impact on who is subsequently identified as gifted and talented in the early years setting.

IMPLICIT BELIEFS

As educators we will all have formed implicit beliefs about what it means to be intelligent. These views will have been formed through our personal experiences, reading, study and feedback from significant others. In the UK public perception of intelligence is further influenced by popular television through programmes such as *The Nation's IQ* and *Mastermind* that claim to search for and locate 'intelligent individuals'. While there can be no doubt that the candidates in such programmes 'know a lot of facts', whether this is the same as being intelligent is open to question. Sternberg (2002) believes that this 'conventional' view of 'intelligence (i.e. memory and analytical abilities) represents only part of the story of intelligence' (2002: 202).

Educators often make judgements about children based on such things as:

- looks
- written work
- behaviour
- motivation
- family history, and
- attitude.

These, at best, provide flimsy and inaccurate pictures of the child. Feeding into this view of the child will be the educator's underlying beliefs about intelligence. If we believe, for example, that young children from areas of deprivation are unlikely to be gifted and talented then we will not look for them and, even if we look, we will not expect to find any. In contrast, if we believe they are to be found in our 'leafy suburbs' then we will be on the look-out for them and not be surprised when we find them. Dweck (1999) has considered these 'personal' theories of intelligence. She has spilt them into two broad categories – an entity theory of intelligence and an incremental theory of intelligence. Possessing an entity view of intelligence will mean believing a person possesses a specific amount of intelligence and nothing you or they can do will change that amount. In other words:

- it's fixed
- you've only got so much of it
- there's not much you can do about how much you've got, and
- educators have very little, if any, influence over it.

Embracing an incremental view of intelligence will mean believing that intelligence is not an 'entity' that resides within a person but is something that can be developed through learning. In other words:

- it can change
- you can become more intelligent
- the more you learn the more you are capable of learning, and
- educators can have a significant impact on your intelligence.

Dweck (1999) suggests that teachers who hold entity views of intelligence are more likely to create a setting in which performance goals are encouraged, where the product of learning is considered important and where assessment and feedback encourage pupils to compare their work to others. On the other hand, teachers who hold incremental theories are more likely to create a setting where learning goals are encouraged, where the focus is on the process of learning and where assessment and feedback encourage improvement based on individual progress.

An understanding of intelligence is vitally important for educators as it goes on to shape the way we identify and assess young children. It moulds our attitudes towards these children, particularly in relation to our expectations of them. It would appear that educators' experiences as pupils and their experiences as educators shape their beliefs about learning and pedagogy (Zeichner and Tabachnick 1981) and that not only do experiences create beliefs but these beliefs, once formed, go on to influence future interactions with others. As discussed earlier, the good news is that we can influence young children's views of themselves so they become interested in learning, but how we influence children's views will depend on our own beliefs about intelligence.

To influence children's views about themselves in a positive way educators need to:

- believe that intelligence is not fixed;
- acknowledge genetics plays a part but not 'write children off' because of who their parents are;
- encourage young children to make mistakes and learn from them;
- praise the amount of effort a child puts in to an activity.

(Sutherland 2005: 12)

BUILDING UP A PICTURE: THE EARLY YEARS SETTING

How then can early years educators ensure that they identify and challenge young gifted and talented learners? One of the difficulties is that when we decide to identify, we are in danger of only finding those we want to find or those that appear on some ready-made checklist. Freeman (1998) suggests that identification through provision may in fact be a more helpful way of considering gifted and talented learners. The Scottish Network for Able Pupils (SNAP) explored this idea and developed a cyclical framework for identification (see Figure 4.1).

Smith and Doherty (1998) suggest four points for reflection within a cyclical process. First, we need to agree a definition of what abilities a gifted and talented young child might demonstrate in a particular curricular area. Having agreed what they might be doing and knowing what to look for, we need to consider the provision on offer. Do we actually offer young children the opportunity to demonstrate the desired ability that might suggest they are gifted and talented? Having offered the opportunity, who is demonstrating these abilities? Could we identify children that seemed to meet our agreed definition at the start? Having identified the children we then need to rethink our original definition. Thus the cyclical process begins again. This cyclical approach takes us away from predetermined checklists and skills, and places provision at the core of the identification procedure.

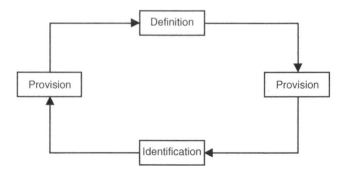

Figure 4.1 The cyclical approach to identification

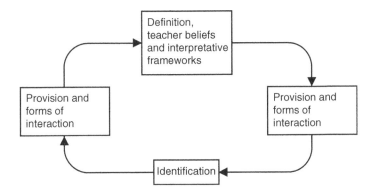

Figure 4.2 Forms of interaction

Further work on this model by Smith and Dakers (2004) saw an additional and perhaps crucial element being added. Having looked at the work of Kennard (1998) in relation to the identification of gifted mathematicians, they suggest that it is not enough to simply reflect on what it means to be gifted. Educators, they argue, also need to think about their own assumptions and beliefs as it is these that will impact on the mediation of the curriculum (see Figure 4.2). In this cyclical process of reflection it now becomes necessary to think not only about activities and resources but also about how these activities and resources will be used with the children. Examination of the interaction the educator has with the children will allow for changes and alterations to be made to both provision and practice. Indeed Smith and Dakers suggest it is 'how teachers organise pupils in their class for learning and how they interact and respond to pupil work [that] becomes crucial' (2004: 11). It will also ensure an inclusive approach to identification so that identification does not rest on some predetermined exclusive list of skills and abilities.

The cyclical nature of the model once again finds us having to re-evaluate our definitions, beliefs and assumptions about gifted children. Smith and Dakers go on to suggest that 'it is only when all these elements converge positively that identification of gifted individuals can occur' (2004: 11).

ASSESSMENT

Inextricably linked to identification is the area of assessment. Staff in the early years setting may draw up a checklist of predetermined skills; children will then undertake tasks that demonstrate proficiency in these skills. These tasks would typically include a range of skills deemed as necessary if success at formal school is to be guaranteed and would include such things as cutting out, colouring carefully and so on. It is likely that these skills will be taught and, for assessment purposes, will be tested. Successful completion of the tasks is taken to indicate that formal school learning is ready to be set in motion and may even be used to predict that the child will be successful as they move through the education system. However, while such skills are important and need to be developed, proficiency in them will not necessarily guarantee school success and it is certainly not an indicator that the child will necessarily be gifted and talented. So if this traditional form of assessment is not helpful in the identification process, how can assessment be used in a way that benefits the learner? Carr (2001) suggests an 'alternative model' of assessment. This model has its roots firmly in the meta-cognitive approach discussed earlier and therefore compliments the ideas of learning dispositions. In line with this alternative model Sutherland (2005: 20) suggests staff should:

- find out what children already know, understand and can do
- discuss with children what the learning goals are for the activity
- discuss with the children what they have done well and what they need to work on, and what they put their progress down to
- allow children to experiment with resources
- look for children who persist with a task, and
- encourage children to express points of view and emotions.

This approach to the gathering of information for assessment purposes is substantially different to the checklist approach described earlier. The learner is placed at the heart of this model and is a major stakeholder in the learning process. Competence in the learning dispositions are much more likely to ensure that the learner will continue to engage in the learning process both formally and informally. It also dovetails well with the cyclical approach outlined in Figures 4.1 and 4.2.

The identification and assessment procedures should help us to build up a holistic picture of the young children in the early years setting. This will help us to gain a broader, all-encompassing view of them and their abilities. The evidence we gather will come from a variety of sources. There are three key contributors to this emerging picture:

1   adults working in the early years setting
2   the parents/guardians of the child, and
3   the child herself.

QUALITY EXPERIENCES FOR YOUNG GIFTED AND TALENTED LEARNERS IN THE EARLY YEARS SETTING

In the UK, learning opportunities offered within the early years setting will be guided by national documentation. The four nations that make up the UK have unique education systems and consequently each has documentation to reflect this. While terminology within each document may differ slightly there are commonalities in terms of the experiences on offer. Not surprisingly, one commonality is the drive for quality educational experiences. However, quality indicators can be hard to define. Different participators will view events in a variety of ways. Children, early years educators, parents, policy makers and society will all have their own agenda when considering issues relating to quality. The European Commission's Childcare Network (ECCN 1990) proposed ten headings which could be used when considering quality: accessibility and usage; environment; learning activities; relationships; parents' views; the community; valuing diversity; assessment of children and outcome measures; cost benefits and ethos (Powney *et al.* 1995: 2–11). The same Network published a further document in 1996 (Quality Targets in Services for Young Children). It states that 'defining quality should be seen as a dynamic and continuous process involving regular review and never reaching a final, "objective" statement' (ECCN 1996: 7). More recently in Scotland, the Standards in Scotland's Schools etc. (2000) Act, the Additional Support for Learning (Scotland) Act (2004) and *Count Us In* (SEED 2003) all recognised the need to ensure that education should be 'directed to the development of the personality, talents and mental and physical abilities of the child to their fullest potential' (Standards in Scotland's Schools, etc (2000) Act, Section 2). There is general agreement that quality early years educational experiences enhance the child's learning and development.

If quality early years educational experiences are an important contribution to a young child's development, it is necessary to consider what early years education is preparing children for, as this will influence the curriculum and activities on offer. Different stakeholders will suggest different answers to this question. Taylor *et al.* (1972) reported that, when asked to rate five possible areas for importance in early years education, teachers ranked them as follows: social, intellectual, home–school, aesthetic, physical. The study found that teachers regarded early years education as preparation for social development as well as intellectual development and the idea that it was preparation for formal schooling was not widely accepted. Clift *et al.* (1980) studied the responses of forty teachers when asked about the purpose of early years education. Their findings corroborate Taylor's findings: social development was the key aim of early years education. Powney *et al.*, in their two-year study into day care and educational provision for children between the ages of two and four, reported that 'many staff viewed the development of social and interpersonal skills, whereby children learn how to learn, as their most important contribution to children's preparation for formal schooling' (1995: 11). Whilst there is agreement that social and interpersonal skills are significant in the process of learning, it is generally agreed that the academic curriculum also has a vital role to play. A study into the role of preschool and preschool teachers in Iceland (Einarsdottir 2003) found that 'preschool teachers are sensing a certain dilemma caused by the changing roles and status of preschools' (p. 114). Tensions between teaching and care-giving were evident and participants in this study felt a need to redefine these two concepts. They also reported that primary schools suggested that 'children were not prepared enough when entering primary school (p. 114). However, the preschool staff were challenging this narrow role that had been assigned by primary schools. Einarsdottir suggests that this challenge coincides with Dahlberg *et al.*'s view of 'childhood institutions which were seen as places for the young child to live in here and now and not seen as places to prepare children for school and learning' (1999: 114). This idea would link well with the view that learning begins long before a child enters an educational institution and will continue long after they leave. During an interview with Loris Malaguzzi, the Director of the Reggio Emilia programme in Italy, it becomes clear that he is against the pressure for early education to prepare young children for school:

> if the school for young children has to be preparatory, and provide continuity with the elementary school, then we as educators are already prisoners of a model that ends up in a funnel […] its purpose is to narrow down what is big into what is small. This choking device is against nature.
>
> (Edwards *et al.* 1993: 86)

If the wider role of the early years curriculum is accepted, then the implications for the identification of young children with abilities must be considered in the light of this. It would also appear that the development of learning dispositions would go some way to address both the social and the academic nature of learning in the early years. This dual approach would capture young children's enthusiasm for learning and propel them towards formal education with the skills and dispositions necessary for full and active participation. If this approach were embraced then it would appear that the best place to challenge gifted and talented learners is the inclusive early years setting.

CONCLUSION

Early years education is but one component of the learning experience of young people. No one constituent part is more significant than the other. Each combines to form a learning matrix for the individual. Within this learning matrix the early years educator must consider the impact their contribution will have, in time, on the others. It is this interface between experiences in the early years, home, formal school and the community that appear ultimately to combine and determine what young children may go on to achieve, do and become.

Whitebread argues that young children are 'accomplished learners, passionate enquirers, loving companions' (2003: 374). If we accept this then it becomes all the more important that we consider the range and quality of experiences and opportunities that we are offering the young children in our care. It is essential that we begin to consider, and perhaps challenge, our attitudes, beliefs and assumptions about ability if we are to ensure opportunity for all. Identifying, acknowledging and challenging the abilities of young gifted and talented learners through the development of learning dispositions will allow staff within the early years setting to begin that journey of learning with the young child. The final destination cannot be predicted. It would seem to me that an inclusive approach to the education of gifted and talented young learners is the only option we have if we want to maximise learning opportunities for all so that the young children in our care become all they can be.

References

Additional Support for Learning (Scotland) Act (2004).

Baker, J. (2003) 'Early specialisation in sport'. *High Ability Studies*, 14 (1), pp. 85–94.

Barynna, I. I. and Vaitsekhovskii, S. M. (1992) 'The aftermath of early sports specialisation for highly qualified swimmers'. *Fitness and Sports Review International*, 27 (4), pp. 132–133.

Carr, M. (2001) *Assessment in Early Childhood Settings*. London: Sage.

Clift, P., Cleave, S. and Griffin, M. (1980) 'The aims, role and deployment of staff in the nursery'. A report of the National Foundation for Educational Research in England and Wales. Windsor, Berks: NFER.

Dahlberg, G., Moss, P. and Pence, A. (1999) *Beyond Quality in Early Childhood Education and Care: Postmodern Perspectives*. London: Falmer Press.

Department for Education and Skills (2000) Foundation Stage.

Dweck, C. (1999) *Self Theories: Their role in Motivation, Personality and Development*. Philadelphia, PA: Psychology Press.

Edwards, C., Gandini, L. and Forman, G. (1993) *The Hundred Languages of Children: The Reggio Emilia Approach to Early Childhood Education*. Norwood, NJ: Alblex Publishing Corporation.

Einarsdottir, J. (2003) 'The role of preschools and preschool teachers: Icelandic preschool educators' discourses'. *Early Years*, 23 (2), pp. 103–16.

European Commission Childcare Network (1996) *Quality Targets in Services for Young Children*. Geneva: ECCN.

Freeman, J. (1998) *Educating the Very Able: Current International Research*. An Ofsted review of research. London: HMSO.

George, D. (1997) *The Challenge of the Able Child* (2nd edn). London: David Fulton.

Gross, M. U. M. (1993) *Exceptionally Gifted Children*. London: Routledge.

Hall, J. (2005) *Neuroscience and Education: A Review of the Contribution of Brain Science to Teaching and Learning*. Glasgow: SCRE.

Katz, L. G. (1992) *What Should Young Children Be Doing?* Urbana, IL: ERIC Clearinghouse on Elementary and Early Childhood Education.

Kennard, R. (1998) 'Providing for mathematically able children in ordinary classrooms'. *Gifted Education International*, 13, pp. 28–35.

McLean, A. (2003) *The Motivated School*. London: Paul Chapman.

Mares, L. (1991) *Young Gifted Children*. Melbourne: Hawker Brownlow Education.

Moyles, J. (1989) *Just Playing? The Role and Status of Play in Early Childhood Education*. Buckingham: Open University Press.

Porter, L. (1999) *Gifted Young Children: A Guide for Teachers and Parents*. Buckingham: Open University Press.

Porter, L. (2005) *Gifted Young Children: A Guide for Teachers and Parents* (2nd edn). Buckingham: Open University Press.

Powney, J., Glissov, P., Hall, S. and Harlen, W. (1995) *We Are Getting Them Ready For Life: Provision for Pre-Fives in Scotland*. Edinburgh: SCRE.

Scottish Consultative Council on the Curriculum (1999) *A Curriculum Framework for Children 3 to 5*. Dundee: SCCC.

Scottish Executive Education Department (2003) *Count Us In*. Edinburgh: HMSO.

Smith, C. M. M. and Doherty, M. (1998) *Identifying Abilities in Individual Curricular Areas*. Glasgow: Scottish Network for Able Pupils.

Smith, C. M. M. and Dakers, J. (2004) 'More able pupils in technology education'. In Dakers, J. and de Vries, M. J. (2003) *Pupils' Attitudes Towards Technology*, conference proceedings from the 13th International Conference on Design and Technology Educational Research, Glasgow, Scotland.

Standards in Scotland's Schools etc. (2000) Act.

Sternberg, R. J. (2002) 'A reflective conversation with Robert J. Sternberg about gifted-ness, gifted education, and intelligence'. *Gifted Education International*, 16 (3), pp. 201–7.

Sutherland, M. (2005) *Gifted and Talented in the Early Years*. London: Paul Chapman.

Tannenbaum, A. J. (1992) 'Early signs of giftedness: research and commentary'. In Klein, P. S. and Tannenbaum, A. J. (eds) *To Be Young and Gifted*. Norwood, NJ: Ablex.

Taylor, P. H., Exon, G. and Holley, B. (1972) *A Study of Nursery Education*. Schools Council Working Paper 41. London: Evans/Methuen Educational.

Whitebread, D. (ed.) (2003) *Teaching and Learning in the Early Years* (2nd edn). London: Routledge Falmer.

Zeichner, K. M. and Tabachnick, B. R. (1981) 'Are the effects of university teacher education "washed out" by school experience?' *Journal of Teacher Education*, 32 (3), pp. 7–11.

Chapter 5

Are we nearly there yet?

Lynne McClure

Different countries provide opportunities for their most able pupils in different ways, or in some cases, not at all. Where such provision does exist it is often separate from mainstream education rather than embedded within it. This chapter is intended to highlight the main stepping stones in the English 'gifted and talented' journey, describe the present status of, and future plans for, the national strategy, and comment on the inherent tensions arising from trying to meet simultaneously the gifted and talented agenda and that of inclusion.

A BRIEF HISTORY OVER TIME

The history of gifted and talented (henceforth G&T) education in England has been a short or a long one depending on which way you look at it and to whom you talk. The change from selective to comprehensive schools in the 1960s and 1970s was based on an equality of opportunity agenda, but discussion actually focussed largely on appropriate provision for the middle and lower sections of the ability spectrum only. When comprehensive schools were introduced nationally, many areas of the country had little idea of how to meet the needs of the most able within a mixed ability context, even though the whole idea of individualisation of teaching and learning was gaining popularity. At this time some local education authorities (LEAs) appointed advisers whose remit included able student provision, and there were the beginnings of initiatives and research projects into defining and providing for gifted children. Local activity tended to be that which provided out-of-school opportunities for exceptionally able pupils, or supported parents and carers of able children who were concerned about the quality and appropriateness of their education. Areas which retained grammar schools were less likely to support such activities as it was assumed that the selective system was a suitable model for teaching the brightest children.

So, prior to the 1990s, there were pockets of practice and research operating in what seemed to be an area of minority interest. When, in 1997, the education of the most able pupils became a national issue, concerned practitioners, academics and parents reacted with delight that a sidelined area of concern was at long last going to become an educational priority. Others, of course, retained a scepticism for any new venture that smacked of elitism.

THE SEEDS OF A NATIONAL STRATEGY

The placing of 'gifted and talented' in the national spotlight took place after various consultations, notably a survey of international provision and research commissioned by Ofsted (the Office for Standards in Education) (Freeman 1998) and a comprehensive consultation to consider current and possible future provision in England, conducted by the House of Commons Education and Employment Committee (1999), and published as *Highly Able Children*. This latter report commented that provision for the highly able was unsatisfactory in the majority of English schools. That strong message gave extra weight to the recently stated government intentions to tackle low attainment and the growing problem of social exclusion, stated in the earlier White Paper, 'Excellence in Schools'. In this way the scene was set for a national strategy for improving able student education.

The vehicle for introducing the strategy was to be Excellence in Cities (EiC), a government-funded initiative that began in 1999 and originally comprised seven mutually supportive components, one of which was the 'gifted and talented' strand. Four areas of the country were identified for the pilot project: a group of central London education authorities and areas around the three conurbations in the Midlands, Manchester and Sheffield. Twenty-five LEAs and 438 secondary schools were involved. In each subsequent year, more areas and schools were to be brought under the 'excellence' umbrella.

The Standards Unit of the DfES (or DfEE as it was then known) was the responsible governmental body. It set up the local management of EiC, which was different to the LEA organisation, sometimes within it and sometimes in parallel, and was usually managed by a steering group consisting of head teachers, strand coordinators and, occasionally, members of the school improvement team. The G&T strand received money, a varying proportion of which was held centrally whilst the rest was devolved to schools in accordance with the steering group wishes. There were specific items for which the money could be used, one of which was to fund the time of a senior member of staff in each school to be a G&T coordinator. Other money was to be used for actions or resources which contributed to in- or out-of-class provision for able pupils. In return for the money, schools were asked to nominate a cohort of G&T pupils and to monitor their progress over time as they benefited from the distinct teaching and learning programme which the school was expected to develop, and which included out-of-hours study support.

Of course in many areas the whole G&T phenomenon was quite new and few local advisers or teachers had any previous experience. And so, in common with the Learning Mentor strand of EiC, the newly appointed coordinators of the G&T strand were to have a distinct training programme. In line with the government Green Paper (DfES 2001) the course for coordinators was to be accredited at a level which supported and encouraged reflective thought and was seen to be the vehicle through which the national strategy was to be both imparted and delivered.

INTENTIONS AND PRINCIPLES

The express intention of the Excellence in Cities initiative was 'To drive up standards in schools in major cities higher and faster to match the standards of excellence found in our best schools' (DfEE 1999). This single statement indicated that the main intention of EiC was school improvement, and all seven strands were expected to contribute towards this aim. Within the holistic aim of EiC, the five principles specific to the G&T strand were as follows:

1   *The development that would make the most difference in the education of the highly able is a change in attitude among teachers and LEAs, but perhaps even more importantly among the public and society at large.* The aim challenged the widely held opinions that a) able pupils would get along fine by themselves and didn't need any exceptional provision (or even possibly not as much as others) and b) that high ability or outstanding skill in a particular field was acceptable on condition that the individual exhibiting such ability was modest about it – summed up by the phrase 'too clever by half'. The intention was to celebrate success and high achievement by making it 'cool to be bright', and to minimise the 'tall poppy' syndrome where exceptional ability was not allowed to be conspicuous.

2   *The emphasis must be on improving provision in mainstream schooling. Most children are educated in maintained primary and secondary schools and it is therefore in mainstream schools that the principal effort should be directed.* This aim was an overt indication that the government's intention was to make G&T an inclusive strategy. Pupils identified as gifted would not be selected to attend particular institutions but would have their needs met in their existing schools.

3   *Although many recognised approaches exist, there is no single 'best way' to meet all these children's needs.* This principle recognised that all schools are different, as are all children, and therefore schools were to be encouraged to be inventive in the ways in which they planned and delivered learning opportunities. The use of the word 'needs' implied that in addition, there might be other aspects of pupils' education to consider, such as social and emotional.

4   *Highly able children must be allowed to enjoy their childhood.* Interestingly this principle does not state that able children should enjoy their school experience, but their childhood. It was taken to mean a) that school provision should be appropriate, meaningful and non-stressful, and b) that whereas out-of-school activities have their place, they should not fill the time of highly able pupils with so much organised activity that they do not have time to relax.

5   *There is already good practice in a range of areas. It is not our role to re-invent the wheel. Our intention is to draw attention to some of the good practice that is currently going on and suggest ways in which it might be spread further.* Within EiC, local schools were organised into clusters – a structure intended to support collaboration and cooperation, and sharing of good practice. The Standards Unit also set up an open website and instigated regular national conferences to which coordinators were invited to contribute. So the principles on which the G&T strand was predicated were intended to support inclusion and embed gifted and talented provision within ordinary schools. The rest of this chapter looks, against the background of these five principles, at where and how intention and practice were related, sometimes leading to positive outcomes and at other times to tension.

CHANGING ATTITUDES

'They will get on anyway; let's put our effort into the ones who need it.'

Coordinators were invited to consider such possibly controversial statements as one of the first activities in their national training programme (WIE 2000 onwards). Hard-pressed teachers trying to meet the inclusion agenda for those at the lower end of the ability continuum had sympathy with the viewpoint. In a context where resources, especially time and additional help, were limited, many felt that spending them on pupils who were already succeeding well could not be justified. Of course the counter-argument of equal opportunities found favour too – that able children are just as entitled to an appropriate education as any other child. But even as late as 2004 Ofsted, evaluating the primary extension of EiC, indicated that

A small number of schools believed that the gifted and talented strand of the programme was not conducive to promoting equal opportunities. Such schools diluted the allocated resources by spending them on generic enrichment activities rather than on raising the attainment of higher-attaining and underachieving pupils.

(Ofsted 2004: 3)

'We don't have any gifted children in our school.'

Even though the House of Commons Education and Employment Committee report used the term 'highly able', the words chosen for the national strategy were 'gifted' and 'talented'. These words have several different meanings in international literature, and certainly were problematic to the teachers who had to reconcile their own everyday use of the terms with the specific EiC definitions:

> 'gifted' learners are those who have abilities in one or more subjects in the statutory school curriculum other than art and design, music and PE;
> 'talented' learners are those who have abilities in art and design, music, PE, or performing arts such as dance and drama.
>
> (DfES 2005)

To get round this, some LEAs and individual schools chose to use the phrases 'highly able' and 'more able' in their policies and planning. Although, on the whole, the terminology has ceased to be such a major issue, there are still eminent thinkers who regard the pedagogic language as unhelpful:

> High achievers have the right to be stretched just as much as anyone else. But if we're not careful, the language of G and T can lead us astray.
>
> (Claxton 2005: 2)

Even if the language question has receded, each new institution joining EiC still struggles with the other part of the EiC definition, which requires each school to define and identify a 'top' 5 to 10 per cent, no matter what the catchment of the school or ability range of the children. The cohort is expected to be representative of the population for the school as a whole in terms of ethnicity, gender, socioeconomic background, etc. and to include a ratio of gifted to talented pupils of about 2:1. This statistical model leads to a relative definition. However, guidance from DfES (2000) provides criteria for identifying ability in different curriculum areas, which leads to an absolute definition. The mix of statistical and criteria-based models has confused coordinators and teachers alike – they were reluctant to label the most able in their class as G&T as, in their opinion, they were often far from meeting the curriculum-specific criteria. Gradually though, schools developed their own unique ways of meeting the DfES prescriptive policy whilst retaining their professional dignity.

But there were other issues too that did not initially help schools and the community as a whole to develop a positive attitude towards the G&T initiative. The focus of G&T was explicitly on ability rather than achievement or attainment, so underachieving pupils were a priority. Teachers initially found identifying such pupils difficult – the very nature of underachievement is that there is little formal evidence to support its identification – and so coordinators and teachers relied on numerical national test data to identify overt rather than latent ability. But the G&T strategy placed the issue of underachievement centre stage and coordinators had to find methods to identify such pupils. Over time they became more practised in using a range of identification strategies including such tests as CATs and MIDYIS (Middle Years Information System), many of which were in place before but had not been used effectively for the top end of the ability range.

Since the nature of ability changes over time, it was likely that the composition of the cohort would too, and children might be added into, or dropped from, the register in successive years. Many schools were uncomfortable about communicating this to parents, a requirement under EiC guidelines. The issue was exacerbated during the transition from school to school, each having different constituencies and therefore different cohorts. Some children found that they were gifted in July and not in the following September.

ABLE CHILDREN IN ORDINARY SCHOOLS

In some cases these issues provided an excuse for the G&T agenda to be perceived as irrelevant, the opposite to the intention. The EiC definition was supposed to ensure that *all* 'ordinary' schools took G&T on board, and, by making specific requirements about the composition of the cohort, that no school could focus solely on academic excellence, or sporting prowess, or ignore groups of children; for example, those for whom English was an additional language. Thus the model was one that included abilities in many different domains, and children from all backgrounds. All schools had a duty to provide for their G&T pupils, and G&T pupils' needs could be met in ordinary schools.

Again though, the message was mixed. Schools were expected to provide a 'distinct and discernibly different' teaching and learning programme for these children. Whilst the inclusion agenda as applied to special needs education led to schools being expected to *reduce* the distinction between a particular group and the rest of the school population, with G&T the expectation was that there would be a distinction which was enhanced. The required out-of-school provision such as study support, master classes and summer schools suggested that all G&T provision could not take place within the mainstream school. Schools with budgets that had to be spent quickly thus spent much of their G&T money on visits and excursions and other exclusive out-of-school provision, rather than in supporting in-class teaching and learning. At the same time charities such as the Ogden Trust were making money available to support exceptional state school pupils who wished to attend independent selective schools, and the government was planning a national academy (NAGTY) to cater exclusively for the top 5 per cent nationally.

CUTTING THE CLOTH TO FIT THE CHILD

> Research shows that the very able are not a homogenous group whether in terms of learning style, creativity, speed of development, personality or social behaviour.
>
> (Freeman 1998: 1–2)

Did the introduction of the G&T initiative encourage the diversity of provision implicit in Freeman's quotation and specified in the third G&T principle? To what extent did the G&T agenda reinforce that of inclusion? The statutory inclusion statement within the National Curriculum documentation states that:

> Schools have a responsibility to ensure a broad and balanced curriculum ... that meets the specific needs of individuals and groups of pupils.
>
> (National Curriculum Online 2005)

and so one could say that, if schools were fulfilling their roles adequately, there would be no need for an initiative aimed specifically at G&T pupils, as they would already be provided with appropriate learning opportunities. However, perhaps one way to answer the question is to consider the three principles for inclusion and how well EiC schools met them for the most able.

The first principle is 'setting suitable learning challenges'. Many G&T books refer to challenge in the classroom as the key, not only to maintaining and improving provision for already achieving pupils, but also to spotting under-achievement. Joan Freeman (1998) refers to the 'sports model' cycle for identifying ability, in which provision both precedes and follows identification – it is only by raising the height of the bar that we can find out how high a child can jump. In other words, it is impossible to identify ability unless the opportunities to exhibit it are provided.

In 2003 the Ofsted evaluation of Excellence in Cities and Education Action Zones stated that: 'The critical issue for most schools is how to affect ordinary classroom practice. Schools need to embed strategies for developing gifted and talented pupils more firmly in the mainstream curriculum' (Ofsted 2003). Since there was no shortage of government and other guidance on providing challenge for G&T pupils in the classroom, we need to examine why it wasn't always being done.

The guidance was usually a variation on the five strategies below:

- broadening the curriculum
- deepening the curriculum
- accelerating through the curriculum
- introducing more independent activity
- facilitating reflection.

(DfES 2000)

Teachers with high levels of subject knowledge have always broadened the curriculum by drawing formally or informally on topics outside the statutory programme of study, or making links between and across different curriculum areas. To make this an effective strategy for increasing challenge for able pupils required preparation time and teacher expertise. Subject specialist staff in secondary schools found this easier to do than teachers in primary schools who taught the whole range of curriculum subjects. Often this type of enrichment took place outside the classroom in after-school clubs, visits or summer schools where it was well received by the pupils but was seen as something separate from regular classroom activity.

Whilst EiC was developing, the topic of thinking skills was also gaining popularity through Carol McGuinness's paper (1999) which compared and contrasted various thinking skills programmes. The phrase 'higher order thinking skills' (HOTS), borrowed from Bloom's taxonomy (Bloom *et al.* 1964), became popular and Bloom's work was commonly used as a framework for deepening the curriculum. All pupils needed to acquire knowledge skills and understanding (Bloom's lower-order levels of knowledge, comprehension, application) but able pupils especially were deemed to benefit from opportunities to synthesise, analyse and evaluate. Again teacher expertise was crucial and whilst subject specialists in secondary and primary schools could offer such challenges without too much preparation, G&T coordinators, expected to support less confident colleagues in planning the teaching and learning programme across a range of subjects, found this challenging.

In the paper 'Acceleration or enrichment?', the United Kingdom Mathematics Trust (UKMT 2003) strongly suggested that accelerating able pupils through the mathematics curriculum was inappropriate for all but a minority of extremely able pupils. The paper suggested that acceleration (doing the same work as everyone else but in a shorter time) should not be entertained lightly and should only be used when pupils were at the stage where they had absolute mastery of their subject, where there was planned continuation and progression, and where pupils had the social and emotional maturity to cope either with working alone, or with older pupils. Successful early entry for GCSE and the number of level 5s (and previously 6s) in SATs have been used by government as an indication of rising standards and so schools have been torn (and still are) between teaching surface, content knowledge, and teaching for deeper understanding. Some schools, however, have taken an independent stance:

> The gifted and talented initiative is divisive and, at this stage in my career, I don't feel threatened by league tables and targets. I am concentrating on the whole child.
>
> (Ofsted in G and T Update 2005: 1)

Bates *et al.* (2003) argue that the emphasis on league tables and targets has led not only to an emphasis on teaching the content but a lack of risk-taking in the classroom, often 'at the expense of actively involving learners in their own learning and raising the awareness of transferable skills' (Bates *et al.* 2003: 2). Shore's research (in Bates *et al.* 2003) indicates that able pupils are capable of reflecting on and monitoring their own thinking processes in increasingly sophisticated ways but, from their action research project, Barrow *et al.* concluded that many of their able pupils 'had not developed the traditional skills in language expression that the school culture expects for demonstrating exceptional thinking and learning ability' (in Bates *et al.* 2003: 2) and therefore were unable to work independently to good effect. In classes where 'independent' learning was interpreted as solitary work on a project, the opportunities to refine linguistic skills were limited. The national strategies (Numeracy and Literacy strategies, later superseded by the Primary Strategy, and the KS3 strategy) had already increased the expectation that pupils would reflect on their work during the plenary session within each lesson. Teachers often found this difficult to manage because of time constraints (DfES 2003) and this was no different for teachers of able pupils.

Coordinators undertaking the national training programme remarked that they had to work hard to help their colleagues understand that increasing challenge in the ways above was intended to replace some of the more tedious work that able pupils had been ploughing through. Teachers' comments were that the curriculum was already over-full and they did not have time to get through the existing scheme of work, let alone entertain additional content.

Back to the principles of inclusion – the second of which is 'responding to pupils' diverse learning needs', in particular by:

- creating effective learning environments
- securing motivation and concentration
- providing equality of opportunity through teaching approaches
- using appropriate assessment approaches
- setting targets for learning.

> 'I used to feel ashamed if I did well in anything because if I told anyone, they'd yell round the class "Oh my God! She got 98 per cent! She's like a total boff!"'
>
> (Eyre 2005)

Perhaps the most effective environment for able pupils is one in which they are free to express themselves without ridicule or prejudice such as this. The G&T strategy heightened awareness that anti-bullying policies, and a school ethos where all pupils' contributions were valued, applied to those at the top end of the continuum as well as those with special needs.

Just as EiC reinforced the thinking skills agenda, it also spawned additional materials and professional development opportunities through which teachers were encouraged to attend to their visual, auditory or kinaesthetic learners, together with the principles of 'accelerated learning', and 'brain-based' techniques for teaching. All of these were in an effort to meet individual pupils' learning needs but were of course not aimed solely at able pupils, although they were frequently advertised as such. More importantly, the G&T guidance helped teachers to work towards offering a range of teaching approaches which took account of pupils' individual strengths and weaknesses. An important part of this for G&T pupils was the emphasis on setting individual targets which acknowledged and built upon previous learning. Some schools devised individual education plans (IEPs) for all those on their G&T register, whilst others reserved them for pupils with dual exceptionalities, such as those able pupils who were also visually or hearing impaired or for whom English was an additional language. Teachers also became more aware that in order to identify their underachieving pupils they had to find ways of assessing ability without disenfranchising students who were, for example, dyslexic but highly able mathematicians, or dyslexic but exceptionally talented at creative writing. There was always the possibility that, as Eyre and Fitzpatrick suggest, the disability may be given more attention than the ability, and expectations of what the child will achieve are reduced (Eyre and Fitzpatrick 2000).

The third principle of inclusion is closely linked to the second – overcoming potential barriers to learning and assessment for individuals and groups of pupils. The Learning Mentor strand of EiC was intended to be one of the vehicles for this and was most effective where the mentors and G&T coordinators worked together to support G&T pupils who were disaffected, or had little parental support. In schools where the two strands existed independently, provision was bound to be less effective.

So schools responded differently to the whole inclusion/G&T issue. I have indicated above instances where the strategy failed to make much of an impression and suggested reasons. But where it had the greatest impact schools took up the challenge and tried new strategies, often within an action research structure. They reported that G&T had invigorated their teaching not only for the most able but across the ability range.

> The findings have allowed the researchers' schools to confidently amend their curriculum and to engage in meaningful professional development centred on children's learning. Most importantly, the research was motivating, fun and authentic for both the teachers and the learners.
>
> (Bates *et al.* 2003)

SCHOOL DAYS ARE THE HAPPIEST DAYS...

In primary schools children are usually taught by one class teacher and the full range of children's abilities, attitudes and activities are known by that one person.

In secondary schools, where a student might work with as many as a dozen different teachers in the course of a week, it is easy for problems over conflicting interests or activities to arise. Many G&T pupils are good all-rounders, likely to be in the school sports teams and orchestra and perhaps to be taking extra classes out of school in an additional language or advanced study in maths or science. One of the roles of the G&T coordinator is to be a 'champion' of G&T pupils and to keep a weather eye out for potential difficulties over conflicting interests or excessive demands on the student.

But equally important is the part the G&T coordinator has in ensuring that the students' emotional and social needs are met, as well as their intellectual or educational ones. Hymer (with Michel 2002) states that truly inclusive G&T provision regards the learner not only as a cognitive processor but as a 'whole person – including cognitive, social, emotional, and physical domains, calling on the experiential, reflective and emotional intelligences' and that rather than 'focussing on the acquisition of content knowledge, emphasises the longer term qualities and dispositions of learning-to-learn'. In schools that were already highly achieving, the G&T initiative provided the 'excuse' to focus on the wider meaning of education:

> I am the head of a highly achieving primary school with excellent results. As a school community we feel strongly that we need to remind ourselves that we are teaching children, not subjects, and that we want our children to emerge from school well-rounded, having developed a love of learning. We are very confident that we meet the needs of children who are highly able in the core subjects but we are keen to improve how we identify and provide for the able children in the other curriculum areas and, more importantly, in school life in general by providing opportunities for leadership, creativity, independent learning and lateral thinking.
>
> (More Able in South Tyneside 2003: 5)

In other areas and over a period of time, whole LEAs have developed a more inclusive definition of gifted and talented. The Barrowise project uses the following:

> a gifted or talented student is one who has a) experienced a degree of facilitated self-reflection on his or her pattern of learning strengths and preferences, and b) identified his or her area(s) of greatest strength(s) within the framework of an enriched learning environment. Strengths would include gifts and talents as identified by the DfES EiC strand and also less easily measurable 'soft' skills and qualities such as interpersonal and intrapersonal skills and other elements crucial to thinking for learning, such as resilience, analysis, wise judgement and discernment, intuition and imagination.
>
> (Hymer, in Bore 2003: 33)

A PROBLEM SHARED...

> All schools have identified a teacher to co-ordinate the work of gifted and talented pupils .On the whole, where the responsible teacher had under-taken the five-day national training course, provision was much more structured and sure-footed.
>
> (Ofsted 2003)

The training programme had a pivotal role in disseminating information and good practice. From a standing start with little or no expertise, areas of the country became G&T strongholds. But there were problems in the initial stages largely because of the unrealistic timescale and lack of planning. Many G&T coordinators found themselves enrolled on a course about which they knew little, and were expected to undertake their role in school without a time allocation (because timetables had already been devised) and allocate their budgets without having time to decide how to use them best. Despite this, local partnerships within clusters evolved and joint initiatives were set up. In an atmosphere where competition between schools had been the watchword, collaboration developed.

On a wider scale, many LEAs set up their own websites which linked to those devised by central government or its agencies, such as Xcalibre – a cross-curricular information site, and the high-ability forum. The government's own site was gradually populated with examples of good practice from Beacon and Specialist schools and others and, in the twice-yearly standing conferences, interested parties came together to discuss successful case studies and future plans. Critics would notice, however, that there was much discussion of good practice but little stringent research to provide evidence that the 'good practice' was having a noticeable effect.

THE SCORE SO FAR

In fact, in his most recent report, David Bell, HM Chief Inspector for Schools, commented that although there is evidence to suggest that the weakest schools have made impressive gains, good schools have got better too, and there has been 'slow progress in reducing the gap in achievement between schools with high and low disadvantage' (HM Chief Inspector of Schools Annual Report 2003). Since the primary aim of EiC was 'to drive up standards in schools in major cities higher and faster to match the standards of excellence found in our best schools', it would appear that, thus far, the aim has not been achieved.

Of course it all depends on how standards are measured. We have rehearsed above the tension between short-term targets to do with faster attainment and added value on the one hand and longer-term targets to do with the quality and depth of learning on the other. Effective pedagogical change is less to do with whether a school is operating within an agreed national policy and more to do with whether the change is sustained and affects the way and to what extent children learn. I would suggest that despite problems with organisational issues, identifying cohorts, budgetary wrangles and the ever-present tension between acceleration and enrichment, the G&T initiative is having an increasingly positive effect on the way teachers think about the teaching and learning taking place in their classrooms and, in the wider context, is beginning to impact on national attitudes towards our most able pupils. Dracup (2004) describes G&T as a 'testbed for universal provision' in that it has enabled teachers to be innovative practitioners and creative thinkers. Laudable future plans to further this include 'making space and time for deep learning and teacher enquiry, and systematising knowledge about learning and teaching gleaned from research on school improvement' – although it is not quite clear yet how exactly this is to be done. What is clear is that in addition the G&T initiative has facilitated some cutting-edge work such as the ground-breaking World Class Tests and Arena, Xcalibre, the G&T arm of the London Challenge and, of course, that of the National Academy for Gifted and Talented Youth.

RETURNING TO THE CONTEXT: COMPETING STRATEGIES NOW AND IN THE FUTURE

As I write, the buzz word in English education is 'personalised learning'. This presumably is the epitome of inclusion and it is interesting to see that many of the phrases within the official documentation echo those of the G&T initiative. Personalised learning will mean:

* *Designing teaching, curricula and school organisation to address the needs of the individual student.* The G&T agenda encompassed all of these and in fact stated that: 'An effective G&T policy will almost certainly require significant changes in the organisation, curriculum and perhaps culture of the school. As a rule of thumb, if the G&T policy is not having this degree of impact, it is probably not working'. (DfES 2005).
* *A learning offer to all children that extends beyond the school context into the local community and beyond i.e. wrap-around schooling.* The G&T guidance suggested that effective provision would be a mixture of in-school and out-of-school activities.
* *An approach to teaching and learning that focuses on an individual's potential and learning skills.* The G&T strategy emphasised building on pupils' prior experiences.

Since there seems to be a large overlap between the two, does this mean that in the near future G&T will be subsumed into a new pedagogy for teaching and learning? The New Relationship with Schools will be totally in place in 2008 and this means that it is likely that many of the traditional levers, such as earmarked funding, will be removed from the G&T strategy. Many fear that the G&T strategy is not yet safely embedded and once the distinctiveness of it disappears, schools will return to the pre-EiC status quo. On the other hand Dracup (2004) suggests that whilst it is true that G&T will be integrated into each of the three national strategies (5–11, 11–14, 14–19) and will not be a distinct and separate strand, there are still plenty of opportunities for G&T to maintain a high profile. The development of G&T quality standards, already being trialled, will emphasise school self-evaluation. Targeted support will continue, in inverse proportion to success, and especially for those schools with relatively poor inspection results. And finally, money will still be available for innovative approaches which may potentially have a wider application than the G&T community.

IN CONCLUSION

> Bright, able, clever, gifted, talented students – whatever we call them – come in all shapes and sizes. There is no such thing as a stereotypical 'gifted child'. More importantly they are simply young people who deserve the same care, support and consideration as any other youngsters.
>
> (Bore 2003: 5)

So – are we nearly there yet? My own opinion is that the kick-start of a national strategy has ensured a great deal of progress in many ordinary schools. However, the changes are not yet secure or embedded in all schools, and have barely had an impact in others. A shift in government policy and funding in order to meet the goals of yet more new initiatives could well jeopardise the future of G&T provision as teachers are forced to concentrate their efforts elsewhere. Are we nearly there yet? Well, we're closer than we were!

References

Bates *et al.* (2003) 'Using teacher-led research as a development tool to challenge preconceived notions about the teaching of gifted and talented students'. Paper given at BERA Annual Conference, Edinburgh.

Bloom, B. J., Krathowhl, D. R. and Masia, B. B. (1964) *Taxonomy of Educational Objectives: The Classification of Educational Goals.* New York: Longman.

Bore, K. (2003) 'A matter of definition'. *Curriculum Briefing,* 1 (2), London: Optimus.

Claxton, G. (2005) Gifted and Talented Update, 21, London Optimus.

DfEE (1999) *Excellence in Cities. London:* DfEE.

DfES (2000) 'Guidance on teaching gifted and talented pupils'. Online advice at http://www.nc.ac.uk (accessed May 2005).

DfES (2001) *Learning and Teaching: A Strategy for Professional Development.* London: DfES.

DfES (2003) *Excellence and Enjoyment – A Strategy for Primary Schools.* London: HMSO.

DfES (2005) http://www.standards.dfes.gov.uk/giftedandtalented.guidanceandtraining/ (accessed May 2005).

Dracup, T. (2004) 'New directions in English gifted and talented education'. Paper presented at European Council for High Ability conference, Pamplona, Spain.

Eyre, D. (2005) 'Reach for the stars'. *Daily Telegraph*, May.

Eyre, D. and Fitzpatrick, M. (2000) 'Able children with additional special needs'. In Benton and O'Brien (eds) *Special Needs and the Beginning Teacher*. London: Continuum.

Freeman, J. (1998) *Educating the Very Able: Current International Research*. London: HMSO.

Her Majesty's Chief Inspector of Schools (2003/4) Annual Report. Available online at http://www.ofsted.gov.uk (accessed May 2005).

House of Commons Education and Select Committee (1999) *Highly Able Children*. London: HMSO.

Hymer, B. and Michel, D. (2002) *Gifted and Talented Learners – Creating a Policy for Inclusion*. London: David Fulton.

McGuinness, C. (1999) 'From thinking skills to thinking classrooms: a review and evaluation of approaches for developing pupils' thinking'. Research Report RR115. London: DfEE.

More Able in South Tyneside (2003) South Tyneside Council.

National Curriculum Online (2005) http://www.nc.uk.net/inclusion.html (accessed May 2005).

Ofsted (2003) *Excellence in Cities and Education Action Zones*. Available online at http://www.ofsted.gov.uk.

Ofsted (2004) *Excellence in Cities: The Primary Extension*. London: HMSO.

Ofsted (2005) In G and T Update, 21. London: Optimus.

UKMT (2003) 'Acceleration or enrichment?' Birmingham: UK Mathematics Trust.

Westminster Institute of Education (WIE) (2000) National Gifted and Talented Coordinator Training Programme, Oxford.

Part II

Can selective interventions be inclusive?

Chapter 6

Submerged talent in inner cities

Inclusion by intervention

Ron Casey and Valsa Koshy

This chapter focuses on aspects of inclusion for gifted and talented pupils in inner-city areas. With supporting evidence obtained from a four-year study, from 1999 to 2003, sponsored by local education authorities and schools, we argue that there is submerged talent in our inner-city schools, and special strategies for identification and specifically designed intervention programmes may be necessary for unlocking the potential of students in these areas. As we suggested in an earlier publication (Casey and Koshy 2002), we believe that potential talents of children from relatively deprived urban areas may be submerged but not eradicated by their circumstances. In order to realise their potential and include them in gifted and talented programmes, two particular aspects need to be addressed: the way we identify gifted and talented pupils and the nature of provision offered to them.

BACKGROUND

Studies carried out by the authors, as part of the work of Brunel University's Able Children's Education Centre with students from inner-city schools during 1996–9, highlighted that many of the students from urban areas were achieving far below their potential. Many of them lacked confidence and were unaware of their abilities and talents, although they demonstrated a high degree of competence in tasks involving problem-solving and other practical activities. The issue of underachievement amongst urban students has been highlighted in the last decade by various agencies. For example, Ofsted (2003: 1) refer to the evidence from their report in 1993, Access and Achievement in Urban Education: 'drawing attention to the disturbing fact that, while standards were rising in the nation's schools, the gap between the average performance and that of pupils in areas of social disadvantage was growing wider'. They maintain that deprivation and disadvantage were closely associated with poor standards, low aspirations and social isolation. The issue of underachievement in England was addressed by the new Labour government in 1999 (DfEE 1999) within the Excellence in Cities initiative, which included a gifted and talented strand specially designed to target provision for able pupils in inner-city areas and improve their achievement. The first six local education authorities (LEAs) which were provided with generous and targeted funding to support gifted and talented pupils were amongst the most deprived areas in inner cities according to Local Index of Deprivation (Department of the Environment, Transport and the Regions 1998). The Excellence in Cities (EiC) initiative has since been extended to 51 LEAs. Its main aim is to raise both the achievement and aspirations of gifted and talented students in urban areas. All schools within the EiC areas are required to identify the top 10 per cent of their brightest pupils to form a gifted and talented cohort and schools are expected to provide special support for these students. Around the same time, another initiative – widening participation of students from relatively deprived areas in universities – was also announced by the government. A major part of the provision for gifted and talented pupils in secondary schools is in the form of enrichment programmes and two- or three-week summer schools run by local authorities or universities.

The problem of underachievement amongst bright students from disadvantaged areas is not just a challenge within the UK. Van Tassel-Baska (1998) highlighted that one of the most neglected populations among the gifted in the United States of America is the gifted disadvantaged. She raises two issues with reference to this particular problem: first is the difficulty in identifying these students as they are often overlooked for special programmes and second, even when they are placed in special intervention programmes, little attention is given to the background socioeconomic factors that may seriously affect their performance and their future achievement.

National developments in England such as Excellence in Cities and Widening Participation provided the backcloth to the launch of our Urban Scholars project, designed to provide strategies for an intervention programme for identified gifted and talented students from areas of social deprivation. The purpose of the four-year programme was to explore the level of the students' achievement and the nature of their attitudes and aspirations, as well as implementing an intervention programme aimed at raising their academic achievement and aspirations. The ultimate purpose of the project was to address the challenge of inclusion of gifted and talented students from disadvantaged backgrounds, so that their life chances may be improved. We hope that the findings of our study, reported in this chapter, will add to the knowledge base on educational inclusion of gifted and talented students. It is our wish that our findings will both influence education policy for inclusion and provide practitioners with some guidance in their efforts to make effective provision for other gifted and talented pupils.

THE URBAN SCHOLARS PROJECT

The Urban Scholars project was set up in May 1999, just before the government initiatives Excellence in Cities and Widening Participation were announced, although these initiatives provided an impetus and context for our study. Forty students were recruited, from schools in two urban areas of London, for the programme. It could be said that we used an 'opportunity sample' (Brown and Dowling 1999) for this project in that we were approached by two LEAs to provide an intervention programme for their higher ability students who were to be identified by their teachers. All 40 students were in Year 8 (aged twelve to thirteen) of their secondary schools. Most of the students were drawn from families with no history of university education and a high percentage of the children were on free school meals, which is an indicator of their poorer financial status. The students were to stay on the programme for four years, following an intervention programme designed on the basis of the ongoing gathering of evidence of what we perceived to be their needs. The intention was that the students stayed within their schools, but were to be provided with an intervention programme which was to be designed and delivered by the university project team. Each year, students were required to attend sessions on nine to ten Saturdays, approximately once a month, and a summer school on the university campus. They would follow a programme which would be designed in response to the perceived needs of the students from the ongoing gathering of data. We were particularly interested in exploring the following questions.

- How were gifted and talented pupils being identified by their schools?
- What was the nature of their ability?
- How did the students perceive their ability?
- What were their attitudes and aspirations?
- What elements would need to be included in an intervention programme?
- Would the intervention programme have any impact on the students' achievement, attitudes and aspirations?

SELECTING CASE STUDY AS A METHODOLOGY

We adopted a case study approach for our investigation as we felt comfortable with the concept of the power of example (Flyvbjerg 2002) for what we were hoping to achieve and disseminate. The intention was not to seek generalisations from our single study, but to highlight aspects which we believe should be applicable to others who are also implementing government policy and striving for the inclusion of gifted and talented students. We believed that our study would act as a documentary rather than provide a set of generalised statements.

The case study methodology was selected as the preferred strategy as it resonated with some of the reasons stated by Yin (2003) for using case studies within research. For example, within our study we were posing questions of 'how' and 'when'. We also needed to be open-minded about the outcomes and also bear in mind that the focus of our study was a contemporary phenomenon within a real context. We were studying the complex topic of provision for gifted and talented students in urban areas. Our intention was to capture and disseminate a real picture through rich descriptions. The unit of analysis for the study was a group of students from schools in relatively deprived urban areas, who had been identified for membership of the gifted and talented groups within their particular schools. As issues of inclusion of gifted and talented students in programmes for effective provision have not been the subject of much previous research in the UK (Smith 2003), our hope is that our findings will make a contribution to a much neglected concept.

GATHERING AND ANALYSIS OF DATA

We will provide only a very brief summary of the range of the methods used to gather data. School coordinators were invited to explain how they identified the cohort of students for the Urban Scholars programme. They were also asked to provide the most recent national test (Key Stage 2) results for their students. Pre-project questionnaires asked students why they thought they had been selected as gifted and talented, and whether they thought they had any special abilities or talents. They were asked to comment on what they thought they would do when they left school and what they believed they needed to do to achieve their aspirations. A small number of students were interviewed to explore the above questions in greater depth and their responses were tape-recorded. The authors and other tutors who were involved in the project kept field diaries and records of significant incidents through observation throughout the four years. Additionally, comments were invited from their schools about any possible changes of attitude or achievement during the students' period of participation in the intervention programme. Students were encouraged to complete written evaluations and accounts of their perceptions of the programme twice yearly. The range of data collected enabled the project team to design an intervention programme which would match the students' learning and affective needs.

Data analysis consisted of studying responses to the questionnaires and noting emerging patterns from interviews, field notes, correspondence from parents, schools and student evaluations.

FINDINGS

During the four years of the project a great deal of data was collected and analysed. In the following sections we present some of our findings which are directly relevant to aspects of inclusion. We are aware that one of the limitations of the study is that it only involved a small number of students providing evidence on which to draw our conclusions. We also acknowledge that we had not used a control group for this study, so any claims we make need to be considered in that context. However, we believe that the issues we raise would be pertinent to those who are concerned with the raising of achievement and aspirations of urban pupils. Our findings are presented and discussed under two main headings: issues relating to the identification of students for gifted and talented programmes, and the design of an intervention programme.

ISSUES RELATING TO IDENTIFICATION

Some students who were selected for the intervention programme had performed well in their national and school tests; their nominations were straightforward. But in many cases, teachers found it difficult to select pupils whose test performances had been average, or even below average, to be included in the gifted and talented programme. The use of terminology – the term gifted to describe their students – created tensions amongst many.

The use of terminology

During conversation Sharon, a form tutor in one school who had the responsibility for nominating students for the Urban Scholars programme, expressed her concern as follows:

> I feel I wish to include the students we believe have 'got it', if you know what I mean, but I feel uncomfortable in labelling them as gifted. Some of the students I wish to nominate have either average or, in some cases, below average test results. Yet I have this gut feeling that they are bright and have not really had many opportunities to demonstrate their potential ability.

Although a small number of educational programmes for the gifted and talented have been in existence for many decades in the UK, there has been no precipitation of a universal acceptance of the semantics of the terminology. The range of social, economic and political perspectives may possibly ensure that a unified definition could never materialise. In a national survey carried out by the authors (Thomas *et al.* 1996), it was found that a significant number of British teachers were reluctant to use the word gifted to describe their brightest pupils. They preferred to use bright or able to refer to children who demonstrated higher ability. Other teachers also shared their tensions about the use of the word gifted to refer to potentially very able pupils.

Labelling of children

There were also difficulties with the concept of labelling children, following the government requirement in England to identify 5 to 10 per cent of the school population as gifted and talented. Amanda, a teacher of Year 8 pupils, articulated her concern:

'I am reluctant to make a list of gifted and talented children and give it to the gifted and talented coordinator and publish it to the parents, because that seems so final and fixed. I cannot make that kind of decision, which may affect some children's perceptions of themselves and may affect their whole future. The percentage divide makes it even more difficult. How do you select 5 – 10 per cent as gifted as if the concept is uniform in all the schools in this local education authority? A comment from one my students made me feel particularly uncomfortable. Darren asked me why he was not being included in the gifted and talented group. He said he was puzzled because he was in the gifted and talented group in his previous school. He wanted to know whether one could be de-gifted after a while.'

The identification of a cohort of children, consisting of 5 to 10 per cent of each annual intake into a school, and referring to them as gifted and talented seems to have posed the greatest challenge, nationally, to teachers. It is interesting to note that in their evaluation of the gifted and talented strand of the Excellence in Cities programme, Ofsted (2001) described identification issues as presenting the most concern for schools and Eyre (2001: 1) maintains that although the gifted and talented programme has enjoyed a good deal of success in raising awareness of the need for enhanced curriculum provision, 'the creation of the cohort has been the most problematic part of the policy'.

For some teachers who worked with us, nominating gifted and talented pupils based on their national and local test results was straightforward, but other teachers felt that there were many students who had potential talent which had not always been translated into high achievement. They wanted to include such students in the intervention programme and sought the guidance from the university which is presented below.

Guidance for identification

Our experience of working with urban students, especially those from relatively poor backgrounds, has suggested that they may not always do well in traditional tests due to a variety of reasons (Koshy and Casey 2003). Alternate methods of assessment are necessary. Our suggestions of guidance for the identification of students whose talent may be submerged due to special circumstances included the following.

- Use multiple sources of data for identification.
- The use of problem-solving is often an effective method of identification of potential talent. In a previous study (Casey and Koshy 2002) we found that students from a relatively deprived area of London outperformed students from a high-achieving school in world-class problem-solving tests, offered for gifted pupils by the Qualifications and Curriculum Authority (http://www.worldclassarena.org).

- Observing pupils working on a cognitively challenging project over a period of time can illuminate potential talent which may not always be revealed in tests. Observing students working in groups with other highly able children may provide indicators of potential. Theoretical support for this comes from Vygotsky's (1978) zone of proximal development, which suggests that test scores may only indicate students' ability to do well within the tested area of development, whereas working with peers and adults may demonstrate what the child's real potential is.

- The power of teacher observation was illustrated for us by a teacher citing the example of an instance of identification of one student – Jack – who regularly failed to complete his work in class and yet was found to have set up a homework business in his school, which involved him selling photocopies of completed homework to his peers. The exceptionally high quality of his work led to him being identified for one of our programmes.

- We also encouraged teachers to follow their *gut feelings* about students' potential, on the basis of our previous experience of teachers' instinctive judgments often proving to be right.

Conceptualising giftedness and talents as developing expertise

Support for flexibility in identification being vital for the inclusion of submerged talent is provided in recent literature from Sternberg (2000: 55) who supports the concept of giftedness as *developing* rather than *developed* expertise. He maintains that giftedness or expertise is not an *end-state*, but a process of continual development; this would suggest that it is not too late for students with unfulfilled potential to be included in programmes for the gifted and talented. Further support for the developing nature of giftedness and a case for the inclusion of students who may not demonstrate academic achievement at a particular time in their life comes from Clarke, who challenges the concept of the genetically inherited, immutable view of intelligence and maintains that it is no longer valid. Based on brain function research, she declares:

> Intelligence must be considered dynamic just as the growth of the functions of the brain is dynamic with higher levels of intelligence actualised only when appropriate challenge is provided.
>
> Clarke (2001: 5)

Of course, other theories of giftedness (Renzulli 1986; Gardner 1983 and 1993; Sternberg 1986) suggest the need for greater sensitivity and flexibility in selecting gifted and talented children from inner-city schools. One of the models which departs from viewing giftedness on the basis of test results alone was proposed by Renzulli (1986) through his three-ring model. The author asserts that no single criterion can be used to determine giftedness and that the interaction of three interlocking rings – *above average ability*, *task commitment* and *creativity* – is a necessary ingredient for creative productiveness. He also makes the distinction between *schoolhouse giftedness,* which can be tested, as opposed to *creative productive giftedness.* In any attempt to define giftedness there must be the assumption that we must provide specialised learning experiences to promote the talent. Our Urban Scholars programme took account of Renzulli's assertion. Further, we also took note of research on human intelligence carried out at Yale University by Sternberg who questions the validity of considering test scores and examination performance as a way to assess giftedness. In his Triarchic Theory of Intelligence, Sternberg (1986) identifies three types of gifted individuals. One type who may excel in academic situations is described as *test smart* and may be little more; another is gifted and particularly adept in *dealing with novelty* and excelling in a synthetic and creative sense; and a third type of gifted person may be *street smart* in external context but at a loss in academic contexts. If we were to achieve the inclusion of submerged talent we had to stress the importance of greater fluidity in the identification process. Further support for a flexible and fluid system of identification is expressed by Gruber (1986), and Csikszentmihalyi and Robinson (1986), who also maintain that talent is not a fixed state, but is an unfolding phenomenon throughout the life span. Giftedness at one point in a person's development can be very different from the giftedness at another point in the same person's development.

DESIGN OF AN INTERVENTION PROGRAMME

For the development and design of an intervention programme we drew on three sources: our previous experience of working with able pupils from urban areas of deprivation, the analysis of emerging data from the Urban Scholars programme and recommendations from authoritative sources on talent development. The underlying principle on which the programme was designed was the promotion of inclusion for the urban scholars through raising their achievement and aspirations. Before presenting the nature of the intervention programme, it may be useful to consider research-based advice offered to us by various authors on desirable features of programmes for gifted students from disadvantaged backgrounds. Frasier (1979) warns us not to assume that children from disadvantaged backgrounds are deprived of love or stimulation, or have a deficit in thought processes. In our programme we did find this to be true. In all cases parents cared for the students deeply and were willing to travel several miles, changing many buses, to bring the students to the university. Many of the parents – about 90 per cent – had not had the opportunity to join higher education and consequently did not know how to go about getting their children into universities and following professions they had not considered prior to their involvement in the Urban Scholars programme. Our own aim was to try and break the cycle of the new generation of children missing out on life chances due to the lack of opportunities of their parents. Van Tassel-Baska (1998) quotes Clasen's advice that ideal pro-grammes for these students should allow for cultural differences in materials, curriculum and, when possible, personnel. We also took note of Fraser's advice that programmes should address the whole child, including the development of basic building blocks for future life performance such as problem-solving, decision-making, seeking assistance, discriminating relevant from irrelevant information, and developing self-direction and control. Such programmes should involve parents in the educational process and provide them with the knowledge, skills and attitudes necessary to nurture their talented children. As many of the students on our Urban Scholars programme were from relatively disadvantaged areas of London, it did make sense to take note of the above guidance.

Van Tassel-Baska's (1998) list of research findings on successful intervention for students from deprived areas was also incorporated into the programme plan-ning. This includes:

- early and systematic response to the needs of these children
- parental involvement in the education programme model
- use of experiential and hands-on learning approaches
- use of activities that enhance self-expression
- use of mentors and role models
- involvement of the community, and
- counselling efforts that address the issue of cultural values in facilitating tal-ent development.

In the following section we present some of the components of the intervention programme, their rationale and the impact as judged by the project team and based on evidence.

Development of basic skills

From the beginning of the programme it emerged that many of the urban scholars lacked the basic skills of arithmetic, grammar and writing. Some reasons for this were suggested by teachers from the schools where the scholars had been nomi-nated. For example, one particular school had had seven changes of mathematics teacher in one term, which could have affected the learning experiences of the students. Other factors – such as lack of motivation, boredom resulting from repetitive work, poor attendance and lack of support at home – were also listed. A catching-up programme planned as sessions in mathematics and English received negative responses from the scholars, who expressed resentment at studying school subjects on Saturdays. Therefore, any such strategies had to be planned as investigations and through real-life projects. It was significant that most students grasped basic skills very quickly, confirming our belief that these students were capable and fast learners. The fact that there was a serious lack of knowledge and basic skills has serious implications in the context of the Widening Participation initiative, widening the participation of students from disadvantaged areas in universities. Based on our findings the targeted students may not obtain the satisfactory grades that prepare them to follow A-level programmes which precede university entrance. Some early remediation may be necessary for inclusion.

Raising motivation

Encouraging students to attend regularly and follow the programme was a challenge for the project team during the initial stages. It took a considerable time – in some cases up to a year – before many of the scholars felt settled into the programme. Initial reactions such as 'It is unfair to have to work on Saturday' and 'I am only here for the lunch' were common. Systematic efforts were made to enhance their motivation. Prizes and rewards – for example, CD and gift vouchers for best efforts and attendance and good reports from schools about improved attitudes and performance – played a significant role in changing many students' attitude to the classes. Students also responded positively to entering competitions and social events. We feel that this feature of the Urban Scholars programme may also have implications for those who organise short programmes designed to encourage students to raise their aspirations and encourage them to move on to higher education. It was significant that five students discontinued the programme during the first year and only one in the subsequent three years (and that was due to moving house).

Development of critical thinking

Students were provided with a course in critical thinking, which was designed to encourage them to think critically, analyse, reason and derive informed conclusions and decisions. It was included in the programme because of its role in contributing to a democratic society (Ennis 1996). The training received was intended to permeate students' thinking in other areas of the curriculum (OCR 2000) as well as real-life situations. As they progressed through the course, there was evidence of students developing confidence in putting forward arguments, developing a questioning attitude and anticipating other people's points of view. The critical thinking sessions were listed as one of the most useful and enjoyable components in the programme. Students' analytical and debating skills were praised by a barrister who attended their presentation of a mock murder trial. Another interesting development was the students abandoning their celebrity aspirations, which were articulated in pre-interview questionnaires, for more realistic ones.

Problem-solving skills

Problem-solving situations were offered both in mathematics and in other areas of the curriculum. The aim was to provide opportunities to produce conjectures, seek relationships between elements within a situation and generate the production of valid solutions. Students were also given opportunities to develop their own algorithms and solve problems without excessive reliance on taught procedures. One area which received very useful response from the students was problem-based learning where groups of students worked on 'real-world' topics, which were also related to school subjects. These sessions proved useful in terms of students appreciating that there are many pathways through a problem and guiding them towards the need for seeking or generating new knowledge. A strong message that came through was the importance of team work in solving problems and the role of cooperation for success.

Development of creativity

The programme responded to the creative attributes of the students which were apparent from the start. The street-smart intelligence displayed by the students supported them in their creative explorations. Subscribing to the view that creativity is not innate or fixed and that it can be developed (Sternberg 2000), students were offered plenty of opportunities for enhancing their creative productivity. The result was an obvious display of playfulness when faced with a challenge, the willingness to take risks and the acceptance that making mistakes and being stuck are honourable states to be in.

Outside speakers

Outside speakers from wide-ranging backgrounds were invited to share their experiences with the Urban Scholars. Some indicators of people's achievements after overcoming difficulties of financial status, language and class problems were highlighted by some speakers. A 'singing doctor' – as the scholars named her because she had to rely on singing in pubs to complete a medical course after losing her parents – and a lawyer who came to England without a fluent knowledge of the English language were amongst those who made an impact on the students. Such visitors encouraged scholars to follow their example and helped to sustain scholars' interest after three years. The outside speakers generally served as good role models who had aspired and achieved in spite of disadvantage and adverse circumstances.

Enrichment projects

From the start of the programme, we had noticed that the Urban Scholars were not used to focused, in-depth work over a period of time. This shortcoming was addressed by asking them to select a topic of personal interest and work on it for an extended period for presentation to an audience, sometimes including an expert from that particular field. As a model for organising our enrichment projects we adopted Renzulli's enrichment triad (1994) which recommends the development of students' early interests and passions through extended projects as a means of talent development. Students were given training in methodologies and were brought into contact with experts in the field to acquire a taste of the authentic experiences of a professional. Each student carried out an extended research project, which provided him or her with research and presentation skills.

Outside support

One area of external support for gifted pupils was through mentors. Special interest mentors were drawn from outside, many of whom gave up much time supporting and scaffolding pupils' special interests and aspirations. The role of adults within the context of the actualisation of talent has been endorsed by Bloom (1985). As talents and interests are quite individual, we sought the support of an expert or someone who was willing to provide support in developing that talent. Csikszentmihalyi (1996) also emphasises the importance of support outside the school in encouraging creative productivity in talented pupils and points out that intrinsic motivation and a passion for pursuing an activity are central to talent development.

Career education

Two aspects which emerged from the questionnaires and interviews at the start of the Urban Scholars programme were: students' lack of awareness of their own abilities and a lack of aspirations to select professional careers which require university education. These findings led us to include discussions on career choices and university education in the programme from the start and these featured throughout the programme. Perrone highlights the need for career education:

> Gifted children from economically disadvantaged backgrounds require early intervention to reduce the limiting effects of a lower social class background and to raise their typically lower levels of career expectations.
>
> (Perrone 1991: 326)

Support for early career advice is also given by Dunham and Russo (1983) who contend that all programmes for disadvantaged gifted children should be integrated with career education so that students can see how education is relevant to the world of work. During the four years of our programme, we organised lectures and workshops on career choices, the preparation of CVs and an early look at UCCA form statements. Workshops for parents about career choices and higher education revealed that many had not thought about these issues. As Olszewski-Kubilius and Scott (1992) point out, middle-class parents begin early to convey expectations to their children that they will attend college. We found that many of our students had no such messages of high expectations, although many of them were capable of joining universities and following successful careers.

A REFLECTION ON OUTCOMES

Our narrative of a four-year trial has given us insights not to be gleaned from books. The multiple facets of our programme and its participants have not enabled us to generate a blueprint for an Urban Scholars programme, but have sketched an outline map. The landmarks are identifiable and a new cohort of Urban Scholars who began their programme in 2004 should provide us with more guidance towards its structure. The teenagers are not homogeneous, though they do share many attributes reflective of an inner-city environment. The parents, though of low income, have shown love of their children in abundance. Inclusion, in a socioeconomic sense, has not been one of life's blessings. The adage that parents want for their children what was denied to them was echoed with gratifying frequency. Membership in gifted and talented cohorts and the transformation of outlook inspired by visiting speakers have injected a sense of inclusion within the education system. Only time will tell whether a greater degree of social inclusion will be enjoyed by Urban Scholars in future years.

CONCLUSION

Procedural difficulties in the formation of gifted and talented cohorts recall the centuries-old conflict between quantitative and qualitative methodologies for assessment and description. Experience indicates it is expedient to view membership of such cohorts in terms of belonging to a multidimensional category. Each dimension corresponds to a specific talent. Improvement of performance along several dimensions – such as mathematics and problem-solving – has been found by our programme. Submerged talent has emerged and received some sustenance. We earnestly hope that social closure will become a diminishing phenomenon as submerged talent emerges along many dimensions during formal education, so that its momentum will sustain it towards inclusion in adult life.

References

Bloom, B. (1985) *Developing Talent in Young People*. New York: Ballentine.

Brown, A. and Dowling, P. (1999) *Doing Research: Reading Research*. London: Falmer.

Casey, R. and Koshy, V. (2002) 'Submerged talent and world-class recognition'. *Assessing Gifted and Talented Children*. London: QCA.

Clarke, B. (2001) 'Some principles of brain research for challenging gifted learners'. *Gifted Education International*, 17, pp. 4–10.

Csikszentmihalyi, M. (1996) *Creativity: Flow and the Psychology of Discovery and Invention.* New York: Harper Collins.

Csikszentmihalyi, M and Robinson, R. (1986) 'Culture, time and the development of talent'. In Sternberg, R. J. and Davidson, J. E. (eds) *Conceptions of Giftedness.* Cambridge, UK: Cambridge University Press.

Department of Environment, Transport and the Regions (1998) *Local Index of Deprivation.* London: DETR.

DfEE (1999) *Excellence in Cities.* London: Department for Education and Employment.

Dunham, G. and Russo, T. (1983) 'Career education for the disadvantaged gifted: some thoughts for the educators'. *Roeper Review,* 5 (3), pp. 26–8.

Ennis, R. (1996) *Critical Thinking.* New Jersey: Prentice Hall.

Eyre, D. (2001) 'An effective primary school for the gifted'. In Eyre, D. and McClure, L. (eds) *Curriculum Provision for the Gifted and Talented.* London: Fulton.

Flyvbjerg, B. (2002) *Making Social Sciences Matter.* Cambridge, UK: Cambridge University Press.

Frasier, M. (1979) 'Rethinking the issue regarding the culturally disadvantaged gifted'. *Exceptional Children,* 45 (7), pp. 538–42.

Gardner, H. (1983) *Frames of Mind.* New York: Basic Books.

Gardner, H. (1993) *Multiple Intelligences.* New York: Basic Books.

Gruber, H. (1986) 'The self-construction of the extraordinary'. In Sternberg, R. J. and Davidson, J. E. (eds) *Conceptions of Giftedness.* Cambridge, UK: Cambridge University Press.

Koshy, V. and Casey, R. (2003) 'Developing mathematically promising students by empowering teachers'. *Gifted and Talented,* 7 (1), 2–28.

Office for Standards in Education (Ofsted) (2001) *Providing for Gifted and Talented Pupils: An Evaluation of Excellence in Cities and other Grant-funded Programmes.* London: Ofsted.

Ofsted (2003) *Excellence in Cities and Education Action Zones: Management and Impact.* London: Ofsted.

Olszewski-Kubilius, P. and Scott, J. (1992) 'An investigation of the college and career counselling needs of economically disadvantaged minority gifted students'. *Roeper Review,* 14, pp. 141–8.

Oxford and Cambridge and RSA (OCR) Examination Board (2000). *Advanced Subsidiary GCE. Approved Specifications.*

Perrone, P. (1991) 'Career development'. In Colangelo, N. and Davis, G. (eds) *Handbook of Gifted Education.* Boston: Allyn & Bacon, pp. 321–7.

Renzulli, J. (1986) 'The three-ring conception of giftedness: A developmental model for creative productivity'. In Sternberg, R. J. and Davidson, J. E. (eds) *Conceptions of Giftedness.* Cambridge, UK: Cambridge University Press.

Renzulli, J. (1994) *Schools for Talent Development: A Practical Plan for School Improvement.* Connecticut: Creative Learning Press.

Smith, C. (2003) 'Can inclusion work for more able learners?' *Gifted Education International,* 18, pp. 201–8.

Sternberg, R. (1986) 'A triarchic theory of intellectual giftedness'. In Sternberg, R. J. and Davidson, J. E. (eds) *Conceptions of Giftedness.* Cambridge, UK: Cambridge University Press.

Sternberg, R. (2000) 'Giftedness as developing expertise'. In Heller, K., Monks, F., Sternberg, R. and Subotnik, R. (eds) *International Handbook of Giftedness and Talent* Oxford: Pergamon.

Thomas, L., Casey, R. and Koshy, V. (1996) 'The education of able and exceptionally able children in England and Wales'. Paper presented at the American Education Research Association Conference, New York.

Van Tassel-Baska, J. (1998) 'The disadvantaged gifted'. In Van Tassel-Baska, J. (ed.) *Excellence in Educating the Gifted*. Denver, CO: Love Publishing.

Vygotsky, L. (1978) *Mind in Society*. Cambridge, MA: Harvard University Press.

Yin, R. (2003) *Case Study Research: Design and Methods*. Thousand Oaks, CA: Sage.

Chapter 7

Maximising potential – both academic and social–emotional

Colm O'Reilly

If we want to include the gifted and talented we must allow them to thrive. An educational environment must be created to allow them to maximise their potential in both academic and social contexts. Terman and Oden (1959) concluded that high ability students often never made use of their superior ability and factors other than their intelligence often affected their life success. Gagné (1993) gave added weight to social and emotional factors being very important in the development of gifted children. Whybra (2000) identified the major needs of gifted and talented children as recognition of their ability and understanding of their social and emotional needs.

In allowing gifted students to maximise potential four issues need to be addressed. First, these students need to be challenged academically: too often in school they are not stretched by the regular curriculum and this can lead to boredom and frustration. By challenging them at a level appropriate to their abilities the students can become stimulated and motivated to achieve to their potential. In 2005 the Department of Education and Science in Ireland[1] produced a report evaluating curriculum implementation in primary schools (DES 2005). The report stated that in almost half of the classes they found that no provision was made for different learning styles and individual needs in mathematics. It was also reported that there was no differentiation within learning tasks for pupils of varying abilities. Second, these students need to be valued in the educational system. Like all students with special educational needs, gifted students need to feel that there is a place for them where they can be encouraged to reach their potential. These students need to be allowed to develop their natural curiosity. Most of these students from a young age may have a thirst for knowledge but their questions can remain unanswered within a regular school system. Too often teachers are governed by curriculum or time restraints that prevent them dealing with the questions that academically talented students may ask in class. Regularly the needs of the gifted are ignored by teachers and they are told that there is not enough time to deal with their queries. In this environment the gifted cannot thrive and will feel discouraged. This can lead to a situation where they stop asking questions and occupy themselves by feeling bored and frustrated. The 2005 report also stated that in almost two-thirds of the classrooms there was an overreliance on whole-class teaching dominated by teacher talk with pupils working silently on individual tasks.

The third issue to be addressed if gifted students are to maximise their potential is that these students need to find a peer group to allow themselves to become more comfortable with their ability. Too often this concept has been misinterpreted by educators or media groups to mean that gifted students have no friends. A stereotype has grown to incorporate a picture of the isolated student who struggles to maintain social relationships and is obsessed with academia. The truth is different as many of these students can become isolated because they are learning at different rates than many of their peers. At an early age they may have an extensive vocabulary which other young children may find difficult to relate to and this can lead to feelings of isolation. The difference when they meet up with peers who share a similar academic ability is huge, as they will find people who they can discuss things with and who they can be comfortable with being themselves. In 1991 when the idea of establishing a programme for gifted students in Ireland was brought up, it was met with opposition from the Department of Education which was reluctant to create an elitist attitude among bright students. Kolloff and Moore (1989) point out that the most critical aspect for students on gifted programmes is to discover that there are young people out there who think like they do, who are interested in the same ideas and who like to learn in similar ways.

Finally, these students need to be accepted as individuals. The 2005 DES report on curriculum implementation stresses an overreliance on the use on a single text book and pupils not becoming sufficiently active in their learning. Too often teachers are asking gifted students to conform to what they want them to be. Their individuality is being crushed as they are being made to fit into mainstream education. Many of these students have a unique way of looking at things and different ways of absorbing new information; this individuality should be celebrated and they should be encouraged to think for themselves. It's difficult for academically talented students to maximise their potential because they may not have outlets to realise their goals. If students are good at sports they are encouraged to improve in these areas and society is accepting of them achieving a high level of proficiency. Music too offers those who are interested the opportunity to excel. But what of those students who are exceptional at maths or other academic endeavours? They do not receive the same opportunities to reach potential because there are very few outlets to allow them to achieve their goals. In Ireland we have used the Talent Search identification model, summer programmes, correspondence courses and Saturday classes to stimulate our talented students. This chapter will look at ways to allow these students to achieve their goals, from identification through to courses and resources that could be made available to them.

HISTORY OF THE TALENT SEARCH

The Talent Search model is used to identify students of high ability. The primary purpose of a Talent Search is to identify those students of exceptional ability who, given present educational practices, are often not identified and consequently are ignored or under-served (Cohn 1991). It is based upon the psychometric approach of using standardised tests of aptitude and achievement. Students whose scores exceed designated criterion are adjudged to be talented or of high ability. It is based on the simple premise of administering a more difficult test to a younger but highly able group.

Stanley (1991) describes the origin of the Talent Search concept. Stanley administered several tests to a highly gifted twelve-year-old student in the 1960s, including the scholastic aptitude test (SAT) and found his results to be quite remarkable. Traditionally, the SAT is used as a criterion for college entrance amongst American teenagers usually aged around seventeen years. Stanley (1990) explains how he believes above-level testing is the answer for identifying these students. While many gifted students will achieve very high scores on tests for their own ages, using an above-level test can measure potential ability in certain areas. It allows the administrator to distinguish between talented students who score at different points on an above-level test. The Talent Search model demonstrated that true potential for specific academic work in maths and verbal areas can be discerned better by administering an above-level test. This can prove much more effective than using a cutoff-point measure which can eliminate some high ability students before they reach full potential. For example, if you use a cutoff IQ measure of, say, 125, what happens to students who score 124 on a given test? There is a danger that these students may be neglected or not allowed to reach full potential. The other benefit of the SAT is that it measures specific areas of aptitude rather than looking at only global intelligence. Research has shown the benefit of the SAT in finding students who benefit from advanced coursework in specific areas (Benbow 1992; Stanley and Benbow 1981). Van Tassel-Baska (1983) spoke of the two important principles demonstrated by the different abilities tapped by SAT testing. First, the more gifted the student, the greater the need for summer programmes, correspondence study and general mentorship. Second, the more gifted the student, the greater the need for existing school services to be extended. The first Talent Search was conducted in 1972 in the catchment area around Baltimore, Maryland. In this first search, 450 students took the SAT Mathematics paper. By 1979 the Talent Search effort had grown to a degree where a separate organisation was necessary. In that year, the Center for the Advancement of Academically Talented Youth (CTY) was founded in Johns Hopkins University. CTY initially conducted a Talent Search for mathematically and verbally precocious youth, using the SAT Mathematics and the SAT Verbal in thirteen Eastern states. Later this was extended to six states in the far West. In 1980, Stanley encouraged the creation of an organisation similar to CTY at Duke

University, North Carolina. This group, the Talent Identification Programme, began a Talent Search in the sixteen states of the South and Midwest. Additional searches began in the University of Denver and Northwestern University, Illinois, so that the four regional Talent Searches now serve all fifty states of the USA. In 1992, the largest Talent Search was the Duke University Talent Identification Program, which identified over 60,000 students. Combining this number with figures from Talent Searches carried out by Johns Hopkins University (approximately 40,000 students), Northwestern University (30,000), and the University of Denver (approximately 5,000) brings the total number of talented students identified to some 140,000.

At Johns Hopkins University, the Talent Search process involves seventh or eighth graders (twelve- to thirteen-year-olds) who score in the top 3 per cent on a nationally normed, in-class achievement test. Students who meet these criteria are nominated to participate further by taking the SAT test. The idea underlying the search is that twelve- to thirteen-year-olds who score highly on the SAT Mathematics have enhanced problem translation ability, and are superior in their capacity to represent and manipulate information in short-term memory (Benbow 1990). The SAT Verbal may be particularly well suited to assessing the verbal reasoning skills of eleven- to fourteen-year-olds, as they are at precisely the stage when verbal skills are integrated with cognitive skills in the conventional Piagetian scheme of development (Piaget 1954). This is a tremendously important time in the intellectual development of the individual. Exposure to the right set of opportunities in a properly designated environment can result in accelerated learning and intellectual development. The use of out-of-age testing makes it possible to distinguish between young students who have reached a high level in tests for their own age group. Students who perform well on these tests are eligible to attend residential summer programmes run by the various universities. Stocking and Goldstein (1992) have shown that the SAT has been of great value in identifying talented adolescents.

In 1992 this model was successfully implemented in Ireland. At this time the Irish Centre for Talented Youth (CTYI) was established at Dublin City University. This was the first time in Ireland that something was put in place for high ability students. The Irish Centre for Talented Youth has a five-fold mission, with the following aims:

1   To identify through national and international talent searches pre-college children who reason extremely well mathematically and/or verbally;
2   To provide talented youth from both Ireland and overseas with challenging and invigorating coursework and related educational opportunities through an annual summer programme, and selected experiences during the school year;
3   To provide teacher training and support services to schools participating in the CTYI programme;

4   To assist parents in advancing talented students by providing access to information and resources;
5   To research and evaluate talent development and the effectiveness of programme models and curriculum provision.

Students establish their eligibility for the CTYI programme by first taking assessment tests in the areas of mathematical, verbal and abstract reasoning with the Centre and achieving certain-age dependent scores. Each year the Centre carries out an annual Talent Search which is a systemic trawl for high ability students in the country, with details being sent to all primary and secondary schools in Ireland, all teachers' centres and libraries etc. Since CTYI's inception in 1992 over 14,600 students have taken part in an assessment at the Centre, with approximately 80 per cent of all secondary schools having at least one student on the programme. It is interesting to note that for many of the most exceptional students on the programme, their initial identification through the Talent Search was the first formal recognition of their ability. Identification itself can be a boost to the self-confidence of the individual involved. The fact that students can see for the first time that having high ability is something useful and is worthy of recognition adds to their self-concept.

CTYI also uses the out-of-level testing advocated in the United States. In this, students take a test which would more usually be taken by students older than them – e.g. thirteen-year-olds take the USA college entry test (Scholastic Aptitude Test) which is taken by seventeen- to eighteen-year-olds. This model has been successfully implemented in Ireland (Barnett and Gilheany 1996). To qualify for the programme students are required to achieve the average score of the older age group.

- 6–12-year-olds – Demonstrate ability at or above the ninety-fifth percentile level
- 13–16-year-olds – Demonstrate ability at or above the ninety-ninth percentile level

The assessment results annually show a very consistent pattern, with the average score of participants aged thirteen to fourteen years being comparable to the average score of seventeen- to eighteen-year-olds on the same test. This is the minimum standard required for qualification for a CTYI course. However, the assessment results annually also show a small number of students reaching exceptionally high scores, e.g. thirteen-year-old students scoring over 700 points in the Scholastic Aptitude Test (SAT I) in both the maths and verbal sections. Such scores are only achieved by approximately 1 per cent of college-bound seniors, thus demonstrating the usefulness of the SAT as a means of identifying talent of a quite extraordinary nature in thirteen-year-old students. SAT scores have been shown to be comparable between Irish and American students (Gilheany 1994).

At primary level around 70 per cent of students taking assessments will qualify for academic programmes, while at secondary level approximately 40 per cent of students will reach the required standard. These figures reflect the large degree of self-selection for such programmes. All secondary students who participate in assessments regardless of the outcome are invited to a number of events such as discovery days, as an acknowledgement of their ability and desire to seek additional challenge. Goldstein and Wagner (1993) believe that these ceremonies represent the first and possibly only opportunity for public recognition many of these exceptional youngsters will receive. Following identification we need to recognise talent. Award ceremonies and discovery days can help the student feel encouraged to try out more academic challenges. Too often in school, students with high ability are not given enough credit from their teachers. A common complaint amongst academically talented youngsters is that teachers do not praise them enough for performing well in class or exams. In many cases there is an expectation on them to do well, and when they do they may not get enough recognition for the work they put in to achieve this result. A frequent scenario for talented adolescents is that in school the teacher will praise the efforts of an average student who does better than expected while ignoring the results of the exceptional child who achieves top marks. These students need more recognition of the effort that they have put in and then they will be encouraged to continue with their endeavours. We need to create an environment where talent is valued and academic achievements are rewarded. This can help to boost confidence and encourage the students to fulfil their potential.

OPTIMAL MATCH

Once the student has been successfully identified and qualifies to participate in a programme suitable for the gifted and talented the question must be addressed as to what the standard should be on such programmes. The optimal match principle (Mills and Tangherlini 1992) is an effective method for teaching these students. Simply stated, an appropriate education experience is one which challenges the individual to perform at a level just beyond his or her cognitive grasp (Redding 1989). Once a student has mastered a subject at a given level he or she must be allowed to proceed to the next stage. An optimal match is the adjustment of an appropriately challenging curriculum to a student's demonstrated pace and level of learning. Robinson (1983) believes that the optimal match assumes the following principles:

- Learning is sequential, developmental and relatively predictable; one can assess a student's progress in mastery of orderly sets of concepts and skills.
- Once a learner has mastered a given level or stage of understanding, it is time to proceed to the next level. Delay will result in boredom, while too rapid a pace will cause confusion and discouragement. An optimal match, an

appropriate challenge, results in conceptual depth, intellectual excitement and growth.

- There are substantial differences in skills and knowledge among children of a given age that primarily reflect differences in their rate of learning. Individual differences characterise not only general intelligence, but more importantly for educational purposes, specific subject areas, e.g. mathematics, foreign languages, literature and science. One student may be more advanced in some domains than in others. Providing for the optimal match involves taking these differences into account.

Mills and Durden (1992) point out that schools should aspire to the ideal of achieving the optimal match between each student's needs and the school system. If the student demonstrates a high level of ability in a particular subject, or a high level of interest and achievement, then these needs exist. If they cannot be adequately met within a school programme, some degree of intervention is needed.

ACCELERATION AND ENRICHMENT

Two of the best-known interventions for academically talented students are acceleration and enrichment. Broadly speaking, acceleration involves moving through the curriculum at a faster pace than would normally be required, while enrichment involves exploring subjects in more depth than would normally be allowed in school. Pressey (1949: 2) defined acceleration as 'progress through an educational programme at rates faster or at ages younger than conventional'. Three assumptions can be identified in this definition. First, it presupposes an educational programme in which content, tasks and skills are defined for each level of instruction. Second, it assumes that there is a pace of instruction that may at least be inferred to be suitable for most students. Third, and most importantly in this context, it assumes that some children are capable of mastering the standard curriculum faster and, thus, are capable of more rapid progress. Pressey's definition sets two criteria for accelerated advancement: higher-than-average achievement, and the ability to master the material at faster rates compared to age-level classmates (Southern et al. 1993). It ties in with both the concept of above-level testing and the optimal match principle.

While acceleration is defined as more rapid than typical advancement within a given curriculum, enrichment can be regarded as a process that extends instruction beyond the bounds of that curriculum. Passow (1958) identified four guidelines for the development of enrichment programmes. He suggested the curriculum be modified in four ways:

- greater depth
- altered tempo or pace

- broader range of materials
- development of process models.

Educational enrichment offers students the opportunity to undertake original research, and to solve problems which would be beyond the interests and abilities of the rest of the class. As there is an indefinite number of possibilities for subject content within an enrichment programme, authors have often used student interest as the major factor for selecting original content. This can be described as vertical enrichment. Renzulli (1977) describes enrichment as the study of content above and beyond the curriculum, and asserts that student interest and learning style should be used to determine the course of study in programmes for the gifted.

ACCELERATION OPTIONS

Sisk (1988) identifies some acceleration options open to students in the United States. These include advanced placement (AP) classes which allow talented students to study college-level courses and receive college credit while still enrolled in high school. Longitudinal studies have shown that AP students are more likely than non-AP students to select an academic career, graduate early and apply to selective colleges (Advanced Placement Program 1991). Another option is that of correspondence courses, taken from major universities while at high school level. This is an excellent opportunity for a student to delve into a subject at a level appropriate to their ability. This also provides opportunities for students from rural areas to have limited access to college facilities. Early entrance to elementary school, or early entrance to college, are other forms of acceleration. Brody *et al.* (1990) found that students who enter college between two and four years earlier than normal make good grades, graduate early and often win awards. Extra load is a form of acceleration where students can take as many high school courses as they wish, which may include time out for students to take college courses, and receive credit. Finally, there are fast-paced classes where students learn content far more rapidly than in traditional approaches.

ACCELERATION OR ENRICHMENT?

Studies of acceleration contain an overall message: acceleration contributes to achievement (see Gallagher 1975; Daurio 1979; Kulik and Kulik 1984). In terms of social and emotional development, no harmful effects have been listed (Keys 1938; Pressey 1949; Hobson 1963; Daurio 1979). There is much debate over whether enrichment or acceleration is the best means of developing the potential of the talented child. Hultgren (1989) did an exhaustive study of the literature on acceleration. He listed advantages of acceleration to include the reduction of boredom for these students and an increase in academic challenge. He also stressed the importance of putting able students with their mental peers. He believes acceleration leads to increased motivation and satisfaction among the highly able students and in the long run promotes a better attitude towards school. The disadvantages of acceleration include a fear of social isolation from a new peer group, an increase in pressure for these students to grow up quickly and a danger that they prematurely complete the available curriculum. Elkind (1988) cautions against the use of the term acceleration to describe interventions designed to enhance and maximise children's intellectual potential and mental growth. Fearing that the term implies something done to the child, rather than an educational accommodation for the child, Elkind prefers the use of the word promotion to describe such interventions. While research may show that acceleration is beneficial and there is little evidence to show negative effects, it is traditionally perceived negatively amongst many parents and teachers. Renzulli (1978) questioned whether progressing through the curriculum at a faster pace than usual met any of the important needs of gifted students. He preferred to advocate enrichment as a means of allowing a student to study a subject in more depth. Stanley (1978) on the other hand believes that enrichment eventually leads to frustration as the talented student will need to accelerate at some stage during the enrichment programme. Daurio (1979) concludes that acceleration seems to be the more feasible method for meeting the needs of gifted students. However, if enrichment exists in the form of original curriculum and problem-solving beyond the boundaries of the regular curriculum, it may be viewed as acceleration (McLeod and Cropley 1989: 195). Fox (1979) observes that the two terms are complementary rather than conflicting. In the case of Ireland, skipping a year in secondary school is usually not an option unless it is the transition year which follows the Junior Certificate which is taken at fifteen years of age. Summer courses and Saturday classes offer fast-paced study in an intensive learning environment. The content matter may be more in-depth than the student would be used to at school, or the student may be exposed to new areas with which they may not be familiar. In this way, these classes are both accelerative and enriching.

SUMMER COURSES AND SATURDAY CLASSES

In these cases gifted students participate in classes that they would not usually get a chance to do in school. For secondary school students in Ireland who attend the Irish Centre for Talented Youth these classes are often pitched at a first-year university standard, and at a faster pace than school. The summer courses also involve students from the CTY programmes in America. As Enerson (1993) points out, programming should stimulate curiosity and investigation while introducing new areas of interest. The instructors are usually university lecturers, and present a course outline for approval by the programme director at CTYI. While the instructor will follow the outline as much as possible during the session, flexibility is encouraged, and the ability to change in midstream is a vital quality in instructors on the programme. It is important that as teachers of talented youth, they have in-depth knowledge of their subject, and that they encourage their students to research independently in their fields of interest.

Summer programmes have been found to be positive experiences for gifted students, offering them opportunities to interact with other equally able students and to further develop their intellectual ability (Van Tassel-Baska *et al.* 1985). The social component is a very important aspect of the summer programme at CTYI and, as Feldhusen (1991) points out, the opportunity to share a common viewpoint or discuss a topic deeply and passionately is not typically available in a forty-minute period.

In the United States, these programmes have long been a fixed element of out-of-school provision for highly able students (Olszewski-Kubilius 1989). CTY's academic programme is based on the following principles:

*   Academically talented students should be provided with the opportunity to learn subject matter and develop skills at a pace and level appropriate to their abilities.
*   Academically talented students require a rigorous and challenging course of studies in the liberal arts, and CTY sees this area as the most valuable embodiment of verbal and/or mathematical ability.
*   CTY combines rigorous and challenging educational coursework with a social experience that encourages the development of a balanced human being.
*   Students' academic accomplishments should be acknowledged and rewarded.

Classes are kept small so that students may interact with one another, for experience shows that students learn as much through intensive interaction with their peers as they do through direct instruction (see Mills and Durden 1992; Tangherlini and Durden 1993). The class size at CTYI allows a pupil–instructor ratio of around fifteen to one, which is much lower than the average class size in both Irish and American schools. The intense nature of the programme means that students are required to put in a very high level of work during the period and for many students this is perhaps the first time that they have ever really been challenged academically. Adjusting to this new challenge allows them to maximise their high academic potential.

SOCIAL AND EMOTIONAL NEEDS

There is evidence to prove that the gifted have significantly higher self-concepts than other students (Tidwell 1980; Ringness 1961; Ketcham and Snyder 1977).

Studies conducted with gifted children have generally found that they obtain higher scores on global self-concept measures compared with non-gifted children (Maddux *et al.* 1982; Davis and Cornell 1985). Hultgren and Marquardt (1986) report that gifted junior high school students perceive themselves to be higher in scholastic competence and judge their conduct to be better than non-gifted students. However, questions must be raised as to the impact of special programmes on these self-concepts. In certain programmes, placement in homogeneous groups can lead to a decrease in self-confidence (Coleman and Fults 1982). A change in school environment which involves a change in friends and social climate can give a negative impact on self-perception (Olszewski *et al.* 1987). But other studies, such as that by Kolloff and Feldhusen (1984), report no differences in self-concept between gifted students who take part in programmes and those who do not. Conflicting opinions may be explained by differences in the programmes. Moreover, these studies were performed on year-round 'pullout' programmes. Kolloff and Moore (1989) looked at residential summer programmes and showed that self-concept does rise using the Piers-Harris children's self-concept scale (Piers 1984), and the ME scale (Feldhusen and Kolloff 1981). Speculation as to why self-concept increases on a summer programme suggests that the students are better able to be themselves in this environment, and there is no need for them to pretend not to be intelligent. There is also an effect operating in which newfound friends and camaraderie act as a factor.

Strop (1985) and Ross and Parker (1980) noted that academically talented adolescents generally feel competent in academic areas, but much less so in social areas. Studies of the CTYI Summer Programme (O'Reilly 1998) yielded some interesting results. This research involved interviewing fifty second-level students who attended a residential summer programme on three separate occasions at CTYI. Most of the respondents were aged sixteen at the time of the research and had started attending CTYI from the age of thirteen. The respondents were asked if they had experienced any social effects from their continued participation in the course. Four significant themes emerged: growth in self-confidence, making new friends, improved communication skills and meeting a variety of new people. Over 85 per cent believed that their self-confidence had improved in some capacity. Many confessed to having been shy originally but feeling much more comfortable with their personality having attended the programme at CTYI. Others reported that they believed they were more understood having experienced the course. Interestingly, three out of ten said that this new self-confidence was restricted to being at CTYI: when these students returned to school, they had difficulty transferring it to a different environment, and in particular relating their CTYI experiences to those at home seems to have been a problem. Many students felt that it was hard to justify to their classmates that they had spent a month of their summer holidays at 'school'. Describing the programme to people who had never even heard of it usually proved a difficult and frustrating task, often culminating in a reluctance even to talk about the experience, let alone share it. As a biology student relates:

> When I told my friends about my first experience at CTYI, they thought I was mad to spend three weeks of my summer holidays in a classroom. It bothered me at first, but then I realised I'd probably have reacted in the same way had I not seen the course for myself and enjoyed every minute of it.

Some 60 per cent said that making new friends had been a major social effect. Enerson (1993) found that while satisfaction with challenging coursework taught by expert teachers and the opportunity to live on a university campus were important, making friends and gaining confidence in one's ability were equally vital. The fact that so many students return to the courses validates this assertion, with the same people meeting up every year. Kolloff and Moore (1989) point out that meeting other students with similar abilities in this type of environment is critical to self-development of the talented student.

Thirty-two per cent of students believed that meeting a variety of new people was an interesting experience. While the numbers on the summer course are increasing every year, they are still at a level where almost everybody on campus can get to know each other. A wide variety of activities and no discrimination amongst age groups means that everyone mixes. The presence of both American and Irish students lends the experience a cross-cultural dimension. Despite the many miles travelled and the boundaries between them, many of these people share similar interests, tastes and goals. Fifty seven per cent felt that their communication skills had improved primarily from their experiences here. Many believed that they were able to establish their own identity at CTYI and that it was different to the perception that their school friends may have had of them. A lot of students felt that they had already been labelled in school and often diagnosed as strange just because that they were intelligent, but that was never a factor at CTYI.

The social benefits of these programmes can not be underestimated. For many students it is the first time that they feel they belong. In school the gifted child can often feel isolated and they need a chance to mix with their academic peers to feel that they are not alone. The sense of relief when they meet people with similar interests to themselves is a huge factor towards them feeling comfortable with their ability.

CONCLUSION

To allow gifted students to maximise their potential academically and socially much must be done to facilitate this. From the identification process to the coursework that is assigned to them, we must provide stimulating options to allow them to develop academically and to create a positive environment to satisfy their emotional needs. As early as the 1940s Hollingworth (1942) maintained that children of high IQ waste most of their time in school. Sadly very little has changed in the intervening period. As educators we need to modify the curriculum in a school setting to include the gifted and talented. This can be through promotion of independent study or asking open-ended questions to allow these students to develop good research skills. We must provide accelerative options to allow them to study at their own pace, and enrichment options to enable them to study subjects at the depth that they require. If this involves putting them together with other students of similar ability we must create an environment where this is possible. Sometimes regular schoolteachers do not have the level of expertise in particular subjects that gifted students require. Knowledge of the subject and the ability to answer questions comfortably about your academic area are two essential requirements for teachers of the gifted and talented. For every pupil to feel included academically, individual needs must be met. Compacting the curriculum in regular schools to cater for the gifted student is a helpful tool but that in itself may not be enough. Extra programmes such as CTYI or similar gifted schemes are necessary for students to achieve their academic potential. The notion of taking them from regular classes and providing extra challenges for them with their academic peers contributes to their overall development and facilitates their inclusion within society. The more acceptable these courses become and the less stigma attached to participating in them, the more we can recognise the important role that gifted students have within the educational system. Full inclusion should recognise individual differences within the system. Gifted students need their individual needs to be catered for so that they can feel valued. Identifying students as having high ability is necessary to make adequate provision for them. Establishing a successful selection criteria is essential for developing programmes for the gifted. The notion of selection of people for a programme can be seen by some commentators as exclusive. There can be problems with identification of the right people for the programme. If one uses testing as a criteria for entry there must be something in place for those who don't qualify for the gifted programme. It is important that these students don't feel excluded and lose motivation towards achieving their potential. Opportunities such as correspondence courses, special events and enrichment materials should be made available to all students if they wish to try new things.

Rogers (1991) demonstrated that enrichment programmes in grouping gifted children together helped prevent emotional isolation by creating true peer groups of students who are the same age socially as well as intellectually. From the initial stage gifted students need to feel that their academic talent is something to be embraced and they should be encouraged to use it to allow them to develop to the best of their ability. This chapter has examined how a high proportion of students who attended a CTYI residential summer programme felt that the experience increased their self-confidence. For the first time many of these students felt comfortable with their high ability. Sometimes, though, this confidence does not transfer back to school. This could be indicative of their feeling that school does not hold as much academic challenge for them and that the gifted student can feel curtailed once they return to their regular environment. At this stage more should be done to include them within the school system. If they have mastered an area of their subject they should be allowed to proceed to the next topic rather than having to wait and repeat the material again and again until everyone has reached the required level. Teachers should be more flexible with their curriculum and vary their teaching methods rather than using the text book exclusively. Programmes for gifted students such as CTYI are necessary to work with the current mainstream curriculum to provide the extra academic and social–emotional challenge that high ability students need. Rather than being perceived to be out of the regular school curriculum they should be seen as an essential tool to maximise the potential of gifted students so they feel part of and included within the overall scheme of things.

Note

1 When Ireland is mentioned in this chapter it refers specifically to the Republic of Ireland.

References

Advanced Placement Program (1991) *AP Yearbook 1991–1992*. New York: College Entrance Examination Board.

Barnett, B. and Gilheany, S. L. (1996) 'The CTY Talent Search – International Applicability and Practice in Ireland'. *High Ability Studies*, 7 (2).

Benbow, C. P. (1990) 'Mathematical talent and females: from a biological perspective'. In W. Wieczerkowski and T. M. Prado (eds) *Hochbegabte Mädchen*. Bad Honnef: K. H. Bock, pp. 95–113.

Benbow, C. P. (1992) 'Academic achievement in mathematics and science of students between ages of thirteen and thirty three: Are there differences among students in the top one per cent of mathematical ability?' *Journal of Educational Psychology*, 84, pp. 51–61.

Brody, L. E., Assouline, S. G. and Stanley, J. C. (1990) 'Five years of early entrants: predicting successful achievement in college'. *Gifted Child Quarterly*, 34 (4), pp. 138–42.

Cohn, S. J. (1991) 'Talent searches'. In N. Colangelo and G. A. Davis (eds) *Handbook of Gifted Education*. Boston, MA: Allyn & Bacon, pp. 166–177.

Coleman, J. and Fults, B. (1982) 'Self-concept and the gifted classroom: The role of social comparisons'. *Gifted Child Quarterly*, 26 (3), pp. 116–20.

Daurio, S. P. (1979) 'Educational enrichment versus acceleration: a review of the literature'. In W. C. George, S. J. Cohn and J. C. Stanley (eds), *Educating the Gifted: Acceleration and Enrichment*. Baltimore, MD: Johns Hopkins University Press, pp. 13–63.

Davis, H. and Cornell, J. (1985) 'The effect of aptitude and achievement status on the self system'. *Gifted Child Quarterly*, 29 (3), pp. 131–135.

Department of Education and Science (2005) *An Evaluation of Curriculum Implementation in Primary Schools – English, Mathematics and Visual Arts*. Dublin: Stationery Office.

Elkind, D. (1988). 'Mental acceleration'. *Journal for the Education of the Gifted*, 11, pp. 19–31.

Enerson, D. L. (1993) 'Summer residential programs: academics and beyond'. *Gifted Child Quarterly*, 37 (4), pp. 169–76.

Feldhusen, J. F. (1991) 'Saturday and summer programs'. In N. Colangelo and G. A. Davis (eds) *Handbook of Gifted Education* (pp. 197–208). Boston, MA: Allyn & Bacon.

Feldhusen, J. F. and Kolloff, M. (1981) 'ME: A self-concept scale for gifted students'. *Perceptual and Motor Skills*, 53, pp. 319–23.

Fox, L. H. (1979) 'Programmes for the gifted and talented: An overview'. In A. H. Passow (ed.) *The Gifted and Talented, their Education and Development*. Chicago: NSSE Yearbook.

Gagné, F. (1993) 'Constructs and models pertaining to exceptional human abilities'. In K. A. Heller, F .J. Monks and A. H. Passow (eds) *International Handbook of Research and Development of Giftedness and Talent*. Oxford: Pergamon Press.

Gallagher, J. (1975) *Teaching the gifted child* (3rd edn). Boston, MA: Allyn & Bacon.

Gilheany, S. (1994) 'Comparison of SAT Scores for Irish and American Students used to identify academic talent of students for Ireland and US'. Presented at the European Council for High Ability, 4th ECHA Conference, Nijmegen, The Netherlands, 8–11 October.

Goldstein, D. and Wagner, H. (1993) 'After school programs, competitions, school Olympics, and summer programs'. In K. A. Heller, F. J. Monks and A. H. Passow (eds) *International Handbook of Research and Development of Giftedness and Talent*, pp. 593–605. Oxford: Pergamon Press.

Hobson, J. R. (1963) 'High school performance of underage pupils initially admitted to kindergarten on the basis of physical and psychological examinations'. *Educational and Psychological Measurement*, 23 (1), pp. 159–70.

Hollingworth, L. S. (1942) *Children Above IQ 180*. New York: World Books.

Hultgren, H. (1989) 'Understanding our gifted'. *Open Space Communications*, 1 (3), pp. 1 and 8–10.

Hultgren, H. and Marquardt, M. (1986) 'A self perception profile of Rocky Mountain talent search summer institute participants'. Paper presented at the Annual Meeting of the American Orthopsychiatric Association, Chicago.

Ketcham, B. and Snyder, R. (1977). 'Self-attitudes of the intellectually and socially advantaged student: Normative study of the Piers-Harris children's self concept scale'. *Psychological Reports*, 40, pp. 111–16.

Keys, N. (1938) 'The underage student in high school and college'. *University of California Publications in Education*, 7, pp. 145–271.

Kolloff, P. and Feldhusen, J. F. (1984) 'The effects of enrichment on self-concept and creative thinking'. *Gifted Child Quarterly*, 28 (2), pp. 53–7.

Kolloff, P. and Moore, A. (1989) 'Effects of summer programs on the self-concept of gifted children'. *Journal for the Education of the Gifted*, 12, 268–76.

Kulik, J. A. and Kulik, C. C. (1984) 'Effects of accelerated instruction on students'. *Review of Educational Research*, 54 (3), 409–25.

Maddux, C., Scheiber, M. and Bass, J. (1982) 'Self concept and social distance in gifted children'. *Gifted Child Quarterly*, 26 (2), 77–81.

McLeod, J. and Cropley, A. J. (1989) *Fostering Academic Excellence*. Oxford: Pergamon Press.

Mills, C. and Durden, W. G. (1992) 'Co-operative learning and ability grouping: An issue of choice'. *Gifted Child Quarterly*, 36 (1), pp. 11–16.

Mills, C. J. and Tangherlini, A. E. (1992) 'Finding the optimal match: Another look at ability grouping and cooperative learning'. *Equity and Excellence*, 25 (2–4), pp. 205–8.

Olszewski-Kubilius, P. (1989) 'Development of academic talent: The role of summer programmes'. In J. L. Van Tassel-Baska and P. Olszewski-Kubilius (eds) *Patterns of*

Influence on Gifted Learners. The Home, the Self and the School (pp. 421–30). New York and London: Teachers' College Press.

Olszewski, P., Kulieke, M. and Willis, G. (1987) 'Changes in the self-perceptions of gifted students who participate in rigorous academic programs'. *Journal for the Education of the Gifted*, X, pp. 287–303.

O'Reilly, C. (1998) 'Effects of summer programmes on academically talented students'. Presented to the European Council for High Ability, 6th ECHA Conference, Oxford, England.

Passow, A. H. (1958) 'Enrichment of education for the gifted'. In N. B. Henry (ed.) *Education for the Gifted: Fifty-seventh Yearbook of the National Society for the Study of Education*, Part 1 (pp. 193–221). Chicago: University of Chicago Press.

Piaget, J. (1954). 'Language and thought from the genetic'. In P. Adams (ed.), *Language in Thinking*. Middlesex: Penguin Education.

Piers, E. (1984) *Piers-Harris Children's Self concept Scale: Revised Manual*. Los Angeles, CA: Western Psychological Services.

Pressey, S. L. (1949) *Educational Acceleration: Appraisal of Basic Problems*. Bureau of Educational Research Monographs No. 31. Columbus, OH: Ohio State University Press.

Redding, R. E. (1989) 'Underachievement in the verbally gifted: Implications for pedagogy'. *Psychology in the Schools*, 26, pp. 275–88.

Renzulli, J. S. (1977) *The Enrichment Triad Model: A Guide for Developing Defensible Programs for the Gifted*. Mansfield, CT: Creative Learning Press.

Renzulli, J. S. (1978) 'What makes giftedness? Re-examing a definition'. *Phi Delta Kappan*, 60 (3), pp. 180–184.

Ringness, T. (1961) 'Self concept of children of low, average, and high intelligence'. *American Journal of Mental Deficiency*, 65, pp. 453–61.

Robinson, H. B. (1983) 'A case for radical acceleration: Programmes of Johns Hopkins University and the University of Washington'. In C. P. Benbow and J. C. Stanley (eds) *Academic Precocity: Aspects of its Development* (pp. 139–59). Baltimore, MD: Johns Hopkins University Press.

Rogers, K. B. (1991). *The Relationship of Grouping Practices to the Education of the Gifted and Talented Learner*. Mansfield, CT: Creative Learning Press.

Ross, A. and Parker, M. (1980) 'Academic and social self-concepts of the academically gifted'. *Exceptional Children*, 47 (1), pp. 6–10.

Sisk, D. (1988) 'The bored and disinterested gifted child: Going through school lockstep'. *Journal for the Education of the Gifted*, 11 (4), pp. 5–19.

Southern, W. T., Jones, E. D. and Stanley, J. C. (1993) 'Acceleration and enrichment: The context and development of program options'. In K. A. Heller, F. J. Monks and A. H. Passow (eds) *International Handbook of Research and Development of Giftedness and Talent*, pp. 387–411. Oxford: Pergamon Press.

Stanley, J. C. (1978) 'Educational non-acceleration: An international tragedy'. *Gifted Child Today*, 1 (3), pp. 54–57.

Stanley, J. C. (1990) *My Many Years of Working with the Gifted: An Academic Approach*. Williamsburg, VA: College of William and Mary, School of Education.

Stanley, J. C. (1991) 'Reflections on my life and how it grew'. In D. L. Burleson (ed.) *Reflections: Personal Essays by Thirty-three Distinguished Educators* (pp. 340–55). Bloomington, IN: Phi Delta Kappa Educational Foundation.

Stanley, J. C. and Benbow, C. P. (1981) 'Using the SAT to find intellectually talented seventh graders'. *College Board Review*, 122, pp. 3–27.

Stocking, V. B. and Goldstein, D. (1992) 'Course selection and performance of very high ability students: Is there a gender gap?' *Roeper Review*, 15, pp. 48–51.

Strop, J. (1985) 'A profile of the needs, characteristics, and preferences of talent search summer institute participants'. Paper presented at the Annual Meeting of the American Educational Research Association, Chicago.

Tangherlini, A. E. and Durden, W. G. (1993) '*Smart Kids: How Academic Talents are Developed in America*'. Geneva: Hogrefe & Huber.

Terman, L. M. and Oden, M. H. (1959) *Genetic Studies of Genius. Vol. 5 The Gifted Group at Mid-life*. Stanford, CA: Stanford University Press.

Tidwell, R. (1980) 'A psycho-educational profile of 1,593 gifted high school students'. *Gifted Child Quarterly*, 24, pp. 63–8.

Van Tassel-Baska, J. L. (1983) 'Statewide replication of the Johns Hopkins Study of Mathematically Precocious Youth'. In C. P. Benbow and J. C. Stanley (eds) *Academic Precocity: Aspects of its Development* (pp. 179–91). Baltimore, MD: Johns Hopkins University Press.

Van Tassel-Baska, J., Landau, M. and Olszewski, P. (1985) 'Towards development of an appropriate math/science curriculum for the gifted learner'. *Journal for the Education of the Gifted*, VIII, 257–72.

Whybra, J. (2000) 'Extension and enrichment programmes: "A place where I could fit in"'. In M. J. Stopper (ed.) *Meeting the Social and Emotional Needs of Gifted Children*. London: David Fulton.

Chapter 8

To group or not to group
Is *that* the question?

Miraca U. M. Gross

Of all the social sciences, education is the field most fraught with sociopolitical metaphors. The educational placement of children who differ significantly from age-peers, either because of physical disabilities or through differences in their capacity to learn, has been, for many decades, a political minefield – partly due to the language we choose to frame our educational philosophies.

Until quite recently, the education of children with physical or intellectual disabilities in the mainstream classroom was termed 'integration'. It is a word with powerful connotations of acceptance, assimilation and belonging, blending children together as members of a community. And, ironically, the very power of the word placed many educators in a quandary. Teachers and administrators who foresaw problems for some children with this practice, and researchers who were aware that 'integration' was by no means the universal panacea that its support-ers claimed, nonetheless found it very difficult to argue against; after all, the antonym for 'integration' is 'segregation' and who would wish to advocate such a process?

Over the years the terminology changed but not the dilemma. Integration is now called 'inclusion'. The antonym for 'inclusion' is 'exclusion'. Who would want to advocate for a child to be excluded?

This chapter looks specifically at the education of gifted and talented pupils. For the purpose of clarity, the definitions developed by Gagné (1995) will be adopted. Gagné defines giftedness as the ability to perform at a level significantly beyond what might be expected for one's age, in any domain of human ability – cognitive, creative, affective or sensorimotor – to a level that would place one in the top 10 to 15 per cent of age-peers. However, giftedness defines outstanding *potential* rather than outstanding performance. This model recognises the exis-tence, and the dilemma, of the underachieving gifted child.

By contrast, Gagné defines talent as *achievement* or performance at a level sig-nificantly beyond what might be expected at one's age. Obviously, numerous fields of performance are associated with any ability domain and, again, a child may be talented in one or many fields of performance. Gagné (2003) notes that through thoughtfully planned, research-based interventions, schools can assist pupils to develop their gifts into talents. Equally, a lack of support, or the active withholding of research-supported interventions, can result in the blocking of talent development.

There has been, over the past twenty years, considerable debate as to whether gifted and talented pupils should be educated ('included') in the mainstream classroom or whether they should undertake part or all of their education in some form of special grouping – from which pupils who do not meet the entry criteria are 'excluded'. Opponents of ability grouping argue that to select gifted pupils for special services which are denied to age-peers of lesser ability is discriminatory and a violation of the principles of equal opportunity (Gross 2004).

It is notable, however, that the domain in which giftedness or talent is sited seems to influence both the degree and intensity of these objections.

ALL GIFTS ARE EQUAL – BUT SOME GIFTS ARE MORE EQUAL THAN OTHERS

Gallagher (1976) relates the story of Mr Palcuzzi, the principal of an American elementary school. Tired of hearing objections to special provisions for gifted children, he decided to bring to a parent–teacher association meeting his own set of proposals. First, he said, gifted pupils should be ability-grouped in their specific areas of talent so that they could learn from, and with, other pupils who shared their abilities and interests. Age-grade barriers should be removed so that gifted fourth- or fifth-grade pupils could learn with sixth-graders if they had the ability and maturity to do so. The curriculum offered to gifted pupils should be differentiated in terms of level, pace and complexity to respond to their faster pace of learning and higher level of skills.

The PTA reaction was mixed. Some were angered by the elitism implicit in the proposal. Others said it was theoretically defensible but would be impossible to implement in practice. How would the programmes be timetabled? And would the funding have to be taken from other programmes?

Programmes would be funded by a levy placed on the parent body, explained Palcuzzi. To ensure their success, a teacher with special qualifications and expertise in the education of talented pupils would be employed. The gifted pupils would travel throughout their local region, learning with, and indeed competing against, gifted pupils from other schools with similar programmes.

The PTA members were horrified. They protested that the proposal was anti-democratic and against the spirit of American education. The establishment of discrete, elitist groups would divide the school and bring it into disrepute.

Palcuzzi sat quietly, nodding in acknowledgement of each of their points. Then he pointed out, gently, that the programme he was proposing, complete with ability grouping, grade advancement and differentiated training, a highly qualified coach, funding levy and inter-school competition was not, in fact, a *new* programme for the intellectually gifted, but an existing programme that the school had been supporting for many years – its programme for gifted basketball players.

Palcuzzi was a thoughtful observer of his community's priorities. The many forms of ability grouping and acceleration which are accepted as viable, valid and indeed advisable for young people talented in sport, athletics and the performing arts (instrumental music, dance and singing, for example) are frequently withheld from academically talented pupils on the grounds that they would stratify the child society, promote elitism, cause dissension, arouse envy or create feelings of inferiority in pupils not selected for these opportunities.

Why do we respond differently to different forms of talent? I suspect that an important element is the degree to which we see the gifts of others to be of immediate practical advantage, or benefit, to ourselves.

It is easy for a school or community to justify expenditure on finding and fostering sporting or athletic potential. Most of us, even if we do not passionately support a particular team, enjoy watching sport played well. Similarly, when we listen to music our pleasure is intensified when the performance is of high quality. We have a lot to gain by fostering the development of sporting or musical talent. Many people, however, see little personal advantage in fostering academic talent.

Whatever the reason, it is common for schools to employ, with pupils talented in sport, athletics and the performing arts, many of the interventions and encouragements that they neglect or refuse to use with academically gifted pupils.

- *Ability grouping* Sports teams and musical ensembles are generally formed on the basis of a certain homogeneity of ability and/or achievement. In general, the higher the level of expertise, the greater the homogeneity of the group that is formed in response.
- *Opportunity for social comparison* Sports teams are matched with each other on the basis of ability and achievement, allowing a facilitative level of healthy competition and social comparison. Music festivals allow talented young musicians and singers to match themselves against others of similar ability. Festinger (1954) showed that realistic self-evaluation is only possible when we are allowed to compare our performance against that of other people whose abilities are similar to ours.
- *Acceleration* Talented young musicians and athletes are permitted to progress at their own pace, training and performing with older pupils when this is appropriate. The repertoire which talented young musicians prepare and perform is chosen on the basis of the performer's maturity and readiness, rather than their chronological age.
- *Mentorships* Highly talented young athletes are often taken under the wing of an older player who will coach them on strategy. Talented young musicians may have the opportunity to take master classes.

- *Sustained and rigorous practice* It is accepted that a structured and rigorous regime of practice, setting ever more demanding goals, is essential if gifted young musicians or athletes are to develop as talented. These pupils' friends understand and support them in this. By contrast, academically talented pupils who passionately commit themselves to developing their talents are often derided as 'swots', 'geeks' or 'brainiacs' – the names vary from year to year and country to country but the social connotation – *uncool* – is unmistakable.
- *Pride in achievement* Talented musicians and athletes are encouraged to feel pride in their gifts and to strive to develop them. However, pride in academic success is often confused with conceit and covertly, or sometimes overtly, discouraged.

This chapter proposes that the issue is not whether we should ability-group academically gifted pupils but how this may most effectively be done. Arguments will be based on what we know about the structure of the inclusion classroom and its effects on gifted pupils' learning and their attitudes towards learning, and on what we know about the academic and socioaffective outcomes of the many forms of ability grouping.

THE SPREAD OF ABILITIES IN THE INCLUSION CLASSROOM

Effective instruction must be based on a recognition of three basic premises of learning.

1   Learning is a sequential, developmental process. Attainment of skills, understanding in different domains of knowledge, and strategies for solving problems, are all acquired gradually, and in sequences that are more or less predictable (Robinson 1983).
2   There are substantial differences in learning status and learning rates among individuals of any given age. Individual differences characterise both the rate of development (i.e. general intelligence) and the acquisition of specific skills (e.g. reading), and even in the earliest years of school we can note a quite remarkable spread of achievement in reading or number work among children in the same school class (Robinson 1983).
3   Effective teaching must involve a sensitive assessment of the individual pupil's status in the learning process, followed by the presentation of problems that *slightly exceed* the level already mastered. (Tasks that are too easy produce boredom; tasks that are too difficult cannot be understood.) Vygotsky (1976) calls this 'target area' the zone of proximal development.

If, as educators, we recognise and accept these three fundamental principles of effective learning and effective teaching, then we must ask ourselves this question:

If it is true that learning is a developmental and sequential process, that there are striking differences in developmental rates among individuals of the same age, and that effective teaching must be grounded where the learner is, then how do we justify an educational system that ignores competence (what pupils are able to do) and achievement (what they have already mastered) and utilises chronological age *as the primary, or only, factor in pupil placement?*

Grouping by chronological age is a relatively modern administrative procedure, introduced within the past hundred years. It was brought in to cope with large numbers of pupils from previously disenfranchised groups entering school systems which had previously catered to comparatively small numbers. Before this time, children had progressed through school on the basis of their mastery of the work of the different grade levels. Acceleration was a common, and accepted, procedure for ensuring that academically gifted pupils were presented with work appropriate to their developmental needs. This also facilitated a certain homogeneity of academic ability within grade levels.

In today's schools, however, we group pupils by chronological age because it seems to be administratively convenient, because we have become accustomed to doing so, and because we wrongly assume that chronological age is an accurate index of academic development. However, sixty years of empirical research has shown us that chronological age is not a reliable indicator of the level that a child can, and should, be working at. Gagné (1986) reports a study conducted by Deslaurier in French-speaking Quebec which investigated the degree to which pupils already know, at the start of the school year, work that theoretically would be introduced that year.

At the start of the school year, Deslaurier administered, to randomly selected Year 5 pupils, the maths test and the French test that would normally be given at the end of the year. The results were disturbing. Fully 3 per cent of the children scored 85 per cent or above on at least one of the tests; a further 3 per cent scored between 80 per cent and 84 per cent, and 7 per cent scored between 75 per cent and 79 per cent. In other words, fully 13 per cent of the pupils knew three-quarters of the year's work in two key subjects areas before year had started. Indeed, Deslaurier found that 45 per cent of these Year 5 pupils already knew more than 60 per cent of the work.

In the United States, a professor of mathematics, Dr James Flanders (1987), analysed the content of three of the best-selling school maths textbook series to see how much new material was taught each year. Giving credit to a book for a 'new page' if *any* new material appeared on that page, Flanders concluded that as early as third grade, pupils were required to revise fully 60 per cent of the work covered in the two previous years, while fully 62 per cent of the work in sixth grade, 65 per cent in seventh grade, and 70 per cent in eigth grade was revision.

Pupils who had mastered work in previous years were 'marking time' in maths for two-thirds of the week.

In 1993 Dr Sally Reis and colleagues at the American National Center for Gifted Education published a startling study which showed that teachers could modify the curriculum for academically gifted pupils by *eliminating* approximately 40 to 50 per cent of the core curriculum in maths, language arts, science and social studies – the proportion of the year's work regularly revised from the previous year – without the pupils suffering any ill effects (Reis *et al.* 1993). Indeed, Reis noted that gifted pupils might well start the school year in January rather than the previous September and compact the year's work into six months!

What can we do for pupils who start the school year already knowing more than half of the work they are to be 'taught' that year? First, schools have to acknowledge that the situation exists, and this is unlikely to happen if we continue to act on the flawed premise that chronological age is a reliable index of what pupils can, or do, achieve.

The span of achievement in mixed ability classes makes individualisation of instruction virtually impossible. In 1998 an Australian study surveying literacy in primary school children found 'a learning gap' equivalent to at least five years of schooling between the top and bottom 10 per cent of children in each Year 3 class surveyed in the study (Coorey 1998). The full achievement range is much wider than that. Although Coorey did not report, in his study, the score ranges of pupils in the lower and upper deciles of the distribution, these pupils were still in the classroom!

Because of the importance of reading as a learning tool, the range of achievement in virtually every subject area increases as a given cohort of pupils moves through school. A Secondary 2 class may include pupils reading, with full comprehension and enjoyment, adult science fiction or historical biography, and pupils who are struggling to read at Primary 4 level.

The teacher's dilemma

The sheer range of pupil achievement in the mixed ability classroom can be daunting for teachers. There is a powerful incentive for them to 'bring the bottom up'. If they are able to enhance the achievement of the slower pupils, not only are they assisting those children but they are also making their own task somewhat easier by decreasing the huge achievement range they have to work with. The aim of inclusion – mainstreaming the slower learners and bringing them closer to the other pupils – is highly congruent with this.

Gifted pupils, however, pose more of a problem. By allowing these children to advance, the teacher is assisting them to move even further ahead of the other pupils, *increasing* the achievement range in his or her class. Often, teachers justify their decision not to give a gifted pupil material that is too advanced for his (or her) classmates by saying, 'I don't want him to get too far ahead of the others'.

Teachers have a genuine concern that pupils, gifted or otherwise, should not be pressured. However, the teacher may also instinctively and subconciously be saying, 'The further away he gets from the others the greater will be my management difficulties. He will be more difficult to "include" in the curriculum that's designed for this class.'

For schools committed to inclusion, there *is* a solution to the dilemma. Include the slower learner in the mainstream classroom. Include the gifted learner, part time or full time, in a group of ability peers.

SOCIAL AND EMOTIONAL ISSUES FOR PUPILS IN THE INCLUSION CLASSROOM

Teachers often argue that gifted pupils should be kept in the inclusion classroom on the basis that, although they differ academically from age-peers, their social and emotional development is generally age-appropriate; yet many years of psychological research have shown this is not so.

It is now generally recognised that the emotional and social maturity of gifted children is much more closely linked to their mental age (their developmental age in terms of their reasoning ability) than to their chronological age (Tannenbaum 1983a; Janos and Robinson 1985; Robinson *et al.* 2002). Lehman and Erdwins (1981), in a study which measured the social and emotional adjustment of third- and sixth-grade children of average intellectual ability, and intellectually gifted third-grade children, found that the gifted grade three pupils scored significantly above their average ability age-mates on all twelve of the measured areas of adjustment. Indeed, the gifted grade three children displayed better social and emotional adjustment than the average ability sixth-grade children on eleven of the twelve measures.

Gifted pupils strongly prefer to learn and socialise with children at their own stage of intellectual and emotional development – and this means either other gifted children or children a few years older (O'Shea 1960; Gross 1992; Silverman 1993; Gross 2004). When access to these preferred companions is restricted, they may either mask their emotional maturity and intellectual talent to be accepted by their classmates (Gross 1989; Benbow and Stanley 1996) or they may become isolates, reluctantly choosing to be alone rather than having to interact constantly with children who are much less emotionally mature and whose interests are so very different to their own. For highly gifted children restricted to the regular classroom with little access to other gifted pupils, lasting social problems and emotional disturbance can result (Silverman 1993; Gross 2004).

Many of the socioaffective qualities that characterise intellectually gifted pupils can set them apart from their age-peers. For example, humour usually creates a bond between classmates; however, children's appreciation of humour is developmental and progresses in stages. Gifted children and adolescents tend to be 'a stage ahead' of their age-peers. In the early years of primary, when their classmates are enjoying visual jokes or scenarios, they may already have developed an enjoyment of puns and wordplay (Silverman 1993; Van Tassel-Baska 1998.) When their classmates have moved on to verbal humour, they may have already advanced to 'situation humour' as expressed in the Monty Python, Blackadder or Seinfeld television series where the joke centres on incongruity of ideas. It is difficult for children to make friendship bonds when they cannot laugh together, and gifted pupils are often regarded as wierd or strange because they laugh at things their age-peers find unfunny or even incomprehensible.

ABILITY GROUPING PROCEDURES USED WITH ACADEMICALLY GIFTED PUPILS

In discussing ability grouping of academically gifted young people, it is important to recognise the difference between 'streaming' or 'tracking' and the other, more commonly used, forms of ability grouping. Tracking/streaming (the terms vary from country to country) generally refers to the practice of designating pupils, at relatively early ages (often around age eleven or twelve) to 'academic' or 'vocational' educational courses. Usually there is minimal opportunity to transfer between streams.

Ability grouping as it is generally practised today is much more flexible and multifaceted. The more commonly used forms are briefly described below, under the names by which they are generally referred to in the research literature – although opponents of ability grouping are prone to use the term 'streaming' as a derogatory synonym for ability grouping of any kind!

- *Special schools*   State-run and private schools for gifted pupils exist in many countries. Schools for pupils talented in the performing arts have existed for many years and arouse almost no controversy; schools for academically gifted pupils arouse rather more debate. As will be outlined later, these schools are highly successful academically and in general have many more applicants than can be accommodated.
- *Full-time classes*   These classes for academically gifted pupils generally exist in primary schools or in the early years of secondary school. In some schools the pupils are educated full-time with their ability peers; in others they join with regular classes for art, music and sport. In some schools the ability grouping is accompanied by acceleration: the gifted class telescopes two years into one, or three years into two, graduating from secondary school a year early (Gross 2004).
- *'Pull-out' or 'withdrawal' programmes*   Gifted pupils leave their regular classrooms for a specified number of hours per week to work with ability peers

from other classes on enrichment and extension material. Pull-out groups may be subject-specific e.g. maths or English, or may comprise pupils with a variety of talents.

- *Cluster grouping*   This refers to the practice of identifying the top six to ten (although Rogers 2002 advises five to eight) pupils at a grade level and placing them in the same (otherwise mixed ability) classroom with a teacher who will develop a curriculum differentiated in level and pace for this group. The cluster may be selected on the basis of single subject talent (e.g. science, maths or art) or general academic ability.
- *Regrouping for specific subject instruction*   This is usually a grade-wide or schoolwide decision where all pupils take a given subject at the same time. Pupils work with ability peers from other classes at the same grade level. In general regrouping occurs for one or more academic subjects and pupils are mainstreamed for other subjects.
- *Cross-grade grouping*   For this procedure, all participating grades take the 'grouped' subjects at the same time. For example, all classes at Primary 3, 4 and 5 will take reading at the same time each day and classes are set by achievement level. Pupils move to the classroom which contains pupils reading at their particular level, regardless of grade. A maths class, for example, may contain pupils from all three grades. Assessment is ongoing and pupils change groups at regular intervals.

Karen Rogers' excellent 2002 text *Re-forming Gifted Education: How Parents and Teachers Can Match the Programme to the Child* contains a comprehensive analysis of the research findings on each of these programme options.

OBJECTIONS COMMONLY PRESENTED TO GROUPING BY ABILITY

As discussed earlier, the objections put forward to grouping academically gifted young people for instruction are seldom made in relation to the grouping of young people gifted in sport, athletics or music. It is noticeable, and disturbing, that the reasons most frequently given by teachers and school administrators for not grouping academically gifted pupils by ability are not supported, and are in many cases contradicted, by empirical research.

1   *'Ability grouping is elitist and adversely effects the self-esteem of those not in the top group.'*   The words 'elite' and 'elitism' are often used much more loosely than they should be. They are value-laden terms which we use in both a positive *and* a negative sense depending on the context. For example, both Britain and Australia have created a sporting elite and that term is used widely to describe and honour high-profile performers. We must therefore

ask outselves: *if* elitist is a positive term in the context of developing sport-ing or athletic talent, then why is it *not* a positive term in the context of the development of intellectual talent? And conversely, of course, if the words elite and elitist are used pejoratively in the context of special programmes for academically gifted pupils, why do our nations commit special funding for elite sports (Australia has even formally defined these: they are the ones we do well in!) and elite athletes? We can't have it both ways.

With regard to the second part of the statement – that grouping gifted pupils adversely effects the self-esteem of pupils not selected: this is an emo-tive argument, but it is not supported by research. Kennedy (1989, 1994) found that children of average and low ability enjoyed having the gifted pupils withdrawn from the classroom; they then had a chance to stand out. Similarly, Fiedler *et al.* describe a primary school pupil's comments when the gifted pupils had left the classroom for their pull-out programme. 'When Bill (the gifted pupil) was in class, it was like the sun shining on a bright, clear day. But when he went out to work with the other gifted kids, it was like when the sun goes over the horizon. The rest of us were like the moon and stars; that's when we finally got a chance to shine' (1993: 7).

Certainly pupils who are not selected for programmes they want to enter will be saddened. It happens when someone fails to make the soccer team. It happens when someone isn't chosen for the choir that will sing in the Eisteddfod. It happens when someone applies for enrolment to a performing arts high school and is rejected. But we don't argue for the disbandment of these programmes on the grounds that they are not all-inclusive!

2   *'Life experiences do not occur in homogeneous settings, and high ability pupils must learn to work with a wide range of people.'* Certainly pupils of any level of abil-ity must learn to work with a wide range of people, but ability grouping hardly denies them that opportunity. Incidentally, if we really examine our lives as adults, it will be seen that very many of our life experiences *do* occur in homogeneous groupings. People tend to socialise with other people with whom they have a certain commonality of interests. Most of us choose, as marriage partners and close friends, people with whom we have a certain degree of intellectual compatibility. This may not be 'politically correct' but it is human nature.

This clustering of like minds and like interests in adulthood is possible only because adults are mobile and can develop their own social groupings. The gifted child who has her primary social group – her school class – selected for her by her school on the basis of chronological age may be placed with a group with whom she has little compatibility on the basis of academic ability, emotional maturity or interests. This may be administra-tively convenient for the school, but it is neither educationally nor psychologically defensible.

3   *'Gifted pupils should be left in the regular classroom as models and mentors for pupils of lesser ability.'* Fiedler *et al.* (1993) point out that this idea is based on three false assumptions: first, that gifted pupils are consistently highly motivated achievers who will inspire others to similar accomplishments; second, that gifted pupils placed in mixed ability classrooms will perform at their peak if they lack regular opportunities to interact with intellectual peers who can stimulate their thinking; and third, that the less able or average pupils will be able to learn effectively from gifted pupils whose modes of thinking and working are so different from theirs. Bandura's (1977) and Schunk's (1987) research finds that children of average and low ability do not, in any case, model on high ability or gifted children; rather, they model on pupils of roughly similar ability to themselves who have succeeded in what they are trying to do – particularly if this has required effort and persistence. In general, gifted pupils are too far removed in ability from the average pupil to be an appropriate role model for these children – and average ability pupils recognise this, and model on pupils whose achievements they can more realistically hope to emulate.

4   *'Ability grouping segregates pupils along ethnic and socioeconomic status (SES) lines.'* When appropriate identification and selection procedures are employed, using objective as well as subjective measures, gifted pupils from low socioeconomic backgrounds and from culturally diverse groups are much more likely to be selected for special programmes than occurs when teacher nomination is used as the primary, or only, selection procedure (Baldwin 1985). Enrolments in Australian academically selective schools and classes, which employ culture-sensitive assessment procedures, reveal that the pupils come from a wide, wide range of cultures and SES backgrounds (Gross 2004).

5   *'Ability grouping makes children conceited about their academic ability.'* As early as 1972, a nationwide report commissioned by Sidney P. Marland, the US Commissioner of Education, showed evidence to the contrary:

> The relatively few pupils who have had the advantage of special programmes have shown remarkable improvements in self-understanding and in their ability to relate well to others, as well as in their academic and creative performance. The programmes have not produced arrogant, selfish snobs; special programmes have extended a sense of reality, wholesome humility, self-respect and respect for others. A good programme for the gifted increases their involvement and interest in learning through the reduction of the irrelevant and redundant.
>
> (Marland 1972: 51)

Silverman (1993) suggests that ability grouping is more likely to reduce conceit and overconfidence in gifted pupils than elicit it. However, if ability grouping does produce conceit in some academically gifted pupils it may be an indication that the pupils are still being underchallenged. Ability grouping of gifted pupils must be accompanied by work that the pupil has to strive to master. Too easy mastery of work offered in a grouped setting may well cause gifted pupils to overestimate their ability.

6   'Research has found no academic advantage to ability grouping.' This belief generally arises from a misconception regarding research undertaken by Slavin (1987, 1990) who investigated the effectiveness of curriculum delivery in grouped settings and claimed that ability grouping made very little difference to the quality of pupils' learning. However, it is important to note that Slavin specifically *excluded* from his analysis any studies focussing on gifted and special education children. His rationale was that those pupils would not benefit from receiving the curriculum developed for pupils of average ability; what he wanted to look at was the interaction between ability grouping and the *standard* curriculum. His expectations were upheld and he found that this central group of children performed equally well whether they were ability grouped or educated in a mixed ability setting. However, the very pupils in most need of differentiated programming were not included in his calculations!

    Research by Kulik (1992), discussed below, found that while the considerable majority of studies investigating the ability grouping of gifted students noted strongly positive academic effects, studies of programmes in which pupils were grouped by ability but were then offered undifferentiated curricula indicated that this approach offers far less advantage to gifted pupils. This finding is sometimes used to argue that 'gifted programmes' provide little educational benefit; however, differential placement without a differentiated curriculum offers little more than a token endorsement of these young people's educational needs. Such a placement cannot realistically be termed a programme for gifted pupils.

7   '*Ability grouping damages gifted pupils' self-esteem.*' The meta-analyses conducted by Kulik (1992), Delcourt *et al.* (1994) and Rogers (1998) of numerous studies on ability grouping (seventy studies in Rogers' synthesis alone) found little evidence to support this assertion.

A large-scale study comparing shifts in self-esteem among more than 1,000 pupils in Australian selective high schools (SHS) and comprehensive (mixed ability) high schools (CHC) found significantly higher self-esteem among SHS pupils (Gross 1997). The *academic* self-esteem of students in both forms of school did experience a dip in the first few weeks of high school (fully congruent with students moving from being top of the age-grade pecking order in primary school to being bottom of the age-grade pecking order in secondary) but recovered as the year progressed. However, although the dip in academic self-esteem was more significant for SHS than for CHS pupils, the SHS pupils still had higher self-esteem scores than did CHS pupils on all aspects of self-esteem (academic, social, home/family, and general self-esteem) and this superiority was maintained at all times during the study (Gross 1997).

Marsh (with Parker 1984) has suggested that the decrease in academic self-esteem sometimes noted when gifted pupils enter ability-grouped programmes is a function of the 'big fish in the little pond' effect (BFLPE) – the realisation, for the first time, that they are no longer the 'best' in the class and that there are pupils even more able than themselves. Yet in Gross's study the CHS pupils experienced a similar self-esteem dip, which suggests that other influences were at work. Perhaps the BFLPE *was* functioning – but as an outcome of the age-grade pecking order phenomenon described above, rather than a function of level of ability.

Indeed, perhaps the self-esteem dip for gifted pupils results less from a change in academic ranking (the BFLPE) than from the opportunity to measure them-selves, for the first time, against academic work which is commensurate with their abilities. William James proposed that self-esteem is a ratio of performance and expectations (James 1910). If our performance is higher than we previously believed we are capable of, our self-esteem will be high. If our performance is less than we have come to expect of ourselves, our self-esteem will be lower.

More than five times as many pupils apply to selective high schools than there are places available. Acceptance into these schools, and exposure to work which offers high levels of academic challenge, may allow intellectually gifted children to realise, for the first time, the full extent of their abilities and, therefore, what they can, or should, expect of themselves. Perhaps the decline in academic self-esteem among SHS students entering ability-grouped programmes, which has been replicated in other studies of gifted students entering ability grouping (e.g. Gibbons *et al.* 1994), reflects these students' realisation, often for the first time, of the gap between their remarkable achievements and their even more remarkable potential. It reflects an understanding that even greater effort is required if they are to realise their potential fully.

The decline is not, therefore, a disturbing *loss* of academic self-esteem, but a realistic appraisal of, on the one hand, what they can do if they try, and on the other, how much further they need to go if they are to become all that they can be.

In Gross's study, self-esteem was shown to be linked to motivational orientation, with pupils who are task-involved (motivated to learn for the love of learning) dis-playing consistently higher self-esteem than pupils who are ego-involved (motivated to learn in order to be better than one's classmates). The few pupils who did experience a disturbing decrease in academic self-esteem during the course of Year 7 (fewer than 5 per cent of the sample) tended to be highly ego-involved. The majority of SHS pupils in this study displayed a task-involved, rather than an ego-involved, orientation – contradicting the community perception that selective schools breed competitiveness. What ability grouped programmes *do* encourage is self-referenced competition – the desire to perform better than one has performed before – which may be misinterpreted by observers as competitiveness against one's classmates.

RESEARCH-BASED ADVANTAGES OF GROUPING BY ABILITY

1   *The academic achievement of gifted pupils in ability grouped settings is consistently and significantly higher than that of ability peers educated in the inclusion classroom.* Overwhelmingly, research shows that gifted pupils in ability grouped settings *in which the curriculum is differentiated in response to their ability* perform significantly better on later measures of school achievement (measures of 'value added') than do their ability-peers in mixed ability settings. Research consistently shows measurable academic gains for gifted pupils across all subject areas, particularly when the grouping is full time (Kulik 1992) and particularly for high ability pupils from minority groups (Page and Keith 1996). Meta-analyses of 'value added' studies of the performance of gifted pupils in ability-grouped classes where the curriculum is accelerated as well as enriched have shown that these pupils gain in grade-level competencies at almost twice the rate of equally gifted pupils retained in the regular classroom (Kulik 1992). The ability-grouped pupils gain, on average, ten months' additional progress over the course of a year. Even pupils in ability-grouped classes whose curriculum consists principally of enrichment were shown to progress at rates 50 per cent higher than ability peers in the mixed ability classroom. These studies found, furthermore, that gifted pupils improved significantly in attitude towards those school subjects in which they were ability grouped.

 Goldring's (1990) meta-analysis of studies on various forms of grouping found that gifted pupils in special classes experienced significant gains in achievement over ability peers retained in the regular classroom, particularly in science and social studies. A further study published in the same year (Berge 1990) confirmed that high ability pupils achieved at significantly higher levels in science instruction using computers when working in small groups of like ability than when they were working individually.

 Educators who argue that ability grouping produces no measurable gains tend to be overinfluenced by the Slavin studies, discussed earlier, and the studies critiqued by Kulik for inadequate curriculum modification.

2   *The quality of gifted pupils' academic achievement is related not only to their access to ability grouping, but to its intensity and duration.* Researchers have noted the different effects of various forms of grouping on academic achievement (e.g.

Rogers 1991, 1998; Kulik 1992; Benbow 1997). A longitudinal study (Delcourt *et al.* 1994) examined a range of academic and socioaffective variables for more than 1,000 academically gifted pupils in a range of educational settings – special schools for gifted pupils, full-time classes, pull-out programmes and small groups of individual students who received a differentiated curriculum within the inclusion classroom As with previous research, this study found that gifted pupils in special programmes perform consistently better than do equally gifted pupils educated entirely in the regular classroom. However, when the achievement of pupils in different forms of ability grouping was compared it was found that gifted pupils in full-time ability-grouped settings (special schools and classes) performed significantly better than did equally gifted pupils who were ability-grouped for only part of the week or who were cluster-grouped or educated individually in the inclusion classroom.

Rogers (1998) found that while homogeneous grouping was more beneficial than mixed ability grouping for pupils at all levels of academic ability, it was much more beneficial for high ability than for low ability pupils. Not only did achievement increase with the degree of ability grouping, but both high ability and low ability pupils benefited from more social interactions when grouped with like-ability peers.

3   *Gifted students in ability-grouped settings have more positive attitudes towards learning, and more realistic attitudes towards their own abilities, than do ability peers in inclusion settings.* Pupils are much more motivated to learn when the level and pace at which the curriculum is pitched is slightly beyond, but not too far beyond, their current level of achievement – Vygotsky's (1976) 'zone of proximal development'. Students in ability-grouped settings are more intrinsically motivated to achieve (Gross 1997; Hoekman *et al.* 1999) and are more interested in sharing and comparing their work with other students. (As Paul, a gifted high school student told this author some years ago: 'If I show my work to other kids in my class either they resent it or they put me down; there's no real common ground. But in the gifted programme everyone shares their work and learns from each other and there's an easy acceptance – no envy, no angst. It's very stimulating but in another way it's very restful because we feel so secure.') A recent empirical study (Gottfried *et al.* 2005) suggests that the higher levels of intrinsic motivation noted in academically gifted students compared to age-peers of average ability may be fundamentally an innate quality. Perhaps the emotional security noted by Paul in the ability-grouped setting allows greater scope for this motivational orientation to flourish.

Delcourt *et al.* (1994) also studied socioaffective issues such as motivational orientation (intrinsic, as might be expected), pupils' attitudes towards learning, and their academic self-perceptions. Gifted pupils in special schools had more positive attitudes towards learning, and were more likely to feel confident about their judgments on issues related to school and learning, than ability peers in any other grouped or ungrouped setting. Interestingly, gifted students in mixed ability classes and part-time grouping had higher perceptions of their own academic abilities than did equally gifted pupils in full-time grouped settings. Contrary to the belief that ability grouping makes gifted pupils conceited, it may be gifted pupils in the inclusion classroom who, having no opportunity to measure themselves against a valid comparison group, have inflated opinions of their own abilities.

THE LEAST RESTRICTIVE ENVIRONMENT

Influenced by a considerable body of research on the positive effects of ability grouping on both the academic and social development of gifted pupils, virtually every recognised authority on the education and psychology of the gifted has recommended that intellectually gifted pupils should be grouped together for a significant proportion of their class time (Hollingworth 1942; Kulik and Kulik 1982, 1997; Tannenbaum 1983b; Borland 1989; Benbow and Stanley 1996; Rogers 1998). Even educators who express concern about the practice of grouping slow-learning pupils by ability (e.g. Oakes 1985; Johnson and Johnson 1989) report the benefits that accrue to gifted pupils when they are grouped for fast-paced, accelerated work.

Given the wealth of research on the positive academic and socioaffective outcomes of ability grouping gifted pupils, and the smorgasbord of grouping options from which to select settings which would suit individual needs, surely the question is not *whether* to group the gifted, but rather *how*?

Decisions regarding pupil placements have, all too often, been based not on educational and psychological principles, but on political expediency and administrative convenience, or on a concern for 'equity' which confuses equal opportunity with equal outcomes. In special education, we seek to place the pupil with special needs in 'the least restrictive environment'. For the gifted pupil, the inclusion classroom may not be the least restrictive environment, while for the highly gifted it is arguably the most restrictive environment we could devise (Silverman 1989; Gross 2004).

If 'inclusion' means placing a gifted pupil, for at least a few hours' structured time each week, together with other pupils who share her abilities and interests and with a curriculum differentiated in response to their learning needs and capabilities, then include me as an advocate of inclusion.

But if 'inclusion' means educating gifted pupils full time in the the mixed ability classroom, ignoring what research shows us about the inadequacies of such a placement both for their learning and for their socialisation, then in the words of the late Samuel Goldwyn, 'Include me out!'

References

Baldwin, A. Y. (1985) 'Programmes for the gifted and talented: Issues concerning minority populations'. In F. D. Horowitz and M. O'Brien (eds) *The gifted and talented: Developmental Perspectives* (pp. 223–49). Washington, DC: American Psychological Association.

Bandura, A. (1977) 'Self-efficacy: Toward a unifying theory of behavioral change'. *Psychological Review*, 84, pp. 191–215.

Benbow, C. P. (1997) 'Grouping intellectually advanced students for instruction'. In J. Van Tassel-Baska (ed.) *Excellence in Educating Gifted and Talented Learners* (pp. 261–78). Denver, CO: Love Publishing.

Benbow, C. P. and Stanley, J. C. (1996) 'Inequity in equity: How "equity" can lead to inequity for high-potential students'. *Psychology, Public Policy and Law*, 2 (2), pp. 249–92.

Berge, Z. L. (1990) 'Effects of group size, gender, and ability grouping on learning science process skills using microcomputers'. *Journal of Research in Science Teaching*, 27, pp. 923–54.

Borland, J. H. (1989) *Planning and Implementing Programmes for the Gifted*. New York: Teachers College Press.

Coorey, M. (1998) 'Notebook'. *The Australian*, 18 May.

Delcourt, M. A. B., Loys, B. H., Cornell, D. G. and Goldberg, M. D. (1994) *Evaluation of the Effects of Programming Arrangements on Student Learning Outcomes*. Charlottesville, VA: National Research Center on the Gifted and Talented.

Festinger, L. (1954) 'A theory of social comparison process'. *Human Relations*, 7, pp. 117–40.

Fiedler, E. D., Lange, R. E. and Winebrenner, S. (1993) 'In search of reality: Uncovering the myths about tracking, ability grouping and the gifted'. *Roeper Review*, 16 (1), pp. 4–7.

Flanders, J. R. (1987) 'How much of the content of mathematics textbooks is new?' *Arithmetic Teacher*, 35, pp. 18–23.

Gagné, F. (1986) *Douance, talent et accélération du préscolaire à l'université*. Montreal: Centre Educatif et Culturel.

Gagné, F. (1995) 'The differentiated nature of giftedness and talent. A model and its impact on the technical vocabulary of gifted and talented education'. *Roeper Review*, 18 (2), pp. 103–11.

Gagné, F. (2003) 'Transforming gifts into talents: The DMGT as a developmental theory'. In N. Colangelo and G. A. Davis (eds) *Handbook of Gifted Education* (3rd edn) (pp. 60–74). Boston: Allyn & Bacon.

Gallagher, J. J. (1976) *Teaching the Gifted Child* (2nd edn). Boston: Allyn & Bacon.

Gibbons, F. X., Benbow, C. P. and Gerrard, M. (1994) 'From top dog to bottom half: Social comparison strategies in response to poor performance'. *Journal of Personality and Social Psychology*, 67 (4), pp. 638–52.

Goldring, E. B. (1990) 'Assessing the status of information on classroom organizational frameworks for gifted pupils'. *Journal of Educational Research*, 83, pp. 313–26.

Gottfried, A. W., Gottfried, A. E., Cook, C. R. and Morris, P. E. (2005) 'Educational characteristics of adolescents with gifted academic intrinsic motivation: A longitudinal investigation from school entry through early adulthood'. *Gifted Child Quarterly*, 49 (2), pp. 172–186.

Gross, M. U. M. (1989) 'The pursuit of excellence or the search for intimacy? The forced-choice dilemma of gifted youth'. *Roeper Review*, 11 (4), pp. 189–94.

Gross, M. U. M. (1992) 'The use of radical acceleration in cases of extreme intellectual precocity'. *Gifted Child Quarterly*, 36 (2), pp. 90–98.

Gross, M. U. M. (1997) 'How ability grouping turns big fish into little fish – or does it? Of optical illusions and optimal environments'. *Australasian Journal of Gifted Education*, 6 (2), pp. 18–30.

Gross, M. U. M. (2004) *Exceptionally Gifted Children* (2nd edn). London: Routledge Falmer.

Hoekman, K., McCormick, J. and Gross, M. U. M. (1999) 'The optimal context for gifted students: A preliminary exploration of motivational and affective considerations'. *Gifted Child Quarterly*, 43 (4), pp. 170–93.

Hollingworth, L. S. (1942) *Children above IQ 180: Their Origin and Development*. New York: World Books.

James, W. (1910) 'The principles of psychology'. In R. N. Campbell (ed.) *The New Science: Self-esteem Psychology*. New York: University Press of America.

Janos, P. M. and Robinson, N. M. (1985) 'Psychosocial development in intellectually gifted children'. In F. D. Horowitz and M. O'Brien (eds) *The Gifted and Talented: Developmental Perspectives* (pp. 149–95). Washington, DC: American Psychological Association.

Johnson, D. and Johnson, R. (1989) 'What to say to parents of gifted children'. *The Cooperative Link*, 5 (2), p. 1.

Kennedy, D. M. (1989) 'Classroom interactions of gifted and non-gifted fifth graders'. Unpublished doctoral dissertation. Purdue University, Indiana.

Kennedy, D. M. (1994) 'Interactions of gifted and non-gifted fifth-graders'. In J. B. Hansen and S. M. Hoover (eds) *Talent development: Theories and Practice* (pp. 227–56). Dubuque, IO: Kendall Hunt.

Kulik, C. C. and Kulik, J. (1982) 'Effects of ability grouping on secondary school students: A meta-analysis of evaluation findings'. *American Educational Research Journal*, 19, pp. 415–28.

Kulik, J. A. (1992) *An Analysis of the Research on Ability Grouping: Historical and Contemporary Perspectives*. University of Connecticut: National Research Center on the Education of the Gifted and Talented.

Kulik, J. A. and Kulik, C. L. C. (1997) 'Ability grouping'. In N. Colangelo and G. A. Davis (eds) *Handbook of Gifted Education* (2nd edn) (pp. 230–42). Boston: Allyn & Bacon.

Lehman, E. and Erdwins, C. (1981) 'Social and emotional adjustment of young intellectually gifted children'. *Gifted Child Quarterly*, 25, pp. 134–8.

Marland, S. P. (1972) *Education of the Gifted and Talented* (2 vols). Washington, DC: US Government Printing Office.

Marsh, H. W. and Parker, J. W. (1984) 'Determinants of student self-concept: Is it better to be a relatively large fish in a small pond even if you don't learn to swim as well?' *Journal of Personality and Social Psychology*, 47 (1), pp. 213–31.

Oakes, J. (1985) *Keeping Track: How Schools Structure Inequality*. New Haven: Yale University.

O'Shea, H. E. (1960) 'Friendship and the intellectually gifted child'. *Exceptional Children*, 26 (6), pp. 327–35.

Page, E. B. and Keith, T. Z. (1996) 'The elephant in the classroom: Ability grouping and the gifted'. In C. P. Benbow and D. Lubinski (eds) *Intellectual Talent: Psychometric and Social Issues* (pp. 192–210). Baltimore: Johns Hopkins University Press.

Reis, S. M., Westberg, K. L., Kulkowitch, J., Caillard, F., Hebert, T., Plucker, J., Rurcell, J. H., Rogers, J. B. and Smist, J. M. (1993) *Why not let high ability students start school in January? The curriculum compacting study*. Storrs, CT: University of Connecticut.

Robinson, H. (1983) 'A case for radical acceleration: Programmes of Johns Hopkins University and the University of Washington'. In C. P. Benbow and J. C. Stanley (eds) *Academic Precocity: Aspects of its Development* (pp. 139–59). Baltimore: Johns Hopkins University Press.

Robinson, N. M., Reis, S. M., Neihart, M. and Moon, S. M. (2002) 'Social and emotional issues facing gifted and talented students: What have we learned and what should we do now?' In M. Neihart, S. M. Reis, N. M. Robinson and S. M. Moon (eds) *The Social and Emotional Development of Gifted Children: What do We Know?* (pp. 267–88). Waco, TX: Prufrock Press.

Rogers, K. B. (1991) *The Relationship of Grouping Practices to the Education of the Gifted and Talented Learner*. Connecticut: National Research Center on the Gifted and Talented.

Rogers, K. B. (1998) 'Using current research to make "good" decisions about grouping'. National Association for Secondary Schools Principals' Bulletin, 82 (595), pp. 38–46.

Rogers, K. B. (2002) *Re-forming Gifted Education: How parents and teachers can match the programme to the child*. Scottsdale, AR: Great Potential Press.

Schunk, D. H. (1987) 'Peer models and children's behavioral change'. *Equity and Excellence*, 23, pp. 22–30.

Silverman, L. K. (1989) 'The highly gifted'. In J. F. Feldhusen, J. Van Tassel-Baska and K. Seeley (eds) *Excellence in Educating the Gifted* (pp. 71–83). Denver: Love Publishing.

Silverman, L.K. (1993) *Counselling the Gifted and Talented*. Denver: Love Publishing.

Slavin, R. E. (1987) 'Ability grouping: A best evidence synthesis'. *Review of Educational Research*, 57, pp. 293–336.

Slavin, R. E. (1990) 'Achievement effects of ability grouping in secondary schools: A best-evidence synthesis'. *Review of Educational Research*, 60, pp. 471–99.

Tannenbaum, A. J. (1983a) *Gifted Children: Educational and Psychological Perspectives*. New York: Macmillan.

Tannenbaum, A. J. (1983b) *Gifted Children: Psychological and Educational Perspectives*. New York: Macmillan.

Van Tassel-Baska, J. (1998) 'Disadvantaged learners with talent'. In J. Van Tassel-Baska (ed.) *Excellence in Educating Gifted and Talented Learners* (3rd edn) (pp. 95–113). Denver: Love Publishing.

Vygotsky, L. S. (1976) *Mind in Society*. Cambridge, MA: Harvard University Press.

What can ordinary schools do to promote inclusion for gifted and talented learners?

Chapter 9

Accommodating gifted learners in regular classrooms

Promises and pitfalls

Michael C. Pyryt and B. Lynn Bosetti

The question of whether the intellectual and social–emotional needs of gifted students can be accommodated in regular classrooms is answered with an unequivocal 'maybe'. Historically, leaders in gifted education have recognised that appropriate programming recommendations for gifted students should be contingent upon their educational and psychological characteristics, understood in the context of the visions and values of the educational community and society at large (Passow 1958). Community attitudes and demographics will necessarily impact the types of services that can be provided for gifted students. In the province of Alberta, in Canada, giftedness is viewed as a multidimensional construct combining the models of Marland (1972) and Gardner (1983). Students can be recognised as gifted by potential or performance in one or more of the following areas: general intellectual ability, specific academic aptitude, creative thinking, social ability, artistic ability, musical ability, kinaesthetic ability (Alberta Learning 2000). The definition is permissive, however. School jurisdictions have the choice of serving all types of giftedness or only one. At its most conservative, giftedness is defined as a score two standard deviations above the mean on an individually administered test of intelligence. This definition places the incidence of giftedness at two in every hundred. To find twenty intellectually gifted students at any grade level would require a school population of 1,000 students at that grade level. A definition that incorporates all seven categories of giftedness would include 10 to 15 per cent of the school population. In practice, school jurisdictions in Alberta are adopting narrow definitions of giftedness. Consequently, the majority of gifted students will find themselves in heterogeneous inclusive classrooms, since the majority will not be identified in the first place and those that are identified will be too few to justify a special programme. It is only in large cities like Calgary that resources for congregrated programming, in which selected gifted students attend specialised centres as a cohort, become feasible. Even in Calgary, nearly half the identified gifted students are served in inclusive classrooms. This chapter will explore ways that inclusive classrooms can provide appropriate challenge for gifted students and factors that lessen the likelihood that inclusive classrooms will nurture the potential of gifted students.

THE PROMISE OF ACCOMMODATING GIFTED STUDENTS IN REGULAR CLASSROOMS

Ward (1962) has generated a clear vision of what the ideal programme for the gifted should entail. It begins with a specification of outcomes based on the roles that gifted individuals will be expected to perform in society. There is an understanding of the characteristics and competencies needed by teachers of the gifted. There is community support for the programme and community members actively participate as mentors. A systematic approach to identification ensures that there are several opportunities for giftedness to be discovered on a system-wide basis. In contrast to current notions of curriculum differentiation, there are distinguishable curricular experiences from which only those selected as gifted would benefit due to the rigour of the curriculum. Accelerative opportunities ensure that gifted students are provided content that matches their achievement regardless of age. Programmes are available throughout all school levels in all subject areas. There is a systematic approach to formative evaluation so that programmes can be improved on an ongoing basis. There is an appropriate allocation of resources for each programme. Finally, the academic achievements of the students are celebrated as passionately as are athletic accomplishments. Ward's principles for programming can serve as the basis for examining the status of gifted programming in a school jurisdiction.

Feldhusen and Robinson-Wyman (1980) provide another lens on the issue of appropriate programming by examining the extent to which the programme meets the basic needs of the gifted. They proposed that gifted students need the opportunity to achieve the expected curriculum goals while being taught at an appropriate pace. Opportunities for developing creative-thinking abilities are important so that gifted learners can cope with future challenges. Positive mental imagery skills would provide mental discipline to help gifted students succeed. The first step in gifted students' self-acceptance is self-awareness of their capabilities. Gifted students need opportunities for career awareness so that they can make effective choices about how to use their gifts, opportunities for self-directed learning so that they will develop responsible autonomy, exposure to a wide variety of information sources, stimulating reading materials and opportunities for learning effective interpersonal skills. Finally, gifted students need stimulation to pursue post-baccalaureate studies. There are a variety of systems and models in gifted education (Renzulli 1986) that have been developed to assist gifted students achieve one or more of these outcomes.

Pyryt (2004) has synthesised the literature on curriculum approaches for gifted students and has developed a parsimonious model for accommodating them in regular classrooms. The approach is called Pyryt's Ps to emphasise the key components of the model. *Pace* involves the opportunity for gifted students to learn at an accelerated pace to address their rapid rate of learning. *Process* enables gifted students to develop higher-order thinking skills such as analysis, synthesis, evaluation, critical thinking, divergent thinking, and creative problem-solving in order to address

Table 9.1 Pyryt Enrichment Matrix

	Pace	Process	Passion	Product	Peers
Language arts					
Maths					
Science					
Social					
Art					
Music					
PE					

their capacity for complex thought. *Passion* incorporates the use of independent inquiry to engage gifted students to pursue areas of interest. *Product* recognises that there are multiple ways that gifted students can represent their knowledge gained through independent inquiry. Finally, *Peers* focuses on ensuring that gifted students develop positive relationships with peers. The Pyryt Enrichment Matrix (see Table 9.1) provides a visual representation of the accommodations made for gifted students across the curriculum. By examining the extent to which curriculum differentiation is occurring in each subject area, teachers in both inclusive classrooms and congregated settings can use the model to enhance learning opportunities. The five Ps represent the promise that the needs of gifted students can be met in regular classroom if appropriate accommodations are made. The following sections elaborate the key components of the model.

Pace

One of the simplest approaches for facilitating accelerating the pace is the use of diagnostic testing followed by prescriptive instruction (DT-PI). This technique was pioneered by Julian Stanley (1978, 2001) especially for mathematically and scientifically gifted students. It begins with pre-testing to determine a student's level of knowledge. The pre-test is normally a standardised achievement test or an end-of-year comprehensive examination. Test results are analysed for errors to determine instructional needs. An instructional programme is designed and implemented to meet these needs. When the teacher is confident that mastery has occurred, the student is re-tested using an alternate form of the initial test. In the DT-PI model, a student proceeds to the next academic level beginning with another comprehensive pre-test (Benbow and Lubinski 1997). This approach has been successfully used to foster acceleration in both mathematics (Bartkovich and Mezynski 1981) and science (Stanley and Stanley 1986). During an intense three-week summer programme, intellectually able students aged eleven to fifteen were able to learn the equivalent of a year of high school biology or chemistry or both using the DT-PI approach. Stanley (2001) suggests that computer programs could greatly facilitate the DT-PI process. Bishop Carroll High School in Calgary successfully uses a variation of DT-PI on a schoolwide basis. The entire high curriculum is broken into modules. Using a mastery learning approach, students complete modules at their own pace and preference. If a student wants to do the entire high school maths curriculum in Grade 10 and the entire high school English curriculum in Grade 12, they would be permitted to do so.

Curriculum compacting developed by Renzulli and colleagues (Reis *et al.* 1992, Renzulli *et al.* 1982, Starko 1986) is also a practical way to shorten the time students spend mastering material. Using this method a teacher identifies curriculum objectives, designs a pre-test, and administers the pre-test to a group of students. The teacher also attempts to avoid repetition and to streamline the teaching of concepts. A plan that specifies the educational alternatives (acceleration or enrichment) that will occur once content mastery has been obtained is drawn up. Often, students are given the opportunity to investigate real-world problems that they are interested in. It is essential to keep good records so that progress is appropriately documented. Using curricular compacting, gifted students can easily achieve content mastery in half the time normally allotted for content attainment (Reis *et al.* 1993).

Another strategy for appropriate pacing is subject-matter acceleration. Students who show strengths in particular subjects such as mathematics or science would accelerate only in those subjects. A variety of strategies can be used to implement subject-matter acceleration. The easiest but riskiest is to allow an individual or small group of students to work on advanced material in their regular classrooms. There is danger that the student may have to repeat the material the following year unless this form of acceleration is written into a student's special education plan, called an individual programme plan (IPP) in Alberta. Another possibility would be for the student to study the subject in the appropriate grade-level classroom. The third-grader with advanced maths skills could take fourth-grade maths in the fourth-grade room. This approach works best when similar subject-matter classes are scheduled at the same time. If done on a schoolwide basis, all students would be working on content appropriate to their needs. A charter school in Calgary has been successfully implementing this approach for over a decade. The use of fast-paced classes provides another possibility for subject-matter acceleration. In such courses, content is covered at a more rapid pace so that at least two years of material is covered in one year. The Study of Mathematically Precocious Youth (SMPY) at Johns Hopkins University has documented the effectiveness of fast-paced classes in mathematics (Bartkovitch and George 1980, George and Denham 1976) and science (Lynch 1990, Mezynski *et al.* 1983, Stanley and Stanley 1986). In Calgary, effective fast-paced maths classes were implemented at F. E. Osborne Junior High School[1] for several years (Pyryt and Moroz 1994). Students completed the junior high maths curriculum and the first senior high maths course while in junior high school. In high school, students successfully completed the second and third required maths classes and had the flexibility in their timetables to pursue additional maths classes or electives of their choice. Finally, subject-matter acceleration can be implemented via distance learning courses. Stanford University's Educational Program for Gifted Youth (Ravaglia *et al.* 1995) is a pioneer in developing distance learning opportunities that allow gifted students to learn at their own pace.

At the high school level, the use of credit by examination is an effective way to accelerate one's progress in all content areas. The Advanced Placement (AP) Program (Hanson 1980) is an excellent example of this approach. Students can earn university credit based on their scores on an AP examination. A score of three on a five-point marking scale will lead to the granting of credit at most universities. Selective universities require a score of four or five before awarding credit. The AP Program offers 34 examinations across 19 subject areas and provides course descriptions for the content that will be assessed on the AP examinations. There are over 110,000 teachers and administrators worldwide involved in AP programmes. Many universities in North America offer graduate credit through summer institutes that prepare secondary teachers to instruct a specific AP course. Longitudinal studies have supported the effectiveness of AP courses for mathematically gifted students. Brody *et al.* (1990) reported that AP credits were the only statistically significant predictor of overall grade point average (GPA), semesters on the Dean's List[2] by earning grades of at least a 3.50 on a 4.00 point scale and graduation honours in their study of early entrants at Johns Hopkins University.

For some gifted students, early entrance to universities (two years earlier than normal), part-time university courses, correspondence courses and distance learning opportunities provide effective acceleration experiences. Students who are identified through academic talent searches (Brody 1998) benefit from early entrance experiences (Brody *et al.* 1988, 1990, Olszewski-Kubilius 1995). Gross and van Vliet (2005) document the benefits of such radical acceleration in their recent review of the literature. In Alberta, the opportunity for early entrance is affected by the opportunities for acceleration at earlier periods. At the University of Calgary, for example, students from Alberta are only eligible for admission when they complete their Grade 12 coursework and diploma examination requirements.

Process

There are numerous approaches to conceptualising process skills. In the original Enrichment Triad Model, Renzulli and Reis (1986) discuss the development of process skills in terms of Type II Enrichment, Group Training Activities. Renzulli and Reis (1986) categorise Type II Enrichment as consisting of cognitive and affective training (creative-thinking skills, creative problem-solving and decision-making, critical and logical thinking, and affective skills), how-to-learn skills (observation, notetaking, interviewing, and organising data), advanced research skills (preparing for Type III investigations, developing library skills, identifying community resources), and communication skills (visual, oral and written). These Type II skills would be especially valuable in helping students develop effective research projects and presentations. This section will highlight some important process skills.

Bloom's (1956) *Taxonomy of Educational Objectives in the Cognitive Domain* is the starting point for conversation about process skills development. Although developed almost a half-century ago, the taxonomy remains a powerful vehicle for differentiating the curriculum. Roberts and Roberts (2005), for example, use Bloom's taxonomy as the cornerstone for developing curriculum units to challenge advanced learners. By organising objectives, instructional activities, questioning techniques and evaluation procedures along Bloom's taxonomy, a teacher can ensure that all students who master content at the knowledge, comprehension and application levels can explore the analysis, synthesis and evaluation levels (Parks 2005). Analysis activities capitalise on gifted students' abilities to make connections. Synthesis activities enable gifted students to transform their knowledge by generating creative products. Evaluation activities help gifted students judge the value of what has been created. The evaluative dimension of Bloom's taxonomy has been enhanced by contemporary developments in the teaching of critical thinking (Ennis 1995, Paul and Elder 2001, Parks 2005, Swartz and Parks 1994). The Center for Gifted Education at the College of William and Mary incorporates critical thinking as a major focus in its award-winning curriculum units (Center for Gifted Education 1999).

Another major component of the process dimension is creative thinking. Techniques for stimulating creativity range from simple brainstorming techniques to more complex, creative problem-solving approaches. Simple divergent-thinking techniques include attribute-listing, general semantics approaches, SCAMPER and morphological analysis. Attribute-listing (Crawford 1954) is an idea-generating technique involving specifying the physical, psychological, social and idiosyncratic characteristics of an object. Based on the ideas of Korzybski (1958), general semantics activities focus on the connection between language, thought and behaviour. General semantics activities involve determining multiple meanings of words such as 'fast' (speedy, gifted, not-eating, promiscuous, fade-proof). In Pyryt's (1999) meta-analysis, activities based on general semantics yielded the highest effect for increasing divergent-thinking ability. SCAMPER is an acronym for Substitute, Combine, Adapt, Magnify/Minify, Put to other uses, Eliminate, Re-arrange. Developed by Eberle (1971, 1984) SCAMPER is a selected example of the use of idea-checklists to generate creative ideas. Morphological analysis is a powerful idea-generation tool. The first step in morphological analysis is identifying the essential elements of a problem, called *parameters*. Using the parameters of people, places, processes and products to address the issue of organising programmes for gifted students, Treffinger (1979) illustrated the power of the approach. Generating fifteen possibilities for each parameter generates over 50,000 unique combinations of ideas to organise programmes for gifted students.

Creative problem-solving (CPS) involves the oscillation of divergent thinking and convergent thinking. In its most basic form, creative problem-solving consists of using five steps to solve a fuzzy problem or 'mess'. Pyryt (1999) provided an example of how the steps in this process can be used to design effective research projects. During *fact-finding*, the student would try to identify the parameters underlying the project (interests, length, available funds, timeframe, resources available). During *problem-finding*, the student would use guiding questions to generate possible problem-statements. During *idea-finding*, the student would generate ideas for potential research projects. During *solution-finding*, the student would generate criteria for judging potential ideas and evaluate the generated ideas against these criteria. During *acceptance-finding*, the student would develop an action plan for implementing the chosen research idea. Numerous resources are available for learning about creative problem-solving (Eberle 1978, Feldhusen and Treffinger 1985, Parnes 1981, 1992, Treffinger 1980, Treffinger *et al.* 1992).

Passion

Allowing students to pursue their academic passions through inquiry is a frequent focus of gifted education programming. Renzulli (1977) incorporated inquiry-oriented experiences into gifted education programming through Type III Enrichment. Individual and Small Group Investigation of Real-World Problems provides the opportunity for students to have self-selected independent inquiry experiences. Renzulli and Reis (1986) describe the qualities of a Type III project as involving problem-finding and focusing, developing a clear management contract, emulating the methodology of a discipline, drafting and revising a finished product, and presenting the product to an appropriate audience. Renzulli and Reis (1997) provide an example of a Type III project in science entitled 'Bobby Bones' which is a life-size model of the human skeletal structure. This project created by fourth graders also involved the development of a taped mini-course which was used by third graders during one of their health units.

Passion can also be enhanced through focus on independence and self-directed learning. Treffinger and Barton (1979) present an approach for fostering independence based on five teaching styles: command, task, peer-partner, teacher–pupil contract and self-directed. The styles vary in terms of who controls the four major components of an instructional system: determination of goals and objectives, assessment of entering behaviour, instructional activities and evaluation plan. In the command style, the teacher maintains complete control over all these dimensions. In the task style, the teacher gives up some control by providing several options for students in terms of initial assessment of entry skills, instructional activities and evaluation of outcomes. In the peer-partner style, the teacher interacts with students and their peer-partners in determining initial assessments, instructional activities and evaluation. In the teacher–pupil contract style, the teacher negotiates with the student in terms of goals and objectives, initial assessment, instructional activities and evaluation. In the self-directed style, the teacher allows the student to control all four components of the instructional system. The transition from command style to self-directed learning is viewed as a gradual process that is implemented over the course of school year.

The Center for Gifted Education at the College of William and Mary has developed a problem-based science curriculum that uses real problems to integrate science process, concepts and systems. The units cover such topics as electricity, nuclear waste, pollution and acid spills. Evaluation data has supported the effectiveness of the William and Mary units for developing science process skills (Van Tassel-Baska *et al.* 1998).

Product

As part of the Schoolwide Enrichment Model, Renzulli and Reis (1985) stressed the importance of identifying students' preferred expression formats as a way of expanding the variety of learning options for students. Renzulli (1994) recommended that teachers interact informally with students to create bulletin boards on how human beings express themselves. Examples generated by students become outlets that students can use to represent the knowledge gained from their inquiry projects. Kettle *et al.* (1998) operationalised the concept of expression preference by developing a promising instrument called My Way ... An Expression Style Inventory. This instrument consists of fifty items organised around ten types of product: artistic, audio-visual, commercial, computerised, dramatised, manipulative, musical, oral, service and written. The initial trial with over 3,500 students representing twenty-four states in the US indicated that the instrument has excellent psychometric characteristics. Karnes and Stephens (2000) provide tools for helping students generate quality products. They recommend that choice of products includes issues such as resource feasibility and audience credibility in addition to mere preferences.

Peers

Giftedness does not guarantee positive peer relationships. One factor that affects peer relationships is one's degree of giftedness relative to one's classmates. Hollingworth (1942) found that gifted children with IQ greater than 180 had difficulty establishing peer relationships. Another factor affecting peer relationships is participation in extra-curricular activities. Coleman (1962) reported that high school students viewed athletic participation as more important than scholarship in gaining peer acceptance. Tannenbaum (1962) found that among high school students in New York, the brilliant, non-studious athlete was rated most favourably while the brilliant, studious non-athlete was rated most unfavourably. Tannenbaum's study was replicated in Calgary with junior high school students (Glover 1993).

A question to consider is 'Who are the peers of the gifted?' Gross (2003a) provides compelling examples of the benefits of using of mental age rather than chronological age as the basis for peer relationships. Inclusive classrooms face the challenge of ensuring that intellectually gifted students have the opportunity to interact with mental-age peers. As a starting point, some junior high schools in Calgary have implemented 'Convocation' programmes in which bright students are brought together for daylong enrichment activities.

Positive peer adjustment can be promoted through interpersonal effectiveness training. Friedman (1978) compiled a list of competencies that are characteristic of effective interpersonal communicators. People who are most likely to be effective in social interaction are: genuine, honest and open about revealing themselves; show empathy, or real understanding of what people think or feel; give warmth, care and support to others; seem confident and relaxed; make appropriate comments to keep conversations going smoothly; are assertive, not dominant or passive; word their ideas clearly and concretely; deal with feelings, express their own and respond sensitively to the feelings of others; are flexible regarding the people and situations with which they can interact comfortably; and are capable of initiating, deepening and terminating relationships appropriately. These competencies have led to the development of self, peer and teacher rating scales that are unidimensional and relatively independent of intellectual ability (Pyryt 1985). Interpersonal skills can be enhanced through modelling, role-playing and practice.

Electronic communication can be a vehicle supporting positive peer relationships. The use of e-mail broadens the social milieu. Through a programme such as BESTS[3] friendships evolve from a collaboration between the Universities of Iowa, Calgary and New South Wales (Assouline et al. 1999). Students in the United States, Canada and Australia have the opportunity to interact with each other electronically. This should reduce some feelings of social isolation if there are no intellectual peers in one's home community. Electronic communication also promotes a greater sense of community since an individual is 'only an e-mail away' regardless of distance. This is comforting in an age of geographic mobility. The use of discussion groups or LISTSERVs also reduces isolation since individuals have the opportunity to communicate with others with similar interests. The various discussion groups in gifted education (families, underachievement, curriculum and miscellaneous issues) can be found on the Hoagies website (http:\\www.hoagies.org). Online course technology also provides the opportunities for synchronous and asynchronous modes. In the synchronous communication mode, individuals all have the opportunity to discuss issues in a selected time setting. In the asynchronous mode, individuals can post and receive information at their leisure. Electronic communication also provides a vehicle for collaboration and productivity and enables individuals to work on projects collaboratively at a distance. Group projects help create interdependence (Strop 2000).

PITFALLS ALONG THE WAY

There are several reasons why the promise of providing appropriate challenge for intellectually gifted learners will be difficult to fulfil. There is a cyclical love–hate relationship between society and the construct of giftedness (Tannenbaum 1993). There is a tension between dreams of excellence and concerns about equality. When 'excellence' is the focus, support for the gifted rises. When 'equity' is the focus, support for the gifted decreases. Colangelo (2003) noted that it is politically easier to ignore individual differences in intelligence rather than appreciate the strong research base related to intelligence testing. In spite of estimates of underachievement among the intellectually gifted as high as 50 per cent (National Commission on Excellence in Education 1983) the prevailing popular attitude is that gifted individuals will make it on their own. Proponents of Gardner's (1983) theory of multiple intelligences often believe that all children are gifted in some way. Giftedness is a normative concept, however. Everyone may have an intra–individual strength; that strength might not be sufficient to be judged as a gift. The following sections will highlight educational barriers, sociopolitical barriers and parental barriers to the promise of effective inclusion for gifted students.

EDUCATIONAL BARRIERS TO EFFECTIVE ACCOMMODATION

Social psychologists have long recognised that when research evidence contrasts with prevailing beliefs, there is a tendency toward ignoring the evidence in hopes of reducing 'cognitive dissonance'. Educators routinely ignore the overwhelming evidence in favour of academic acceleration (Colangelo *et al.* 2004, Daurio 1979, Gallagher 1996, Gross and van Vliet 2003, Kulik and Kulik 1984, Shore *et al.* 1991). In doing so, educators often dismiss an essential strategy for challenging the intellectually gifted. Similarly, educators tend to prefer the criticisms of ability grouping by Oakes' (1985) ethnographic study to the positive meta-analytic results obtained by Kulik and Kulik (1984). As a result, educators may limit the opportunities for gifted students to interact with intellectual peers. There is also a tendency to dismiss mastery learning paradigms as too mechanistic as educators favour constructivist approaches to teaching and learning.

By far the most important barrier to effective accommodation of gifted students in regular classrooms is the inability of the typical classroom teacher to effectively differentiate. Westberg *et al.* (1993) observed classroom practices in forty-six heterogeneous classes on two school days and reported that no differentiation for gifted students occurred in 84 per cent of the classes observed. It should not be surprising that many classroom teachers don't have the skills to differentiate instruction for gifted students since coursework in gifted education, if available, is not required of teacher training programmes. Leroux

(2000) surveyed fifteen universities across Canada regarding gifted education coursework in teacher education preparation programmes and found the extent of training was a module in gifted education as part of a survey of special education courses. It is clear that effective teachers of the gifted who possess specialised knowledge related to curriculum, differentiate and are sensitive to the affective needs of gifted students (Croft 2003, Frank 2003, Hansen and Feldhusen 1994, Feldhusen 1997). The widening variability in the inclusive classroom affects a teacher's ability to differentiate instruction. Gagné (2005) examined developmental standard score norms on a standardised achievement test and reported that the achievement gap within grade levels between highest and lowest achievers often exceeded the eight-year gap between the average first and ninth grader.

One can also use the concept of mental age to describe potential variability within a classroom (Gross 2003b). A twelve-year-old with an IQ of 133 would have a mental age of 16. A twelve-year-old with an IQ of 68 would have a mental age of eight. Thus, in the typical inclusive classroom with one student with intellectual gifts and one student with cognitive delays, there is an eight-year gap in cognitive functioning. The gap widens dramatically when exceptionally gifted students are added to the equation.

ACCOUNTABILITY CONSTRAINTS ON EXCELLENCE

The accountability movement that has dominated public education for the past decade is another barrier to appropriate education for intellectually gifted students. Moon *et al.* (2003) conducted a mixed-method investigation of the impact of standardised testing teaching practices in the United States. In Phase One, a nationally representative sample of 1,289 elementary school teachers completed a survey of classroom practices. About 30 per cent of these teachers rated their classrooms as functioning above grade level. In these classrooms, teachers report spending the entire month before the test having students complete worksheets on test-related content, providing instruction on test-taking strategies, reviewing and completing previously released versions of the test, and practising completing the types of items on the test. During the first six months of the year, teachers also spend several weeks implementing these practices. In classrooms where students are functioning above grade level, more than half of the teachers reported that they teach to the test and omit content that is not on the state test. Instructional practices that are reportedly used the least in classes where students are functioning above grade level are: instruction in fine and performing arts, topics not covered by the state tests, and enrichment. Teachers report matching their assessment approaches to the state testing formats. The assignment of long-term projects is a rare occurrence. Even in schools where the achievement of students is above grade level, teachers report that there is strong administrative focus on improving test scores. Teachers perceive pressure to change teaching strategies, and fear private reprimand and reassignment if students perform poorly on standardised tests. The quantitative data was supplemented with qualitative data based on purposive sampling of teachers and students in three states. The data was collected through focus groups of teachers and students, individual interviews of teachers and students, and classroom observations. Qualitative results parallel the quantitative findings.

In the US, the passage of the 'No Child Left Behind Act' of 2001 has had a detrimental effect on attempts to provide appropriate programming for gifted students (Schemo 2004). Since resources from the US Government are contingent upon increasing the percentage of students achieving state proficiency standards, school jurisdictions are reducing the resources available for challenging gifted students. Tomlinson (2002) noted the 'No Child Left Behind Act' provides no incentive to challenge students who have met limited expectations of proficiency. Once again, the scales are tipped to promote a narrow view of equity. Focusing on equality of outcome rather than equality of opportunity is a prescription for mediocrity (Gallagher 1996).

ASSUMPTIONS ABOUT HOW PARENTS CHOOSE SCHOOLS

Western industrialised nations have embraced forms of school choice and parental autonomy as mechanisms to revitalise public education and reassure middle-class voters that they will have access to quality education (Ball 2003, Brown 1997, Savage 2000, Thrupp 2001). The assumption is that once parents and students are free to choose among expanded educational options, schools will differentiate themselves both philosophically and practically in offering 'better quality' education than their competitors. School choice and parent autonomy in part stem from dissatisfaction with comprehensive schools, perceived low educational standards in public schools, and poor student performance among minority and socioeconomically disadvantaged groups. For example, those on the right espouse the view that the 'spirit of competition and excellence has been sacrificed in order to make the educational system conform to a socialist notion of social justice', resulting in a system that promotes mediocrity in the name of social justice, over merit and standards of excellence (Brown 1997). For those supporting this view, comprehensiveness has come to epitomise all that is wrong with public education (Thrupp 2001). They hold a disdain for collective forms of educational reform and instead embrace the competition of the free market and individual liberty in matters of education and schooling (Brown 1997). The result is that some factions of the middle classes have opted out of public education through increased use of private sector provisions, while others have successfully colonised particular parts of public education in ways that make them safe for their children (Whitty 2001). This is evidenced by the increase in specialist schools, charter schools and private schools with tuition fees that are within the reach of the aspiring middle class.

EDUCATION FOR ECONOMIC AND SOCIAL PROSPERITY

There is increased rhetoric among government, business and industry regarding the political and economic significance of highly qualified knowledge workers who can compete in an increasingly global labour force, and contribute to maintaining positional advantage in the global economy. For example, the Federal Government of Canada has articulated 'Canada's Innovation Strategy' in two White Papers: *Knowledge Matters: Skills and Learning for Canadians* (Government of Canada 2002a) and *Achieving Excellence: Investing in People, Knowledge and Opportunity* (Government of Canada 2002b). In these documents they view knowledge as a strategic national asset and enhancing the level of education and skill set of citizens as a national priority. This indicates the importance of education as a determinant of future life chances, and contributes to the creation of a credential society (Savage 2000).

Increased globalisation and a significant shift from a meritocratic society (advancement based on ability and effort) to a credential society (advancement based on accumulation of academic qualifications) has increased anxiety among middle-class parents regarding their ability to maintain their place in society and secure educational advantage for their children. Career advancement through the labour market has become increasingly risky and parents have become more prudent in selecting schools (Bourdieu and Boltanski 1977, Brown 2000, Avis 2003, Hill and Guin 2003). Many believe that the educational success of their children is too important to be left to the chance outcome of a formally open competition and instead seek competitive advantage for them through independent or specialist schools. Brown (1997) argues that 'old' and 'aspiring' middle-class parents are 'undermining the principle of "equality of opportunity" in the sense that educational outcomes should be determined by the abilities and efforts of pupils, not the wealth and preferences of parents' (p. 402). Brown (2000) refers to this as a 'parentocracy', in which educational markets respond to the self-interests and desires of parent-consumers rather than stakeholder groups. Actively choosing a 'good school' becomes a moral imperative for many middle-class parents – and not doing so is viewed as failing their parental duties (Thrupp 2001). This indicates a move away from the 'duality of standpoints' that are the 'basis of practical ethics and moral stability – that is the nexus of equality and partiality – towards an ethics of the "personal standpoint" that privileges the personal interests and desires of individuals' over impersonal values and concern for the collective good (Ball 2003).

RATIONAL CHOICE

Most school choice plans are based on the assumption that all parents will engage in school selection in a similar goal-oriented and self-interested fashion. The belief is that parents are 'utility maximisers' who make decisions from clear value preference based on rational calculations of cost, benefits and probabilities of success of options; that they are able to demand action from local schools and teachers; and that they can be relied upon to pursue the best interests of their children (Bosetti 2004, Hatcher 1998, Wells 1997). However, recent research demonstrates that this perspective underestimates the role of human agency, the freedom and ability of parents to act independently, and the social and cultural practices that influence or guide their decision-making (Wells 1997). Parents are often predisposed to make decisions based on their habitus, informed by practical wisdom, a logic of necessity, their lived experience, social class, ethnicity, parents' education, and deeply internalised values that have been passed down through generations (Bourdieu 1990, Wells 1997, Ball 2003). This is not to suggest that parents are irrational in their decision-making, but that their values and habitus serve as a filter to determine what factors, priorities or utilities they seek to maximise in their choice of schools.

Rational action theorists (Goldthorpe 1996, Erikson and Jonsson 1996) explain that the social location of families and their aspirations for their children influence how they interpret the costs and benefits of selecting a school and the extent to which it will enhance the success for their children. For example, some middle-class families view education as an investment good. They want to ensure that their children acquire the necessary educational credentials and social connections to preserve or improve their class position. Attending what they perceive to be high-status schools may provide social and academic advantage for their children in terms of winning scholarships, gaining admission to particular post-secondary institutions, and developing influential social networks. The benefits of education are greater for children from middle-class families as compared to lower-class families, because of the 'social distance' they have to travel to attain their aspirations. Lower-class children can maintain or improve their class position by completing high school; however, middle-class children are at greater risk of social demotion if they do not attain some post-secondary education. Since children of middle-class parents are at higher risk and have further to fall down the social ladder, they are more inclined to take action to secure their social location (Savage 2000, Hatcher 1998, Brown 2000). This in part explains why middle-class parents tend to be more anxious about education, and are more likely to engage in educational markets. Goldthorpe (1996) concludes that despite the expansion of educational choice, class differences remain because there is little change in the relative cost–benefit balances for different classes.

CONCLUDING STATEMENT

It is possible to accommodate gifted students in regular classrooms provided that teachers allow gifted students to learn at an appropriate pace, develop their critical and creative thinking skills, pursue their passions, represent their knowledge in a variety of ways, and interact with mental-age peers. Factors such as societal attitudes, governmental policies, teacher competencies and parental demands limit this possibility.

Notes

1 Frank Ernest Osborne was a former mayor of Calgary.
2 In the US, most universities recognise excellence each semester by the acknowledgement of Dean's List on one's transcript. The criterion for making the Dean's List is normally 3.50 GPA.
3 BESTS is an acronym for Belin-Blank Exceptional Student Talent Search conducted in collaboration with the Belin-Blank Center at the University of Iowa.

References

Alberta Learning (2000) *Teaching Students who are Gifted and Talented*. Edmonton: Alberta Learning Special Education Branch.

Assouline, S. G., Colangelo, N., Gross, M. U. M. and Pyryt, M. C. (1999) 'International talent search results: a comparison with TIMMS'. Presented at the National Association for Gifted Children, Albuquerque, 3–7 November.

Avis, J. (2003) 'Re-thinking trust in a performative culture: the case of education'. *Journal of Education Policy*, 18 (3), pp. 315–32.

Ball, S. (2003) *Class Strategies and the Education Market: the Middle Classes and Social Advantage*. London: Routledge/Falmer.

Bartkovich, K. G. and George, W. C. (1980) *Teaching the Gifted in the Mathematics Classroom*. Washington, DC: National Educational Association.

Bartkovich, K. G. and Mezynski, K. (1981) 'Fast-paced precalculus mathematics for talented junior-high students'. *Gifted Child Quarterly*, 25 (2), pp. 73–80.

Benbow, C. P. and Lubinski, D. (1997) 'Intellectually talented children: How can we meet their needs?' In N. Colangelo and G. A. Davis (eds), *Handbook of Gifted Education* (2nd edn) (pp. 155–69). Boston: Allyn & Bacon.

Bloom, B. S. (ed.) (1956) *Taxonomy of Educational Objectives. Handbook I: Cognitive Domain*. New York: McKay.

Bosetti, L. (2004) 'Determinants of school choice: understanding how parents choose elementary schools in Alberta'. *Journal of Education Policy*, 19 (4), pp. 387–405.

Bourdieu, P. (1990) *In Other Words: Essays Towards a Reflexive Sociology*. Stanford, CA: Stanford University Press.

Bourdieu, P. and Boltanski, L. (1977) 'Changes in social structure and changes in the demand for education'. In S. Giner and M. Scotford-Archer (eds) *Contemporary Europe: Social Structure and Cultural Change* (pp. 197–227). London: Routledge and Kegan Paul.

Brody, L. E. (1998) 'The talent searches: A catalyst for change in higher education'. *Journal of Secondary Gifted Education*, 9 (3), pp. 124–33.

Brody, L. E., Lupkowski, A. E., and Stanley, J. C. (1988) 'Early entrants to college: A study of academic and social adjustment during freshman year'. *College and University*, 63 (4), pp. 347–59.

Brody, L. E., Assouline, S. G. and Stanley, J. C. (1990) 'Five years of early entrants: predicting achievement in college'. *Gifted Child Quarterly*, 34 (4), pp. 138–42.

Brown, P. (1997) 'The "third wave": education and ideology of parentocracy'. In A. H. Halsey, H. Lauder, P. Brown and A. S. Wells (eds) *Education: Culture, Economy and Society* (pp. 393–408), Oxford: Oxford University Press.

Brown, P. (2000) 'Globalisation of positional competition'. *Sociology*, 34 (4), pp. 633–54.

Center for Gifted Education (1999) *Guide to Teaching Language Arts Curriculum for High Ability Learners*. Williamsburg, VA: Center for Gifted Education, The College of William and Mary.

Colangelo, N. (2003) 'Introduction and overview'. In N. Colangelo and G. A. Davis (eds) *Handbook of Gifted Education* (3rd edn) (pp. 3–10), Boston: Allyn & Bacon.

Colangelo, N., Assouline, S. G. and Gross, M. U. M. (2004) *A Nation Deceived: How Schools Hold Back America's Brightest Children*. Iowa City: The Connie Belin and Jacqueline N. Blank International Center for Gifted Education and Talent Development, The University of Iowa.

Coleman, J. S. (1962) *The Adolescent Society*. New York: Free Press.

Crawford, R. P. (1954) *The Techniques of Creative Thinking*. New York: Hawthorn Books.

Croft, L. J. (2003) 'Teachers of the gifted: gifted teachers'. In N. Colangelo and G. A. Davis (eds) *Handbook of Gifted Education* (3rd edn) (pp. 558–71). Boston: Allyn & Bacon.

Daurio, S. P. (1979) 'Educational enrichment versus acceleration – a review of the literature'. In W. C. George, S. J. Cohn and J. C. Stanley (eds) *Educating the Gifted: Acceleration and Enrichment* (pp. 13–63). Baltimore, MD: Johns Hopkins University Press.

Eberle, R. F. (1971) *SCAMPER: Games for Imagination Development*. Buffalo, NY: DOK Publishing.

Eberle, R. F. (1978) *CPS for Kids*. Buffalo, NY: DOK Publishing.

Eberle, R. F. (1984) *SCAMPER on for Creative Imagination Development*. Buffalo, NY: DOK Publishing.

Ennis, R.H. (1995) *Critical Thinking*. Englewood Cliffs, CO: Prentice-Hall.

Erikson, R. and Jonsson, J. O. (1996) 'Introduction: explaining class inequality in education: the Swedish test case'. In R. Erikson and J. O. Jonsson (eds) *Can education be Equalized? The Swedish Case in Comparative Perspective* (pp. 1–65). Boulder, CO: Westview Press.

Feldhusen, J. F. (1997) 'Educating teachers to work with talented youth'. In N. Colangelo and G. A. Davis (eds) *Handbook of Gifted Education* (2nd edn) (pp. 547–52). Boston: Allyn & Bacon.

Feldhusen, J. F. and Robinson-Wyman, A. (1980). 'Super Saturday: design and implementation of Purdue's special program for the gifted'. *Gifted Child Quarterly*, 24 (1), pp. 15–20.

Feldhusen, J. F. and Treffinger, D. J. (1985) *Creative Thinking and Problem Solving in Gifted Education* (3rd edn). Dubuque: Kendall-Hunt.

Frank, J. (2003) 'Teachers of the gifted: A literature review'. *AGATE*, 16 (1), pp. 17–31.

Friedman, P. G. (1978) 'Social giftedness: description and development'. Delivered to the National Association for Gifted Children, Houston, 1–3 November.

Gagné, F. (2005) 'From noncompetence to exceptional talent: exploring the range of academic achievement within and between grade levels'. *Gifted Child Quarterly*, 49 (2), pp. 139–53.

Gallagher, J. J. (1996) 'A critique of critiques of gifted education'. *Journal for the Education of the Gifted*, 19 (2), pp. 234–49.

Gardner, H. (1983) *Frames of Mind*. New York: Basic Books.

George, W. C. and Denham, S. A. (1976) 'Curriculum experimentation for the mathematically talented'. In D. P. Keating (ed.) *Intellectual talent: Research and Development* (pp. 103–31). Baltimore, MD: Johns Hopkins University Press.

Glover, M. A. (1993) 'Adolescents' attitudes toward intellectually gifted students'. *AGATE*, 7 (2), pp. 28–35.

Goldthorpe J. (1996) 'Class analysis and the reorientation of class theory: the case of persisting differentials in educational attainment'. *British Journal of Sociology*, 47 (3), pp. 481–505.

Government of Canada (2002a) *Achieving Excellence: Investing in People, Knowledge and Opportunity. Canada's Innovation Strategy*. Ottawa: Industry Canada.

Government of Canada (2002b) *Knowledge Matters: Skills and Learning for Canadians. Canada's Innovation Strategy*. Ottawa: Human Resource Development Canada.

Gross, M. U. M. (2003a) *Exceptionally Gifted Children* (2nd edn). London: Routledge/Falmer.

Gross, M. U. M. (2003b) 'Nurturing the talents of exceptionally gifted individuals'. In K. A. Heller, F. J. Mönks and A. H. Passow (eds) *International Handbook of Research and Development of Giftedness and Talent* (pp. 473–90). Oxford: Pergamon.

Gross, M. U. M. and van Vliet, H. E. (2003) *Radical Acceleration of Highly Gifted Children: an annotated bibliography of international research on highly gifted children who graduate from high school three or more years early*. Sydney: Gifted Education Research, Resource and Information Centre, The University of New South Wales.

Gross, M. U. M. and van Vliet, H. E. (2005) 'Radical acceleration and early entrance to college: a review of the literature'. *Gifted Child Quarterly*, 49, (2), pp. 154–71.

Hansen, J. B. and Feldhusen, J. F. (1994) 'Comparison of trained and untrained teachers of the gifted', *Gifted Child Quarterly*, 38, (3), pp. 115–23.

Hanson, H. P. (1980). 'Twenty-five years of the Advanced Placement Program: encouraging able students'. *College Board Review*, 115, pp. 8–12, 35.

Hatcher, R. (1998) 'Class differentiation in education: rational choices?' *British Journal of Education*, 19 (1), pp. 5–24.

Hill, P. and Guin, K. (2003). 'Baseline for assessment of choice programs'. *Educational Policy Analysis Archives*, 11 (39), pp. 1–32.

Hollingworth, L. S. (1942) *Children above 180 IQ*. Yonkers-on-Hudson, NY: World Books.

Karnes, F. A. and Stephens, K. R. (2000) *The Ultimate Guide for Student Product Development and Evaluation*. Waco, TX: Prufrock Press.

Kettle, K. E. Renzulli, J. S. and Rizza, M. G. (1998) 'Products of mind: exploring preferences for product development using My Way … An Expression Preference Instrument'. *Gifted Child Quarterly*, 42 (1), pp. 48–61.

Korzybski, A. (1958) *Science and Sanity* (5th edn). Lakeville, MN: International Non-Aristotelian Library Publishing.

Kulik, J. A. and Kulik, C. L. C. (1984) 'The effects of accelerated instruction on students'. *Review of Educational Research*, 54 (3), pp. 409–25.

Leroux, J. (2000) 'A study of education for high ability students in Canada'. In K. A. Heller, F. J. Mönks, R. J. Sternberg and R. F. Subotnik (eds) *International Handbook of Giftedness and Talent* (2nd edn) (pp. 695–702). Oxford: Pergamon.

Lynch, S. J. (1990) 'Fast paced science for the academically talented: issues of age and competence'. *Science Education*, 74 (6), pp. 585–96.

Marland, S. P. (1972) *Education of the gifted and talented: Report to the Congress of the United States by the Commisioner of Education*. Washington, DC: U.S. Government Printing Office.

Mezynski, K., Stanley, J. C. and McCoart, R. F. (1983) 'Helping youths score well on AP examinations in physics, chemistry, and calculus'. In C. P . Benbow and J. C. Stanley (eds) *Academic Precocity: Aspects of its Development* (pp. 86–112). Baltimore, MD: Johns Hopkins University Press.

Moon, T. R., Brighton, C. M. and Callahan, C. M. (2003) 'State standardized testing programs: friend or foe of gifted education?' *Roeper Review*, 25 (2), pp. 49–60.

National Commission on Excellence in Education (1983) *A Nation at Risk: the Imperative for Educational Reform*. Washington, DC: US Government Printing Office.

Oakes, J. (1985) *Keeping Track: How Schools Structure Inequality*, New Haven, CT: Yale University Press.

Olszewski-Kubilius, P. (1995) 'A summary of research regarding early entrance to college'. *Roeper Review*, 18 (2), pp. 121–5.

Paul, R. and Elder, L. (2001) *Critical Thinking: Tools for Taking Charge of your Learning and your Life*. Upper Saddle River, NJ: Prentice-Hall.

Parks, S. (2005) 'Teaching analytical and critical thinking skills in gifted education'. In F. A. Karnes and S. M. Bean (eds) *Methods and Materials for Teaching the Gifted* (2nd edn) (pp. 249–84). Waco, TX: Prufrock Press.

Parnes, S. J. (1981) *The Magic of your Mind*. Buffalo, NY: Bearly Limited.

Parnes, S. J. (ed.) (1992) *Sourcebook for Creative Problem Solving*. Buffalo, NY: Creative Educational Foundation.

Passow, A. H. (1958). 'Enrichment of education for the gifted'. In N. B Henry (ed.) *Education for the Gifted: Fifty-Seventh Yearbook Part 2 of the National Society for the Study of Education* (pp. 193–21). Chicago: University of Chicago Press.

Pyryt, M. C. (1985) 'The structure of social intelligence'. Presented to the World Council for the Gifted and Talented. Hamburg, 5–9 August.

Pyryt, M. C. (1999) 'Effectiveness of training children's divergent thinking: a meta-analytic review'. In A. S. Fishkin, B. Cramond and P. Olszewski-Kubilius (eds) *Investigating Creativity in Youth* (pp. 351–65). Cresskill: Hampton Press.

Pyryt, M. C. (2004) 'Adventures in curriculum differentiation: using the Pyryt Enrichment Matrix'. Presented to the Council for Exceptional Children, New Orleans, 14–17 April.

Pyryt, M. C. and Moroz R. M. (1994) 'Evaluating an accelerated mathematics program: a Centre of Inquiry approach'. In E. A. Hany and K. A. Heller (eds) *Competence and Responsibility: The Third European Conference of the European Council of High Ability* (Volume 2) (pp. 351–54). Göttingen: Hogrefe & Huber.

Ravaglia, R., Suppes, P., Stillinger, C. and Alper, T. M. (1995) 'Computer-based mathematics and physics for gifted students'. *Gifted Child Quarterly*, 39 (1), pp. 7–13.

Reis, S. M., Burns, D. E. and Renzulli, J. S. (1992) *Curriculum Compacting: the Complete Guide to Modifying the Regular Curriculum for High Ability Students*. Mansfield Center, CT: Creative Learning Press.

Reis, S. M., Westberg, K. L., Kulikowich, J., Caillard, F., Hébert, T., Plucker, J., Purcell, J. H., Rogers, J. B. and Smist, J. M. (1993) *Why Not Let School Start in January?: The Curriculum Compacting Study*. Storrs: National Research Center on the Gifted and Talented, University of Connecticut.

Renzulli, J. S. (1977) *The Enrichment Triad Model: A Guide for Developing Defensible Programs for the Gifted and Talented.* Mansfield Center, CT: Creative Learning Press.

Renzulli, J. S. (ed.) (1986) *Systems and Models for Developing Programs for the Gifted and Talented.* Mansfield Center, CT: Creative Learning Press.

Renzulli, J. S. (1994) *Schools for Talent Development: A Practical Plan for Total School Improvement.* Mansfield Center, CT: Creative Learning Press.

Renzulli, J. S. and Reis, S. M. (1985) *The Schoolwide Enrichment Model: A Comprehensive Plan for Educational Excellence.* Mansfield Center, CT: Creative Learning Press.

Renzulli, J. S. and Reis, S. M. (1986) 'The enrichment triad/revolving door model: A schoolwide plan for the development of creative productivity'. In J. S. Renzulli (ed.) *Systems and Models for Developing Programs for the Gifted and Talented* (pp. 216–66). Mansfield Center, CT: Creative Learning Press.

Renzulli, J. S. and Reis, S. M. (1997) 'The schoolwide enrichment model: new directions for developing high-end learning'. In N. Colangelo and G. A. Davis (eds) *Handbook of Gifted Education* (2nd edn) (pp. 136–54). Boston: Allyn & Bacon.

Renzulli, J. S., Smith, L. H. and Reis, S. M. (1982) 'Curriculum compacting: an essential strategy for working with gifted students'. *The Elementary School Journal*, 82 (3), pp. 185–94.

Roberts, J. L. and Roberts, R. A. (2005) 'Writing units that remove the learning ceiling'. In F. A. Karnes and S. M. Bean (eds) *Methods and Materials for Teaching the Gifted* (2nd edn) (pp. 181–210). Waco, TX: Prufrock Press.

Savage, M. (2000) *Class Analysis and Social Transformation.* Buckingham: Open University Press.

Schemo, D. J. (2004) 'Schools facing tight budgets leave gifted programs behind'. *New York Times*, 2 March.

Shore, B. M., Cornell, D. G., Robinson, A. and Ward, V. S. (1991) *Recommended Practices in Gifted Education.* New York: Teachers College Press.

Stanley, J. C. (1978) 'SMPY's DT-PI model: Diagnostic testing followed by prescriptive instruction'. *Intellectually Talented Youth Bulletin*, 4 (10), pp. 7–8.

Stanley, J. C. (2001) 'Helping students learn only what they don't already know'. In N. Colangelo and S. G. Assouline (eds) *Talent Development IV: Proceedings from the 1998 Henry B. and Jocelyn Wallace National Research Symposium on Talent Development* (pp. 293–9). Scottsdale: Great Potential Press.

Stanley, J. C. and Stanley, B. S. K. (1986) 'High-school biology, chemistry, or physics learned well in three weeks'. *Journal of Research in Science Teaching*, 23 (3), pp. 237–50.

Starko, A. (1986) *It's About Time: Inservice Strategies for Curriculum Compacting.* Mansfield Center, CT: Creative Learning Press.

Strop, J. (2000) 'The affective side of the internet'. *Understanding Our Gifted*, 12 (3), pp. 28–9.

Swartz, R. J. and Parks, S. (1994) *Infusing the Teaching of Critical and Creative Thinking into Content Instruction.* Pacific Grove, CA: Critical Thinking Press and Software.

Tannenbaum, A. J. (1962) *Adolescent Attitudes Towards Academic Brilliance.* New York: Teachers College Press.

Tannenbaum, A. J. (1993) 'History of giftedness and gifted education in world perspective'. In K. A. Heller, F. J. Mönks and A. H. Passow (eds) *International Handbook of Research and Development of Giftedness and Talent* (pp. 3–27). Oxford: Pergamon.

Thrupp, M. (2001) 'Education policy and social class in England and New Zealand: An instructive comparison'. *Journal of Education Policy*, 16 (4), pp. 297–314.

Tomlinson, C. A. (2002) 'Proficiency is not enough'. *Education Week*, 6 November.

Treffinger, D. J. (1979) '50,000 ways to create a gifted program'. *G/C/T*, 2 (6), pp. 18–19.

Treffinger, D. J. (1980) *Encouraging Creative Learning for the Gifted and Talented: A Handbook of Methods and Techniques*. Ventura: Ventura County Superintendent of Schools Office.

Treffinger, D. J. and Barton, B. L. (1979) 'Fostering independent learning'. *G/C/T*, 2 (7), pp. 3–6, 54.

Treffinger, D. J., Isaksen, S. G. and Dorval K. B. (1992) *Creative Problem Solving: An Introduction* (rev. edn). Sarasota, FL: Center for Creative Learning.

Van Tassel-Baska, J., Bass, G., Ries, R., Poland, D. and Avery, L. D. (1998) 'A national study of science curriculum effectiveness with high ability students'. *Gifted Child Quarterly*, 42 (4), pp. 200–11.

Ward, V. S. (1962) *The Gifted Student: A Manual for School Improvement*. Atlanta, GA: Southern Regional Education Board.

Wells, A. S. (1997) 'African-American students' view of school choice'. In A. H. Halsey, H. Lauder, P. Brown and A. S. Wells (eds) *Education: Culture, Economy and Society* (pp. 422–38). Oxford: Oxford University Press.

Westberg, K., Archambault, F. X., Dobyns, S. M. and Salvin, T. J. (1993) 'An observational study of classroom practices used with third- and fourth-grade students'. *Journal for the Education of the Gifted*, 16 (2), pp. 120–46.

Witty, G. (2001) 'Education, social class and social exclusion'. *Journal of Education Policy*, 16 (4), pp. 287–295.

Chapter 10

Structured tinkering

Improving provision for the gifted in ordinary schools

Deborah Eyre

Structured tinkering is a systematic approach to the modification of the basic school curriculum to meet the needs of gifted and talented pupils. The approach builds on curriculum planning techniques and classroom differentiation techniques, and encourages individual teachers to determine the areas and methodologies for curriculum improvement. It foregrounds the role of the teacher and provides them with the skills to engage in critical reflection and systematic data collection so as to make informed choices on behalf of their class or department. This chapter explores the rationale for the development of such an approach, gives details of its methodology and highlights some of its outcomes.

The idea that gifted and talented children need particular consideration during their schooling is one that has only recently been formally recognised. Yet, it has long been recognised that one of the greatest challenges for any teacher is to manage the learning needs of the various children in their class, especially when those pupils have very differing abilities.

This situation in England has changed markedly since 1997 when a newly elected government declared the needs of the gifted to be an educational priority with the development of a national strategy and an explosion of work and research in this field. A review of current practice was undertaken by the House of Commons Education Select Committee (1999) and reported that provision for the highly able was unsatisfactory in the majority of English schools. The Department of Education and Employment, in its evidence to the Committee, stated bluntly that: 'Action is needed to improve the quality of provision.'

Subsequent years have seen the implementation of a systematic national strategy, underpinned by five principles identified in the Select Committee report:

- The development that would make the most difference in the education of the highly able is a change in attitude amongst teachers and local education authorities, but perhaps even more importantly among the public and society at large.
- The emphasis must be on improving provision in mainstream schooling.
- There is no single 'best way' to meet all these children's needs.

- Highly able children should be allowed to enjoy their childhood.
- There is already good practice in a range of areas.

The National Strategy can be summarised as follows:

- Support the most gifted and talented in the country and in each school, particularly in disadvantaged areas.
- Provision building on pupils' particular strengths and weaknesses, making sure they too receive a broad and balanced education.
- Combine in-school learning with complementary opportunities out of school hours.
- Provide more opportunities for pupils to progress in line with their abilities, rather than their age and, where possible, achieve mastery, rather than superficial coverage in all subjects.
- Blend increased pace, depth and breadth in varying proportions according to the ability and needs of pupils. We want teachers to consider express sets, fast-tracking and more early entry to GCSE and advanced qualifications.

(DfES 2001)

THE ENGLISH MODEL

There is very little that could be said to be unusual about the National Strategy as such, but perhaps more unusual is the way it is being implemented. This method of implementation is referred to as the English model. The English model focuses on integration – integration in two ways.

- Gifted education is an integral part of general education policy.
- The actual approach used integrates pupils with their peers as much as is possible.

This approach to gifted education builds on the general education structure rather than placing gifted education outside of it. However, integrated education does not suggest that all provision for gifted pupils must be delivered in the regular classroom or indeed in the regular school – just as much as possible. When specialist provision is needed then it must be made available, and lack of availability in school should not be a barrier to the progress of the individual. The key elements of the English model are:

1   A *high-quality basic system*. The core of gifted education in the integrated model is through day-to-day classroom provision as part of a high-aspiration and high-attaining education system. The standard school system should recognise individual differences and every school should plan on the basis

of meeting a variety of needs, personalising the curriculum. This means schools should routinely plan to meet the needs of their most able as well as their least able. All schools should deploy a range of pupil grouping approaches that reflect the needs of their pupils. Sometimes pupils will be grouped by ability and sometimes in mixed ability classes. School flexibility for the gifted should include the ability to progress more rapidly than others in the peer group, including taking external examinations early.

2   *Fulfilment of individual potential through diversity of provision.* One of the key influences on modern education policy is *diversity* of opportunity to meet a wide range of needs. Here provision is dictated by the needs of the child rather than by what the host school can offer.

    a)   schools – different types of school catering for different types of aptitude;

    b)   pathways – different pathways for individuals within the general school, enabling students to develop areas of particular strength;

    c)   wider schooling – a focus on wider schooling with the host school forming only one part of the education process. Here schools have a role in 'shopping' for the provision that will help their students make the most of their expertise.

3   *Equality, social justice, meritocracy.* The English model for gifted education balances equality and meritocracy. Whilst it is concerned with meritocracy, it recognises that the creation of better opportunities will not in itself ensure that gifted children from under-represented groups rise through the system. In the English model, special attention is paid to those from under-represented groups. This is achieved in part by working through the school system to improve the general education offered, but also by each school using data to identify individual gifted students from under-represented groups and intervening to offer them access to the high quality opportunities and the support they need to help them realise their potential. This is achieved using a combination of school-based systems and access to wider schooling opportunities.

4   *A global perspective for the twenty-first century.* A major reason for a dedicated educational focus on gifted and talented pupils is their potential to play a leading role in their adult lives. The gifted education strategy is the catalyst that makes sure that this generation of gifted young people has the opportunity to develop their talents. This is a joint endeavour between educationalists and the wider business and voluntary community. The English model works across boundaries in pursuit of expertise, mobilising all sectors to support education.

Structured tinkering relates directly to point one in the English model and to provision for gifted and talented pupils within the ordinary classroom. This element of the English model, whilst highly desirable, is also the most difficult to achieve. It requires all teachers to be teachers of the gifted and to have both the subject knowledge and the teaching skills to make that a reality.

TRADITIONAL WAYS OF DESIGNING A CURRICULUM FOR GIFTED LEARNERS

Whilst England may be new to the field of gifted education, designing an appropriate educational curriculum for gifted and talented pupils has been the focus of much research over a period of very many years. Extensive studies in the USA by Gallagher (1985), Joyce and Weil (1986, cited in Maker and Neilson 1995), Van Tassal-Baska (1992) and Maker and Nielson (1995) have produced some measure of agreement regarding the key characteristics of effective curricular provision. In addition, such colleagues as Renzulli and Reis (1985) have designed models for teaching the gifted which are deliberately located in the general school context rather than for the optimum conditions provided by separate gifted programmes.

Whilst the models advocated in these studies are very different in many ways, they are united by the broadly rationalist approach that underpins them: the 'one size fits all' approach. Certain factors are assumed to be static whereas, in reality, they are fluid. These are related to the following areas:

* the nature of gifted children
* the context in which they are taught
* the teachers who are teaching them.

In addition, in the work of some researchers, assumptions are also made about the core curriculum that is being taught. Maker and Neilson, for example, in their otherwise helpful book on curriculum models (1995), refer to the way in which changes to the curriculum can be categorised by changes to content, process, product or climate but still assume that starting points will be similar.

A fundamental flaw, then, in these approaches is the lack of attention to individual needs, to context and to teaching skill. These have proved in practice to be very significant factors in securing appropriate provision for the gifted and therefore deserve careful thought. Comprehensive research evidence suggests that gifted pupils are diverse in nature and personality. Recent work on learning styles (Riding and Rayner 1998) would suggest that preferences in learning styles are not related to ability but rather to personality, so any approach to teaching the gifted would need to incorporate opportunities that respond to the full range of learning styles, rather than assuming that one style of learning best meets the needs of the gifted. The learning context is also a critical factor in determining effective provision. Schools have their own 'personality' and approaches that work well in some schools will not work so effectively in others. Finally, teachers are as diverse as their pupils – some are capable of delivering a more complex and interactive curriculum than others.

Perhaps the most significant barrier to effective discussion of 'one size fits all' curriculum provision for the gifted is the first – the nature of giftedness itself. Freeman sums up the research as follows:

> Research shows that the very able are not a homogeneous group, whether in terms of learning style, creativity, speed of development, personality or social behaviour.
>
> (Freeman 1998: 2)

It is therefore difficult to conceive of a curriculum or even a model of teaching which is likely to be effective for everyone in this diverse and disparate group. In a practical sense teachers see this diversity in their own classrooms on a daily basis. They recognise that the gifted pupils in their classes come in all shapes and sizes. There are those who like to concentrate for long periods of time and those who like to jump from one topic to another with great rapidity. There are those who like to write extensively and those who dislike any kind of written recording; those who are very confident in their ability to master challenges and those who fear mistakes and lack confidence in their ability; those who prefer their work carefully structured and those who find such constraints onerous and prefer the freedom to develop tangentially. Reading or learning about curricular approaches to teaching the gifted that assume a general similarity amongst gifted pupils is at odds with teachers' own experience and therefore not compelling for the thinking teacher. A model of teaching that is appropriate for all gifted pupils is unlikely, and most thinking teachers recognise that any model, however carefully constructed, can only be a starting point which needs adaptation to fit the needs of individuals.

A second limitation on curriculum planning models for the gifted relates to the issue of organisational context. Once again, assumptions are made regarding a notional or mythical school. Reality suggests that schools are radically different in their make-up, ethos, geography, catchment, etc.; the typical school simply does not exist. What works well in one school may not work well in others. For example, rigid curriculum systems where pupils are taught as a single group using the same material are very different from schools where differentiated provision is a feature of every lesson. Equally, schools where pupils only use the library or computers at set times and under strict supervision are very different from those where pupils have free access to such facilities. These differences in school philosophy and overall approach have a significant impact on the teaching and learning opportunities. Designing an optimum curriculum to suit all contexts is impossible and one might even say a futile pursuit. The best that one might aim for, is recognition that a set of general principles of the kind quoted in the 'Effective Schools' literature (Sammon *et al.* 1996), can also be created to describe effective provision for their gifted and talented pupils.

Finally, most approaches to curriculum design fundamentally fail to recognise the importance of the individual teacher in considering curriculum design. Like gifted pupils, teachers are a diverse group with different styles or approaches which are linked to their personality characteristics. Some teachers do teach the set curriculum uncritically making only minor and superficial modifications to meet the needs of individuals, but others are highly reflective and modify the curriculum radically to accommodate individual needs. Assessment of teacher performance is itself, of course, an interesting subject for debate. Is a good teacher one who delivers the set curriculum well, or one who can use their professional judgment to adjust the curriculum as required?

To summarise then: accepted approaches to curriculum design for gifted pupils often appear mechanistic and arguably too rigid to deliver a curriculum flexible and creative enough to meet the diverse needs of gifted pupils. Therefore an altogether different starting point might need to be considered.

My approach offers an alternative. It places the teacher at the heart of the process, rather the curriculum designer, and encourages individual teachers to determine the areas and methodologies for improvement. The teacher takes charge of modifying the curriculum and of incorporating the teaching and learning approaches most likely to benefit their pupils.

MODIFYING THE EXISTING CURRICULUM TO MEET THE NEEDS OF GIFTED CHILDREN

At the heart of integrated provision is the modification of the existing curriculum to add greater challenge for the most able. This approach is cost effective, culturally acceptable and can readily address issues of curriculum continuity and progression. There are various ways to do this, the most obvious one being the Renzulli and Reis (1985) model curriculum compacting but this is only one way to approach curriculum modification – and a crude one at that. A more sophisticated approach would be to take the basic school curriculum, which in most countries is configured as a spiral curriculum, and to thread through it opportunities for enrichment of the curriculum, extension of the curriculum and acceleration (breadth, depth and pace). Whilst this kind of approach is attractive, a possible difficulty is its complexity. Either a detailed mapping exercise would be needed to modify the basic curriculum, or responsibility for curriculum modification would need to move away from the university-level curriculum designer and into the hands of the teachers on the ground. Given the differences in pupils and context, the latter approach has much to commend it and is the basis for structured tinkering.

If the basic curriculum in a school is modified in this way then some of the spin-offs are interesting and perhaps unexpected. Evidence from Sternberg (1986), Gardner (1983, 1999 and 2000) and others indicates that the idea of a clearly defined, ring-fenced group of pupils who can be defined as 'the gifted' may be erroneous. Some pupils may be gifted in the broad range of areas traditionally associated with giftedness; others may be outstanding in a limited range of domains. Working with modifications to the basic school curriculum allows individuals to move in and out of gifted provision quite naturally, and without adverse effects on self-esteem. A pupil may be experiencing modified provision in one area of the curriculum but not in others.

The volume of pupils with significant abilities and talents is also an issue here. Work in English schools in the 1980s (Denton and Postlethwaite 1985) suggested that if a school identified pupils (top 10 per cent) with specific abilities and talents as well as general ability, then the proportion of the total school cohort who might be considered gifted was substantial – up to 40 per cent. If a school's provision sets out to nurture talent then it must accommodate all those who exhibit significant ability, whether this manifests itself in a wide range of areas or a single domain. This has serious implications for curriculum design: either it must be an integral part of regular school provision or a complex system of additional programmes would need to be created. An integrated approach may be said to be organisationally more feasible for an individual school than the creation of individual education plans for nominated pupils.

Working directly with schools over a twenty-year period to implement this approach highlighted a series of broader educational implications (Eyre 1997). Where a whole-school approach to curriculum modification was used as the basis of provision for the gifted, a measurable improvement in overall school attainment could be observed (HMI 1992). Small-scale research (Eyre et al. 2002) suggests that this is likely to be because when a teacher offers additional opportunities within the ordinary classroom they will, for administrative reasons, make them available to as wide a group of pupils as possible, so extending the cohort of those likely to benefit. Rather than creating set groupings within the classroom the teacher is likely to plan for a top group but, where possible, introduce the same work to other pupils by adding additional support to enable access. Detailed research into how this phenomenon operates in practice has yet to be undertaken, but the evidence is sufficiently compelling for the DfES to see a focus on gifted pupils as a key factor in raising general standards in schools.

STRUCTURED TINKERING

So what is structured tinkering exactly? Structured tinkering is a systematic approach to the modification of the basic school curriculum to meet the needs of gifted and talented pupils. The approach builds on curriculum planning techniques and classroom differentiation techniques, and encourages individual teachers to determine the areas and methodologies for curriculum improvement. It foregrounds the role of the teacher and provides them with the skills to engage in critical reflection and systematic data collection so as to make informed choices on behalf of their class or department. This in turn creates a classroom that is responsive to differing individual needs and circumstances as well as to the generic learning needs of gifted pupils.

Hickey (1988) found that internationally educators of gifted and talented pupils converged in having three main goals for gifted programmes:

1   To provide a learning environment that will permit and encourage the capable student to develop their individual potential while interacting with intellectual peers.
2   To establish a climate that values and enhances intellectual ability, talent, creativity and decision-making.
3   To encourage the development of, and provide opportunities for, the use of higher levels of thinking (analysis, synthesis and evaluation).

Structured tinkering shares these goals and makes it the responsibility of the teacher to achieve them on behalf of their pupils.

The set of basic assumptions underpinning the structured tinkering approach is as follows:

*   Gifted pupils are a diverse and disparate group and therefore optimum provision will vary from child to child.
*   The best provision for gifted pupils is made by extending that which is available to all children rather than providing a completely different curriculum for gifted pupils.
*   Schools and teachers vary in their capacity to deal effectively with gifted pupils.

Structured tinkering builds on the ideas of the philosopher Karl Popper (1944, cited in Miller 1987: 304), who states the following: 'Piecemeal tinkering combined with critical analysis is the main way to practical results in the social as well as natural sciences.'

In this approach the teacher is at the heart of the process, using their professional skills to design a curriculum suited to the needs of the gifted pupils in their school and community. The strengths of this approach lie in the way it uses existing teaching skills and knowledge of how children learn, and applies them to the education of the gifted rather than separating the education of the gifted from the education of other children. This does not diminish the importance of work on teaching gifted children but simply locates it within, rather than outside, the broader educational field.

STRUCTURED TINKERING HAS A THREE-STAGE CYCLE

1   The teacher recognises that it is their role to adapt classroom provision to meet the needs of the gifted. Here the teacher accepts that they, not the pupil, are the expert and they need to take responsibility for designing the provision for this group within the class. Usually teachers begin by suggesting that they do not know how to teach the gifted. In reality gifted children are first and foremost children and most of their learning needs are the same as for others of their age. So most of what they need is the same as their peers. The teacher already knows how to provide that. The problem for teachers is what else should be provided? Popper suggests that we all have an interpretative framework which helps us to solve such problems. In the case of teachers some of that framework is established in pre-service or in-service training and then refined through teaching experience. The more reflective the teacher the more such a framework is refined. In schools which are good 'learning institutions', as outlined in the work of Sammons *et al.* (1996), interpretative frameworks should be very sophisticated and teachers are well able to achieve this.

2   The teacher becomes familiar with the general theories, models and principles underlying effective teaching of the gifted, and broad strategies which may be useful in this respect. This might include a clear understanding of the complexity of definition and identification as well as knowledge of teaching models and generic approaches. Researching what has been tried by others, and what is thought by curriculum designers and educational researchers to be effective, helps the teacher to identify possible ways to improve their own practice and also helps to highlight areas of their current practice which are already particularly good. This process helps to provide an answer to the 'what else' question.

3   The teacher, or team of teachers, select an area of their practice that they consider could be made more effective for the gifted pupils and try to improve it using action research methodology (tinkering). This process is carefully monitored and permanent adjustments made based on defendable findings. The process becomes a regular event with teachers considering different aspects of their practice as the focus for investigation. This is more than just experimenting: it is systematically defining the problem, intervening to bring about beneficial change and then deciding if the result is really an improvement.

This approach is very appealing to teachers because it recognises their professional skill. It also recognises the complexity of teaching and learning and attempts to take account of it. Finally, whilst individual changes using this method may not be great, they are real changes – unlike what Popper refers to as utopian engineering in which grand schemes are envisaged but rarely implemented. In teaching, much in-service work is based on grand schemes and there is ample research to demonstrate that in-service frequently fails to change practice. Structured tinkering takes small steps, but over time leads to significant change.

Stage 1: Practitioner research methodologies

In order for teachers to participate effectively in structured tinkering they need to learn how to assess the strengths and weaknesses of their current provision, how to make changes in their classroom and how to monitor the effectiveness of these changes. They need a process 'tool kit'. Change is, in itself, not difficult to achieve but judgments also need to be made regarding whether such change has actually been beneficial. Practitioner or teacher research is a useful way to achieve this. Practitioner research is not a new idea – it is well developed in the research methodology for social sciences. Action research, case study research and evaluation have all been used extensively and the arguments related to the value, and problems, of insider research are well rehearsed (Robson 1993). What makes this approach particularly suitable for exploring the education of able/gifted pupils is that it focuses not on the grand solution but on the limited but significant change. It also provides methodology for understanding existing practice and identifying its strengths and weaknesses.

Practitioner research is a useful vehicle for enabling teachers to adopt structured tinkering in a systematic and rigorous way. One of the problems in teachers 'tinkering' with the curriculum in an ad hoc or unstructured way is that in a busy classroom it is not always possible to be fully aware of what is occurring. An intervention or change may, on a superficial level, appear to be effective but in reality be less so. Of course the reverse may also be true. Introduction to the systematic use of research tools also helps the teacher to be more rigorous in their data collection and more critical in their analysis.

Stage 2: Auditing existing provision

A key feature of structured tinkering is that the implementation of change does not occur until the teacher or teachers have gained a clear understanding of the nature of the problem or barrier inhibiting effective provision. Such barriers may relate to the social climate in the classroom or school, to the curriculum planning or assessment processes, to pupil grouping or access to opportunities. Whatever is the issue, it needs to be examined carefully before any intervention takes place. A typical example of this might be a focus on pupils thinking for themselves and articulating their ideas. It may be that the teacher thinks that the children are not capable of independent thinking and the articulation of personal views. Interviews with pupils may highlight the fact that few opportunities exist to demonstrate this skill so whilst some may be able to do it they rarely get the chance. Others could maybe learn how to do it but haven't tried as yet. Understanding the nature of the problem is crucial if interventions are to bring about real improvements.

Stage 3: Devising a personal repertoire

In order to devise an intervention which might lead to improvement teachers need to secure an understanding of what might be seen as optimum provision. In traditional curriculum design models (e.g. Renzulli's triad model, 1977), the model provides both the goal and the process. In more flexible approaches (e.g. Van Tassel-Baska 1994) goals for an effective programme provide a framework around which activities can be devised: cognitive, affective, social/behavioural and aesthetic. In structured tinkering, the teacher is encouraged to become familiar with a variety of possible approaches to effective provision. A range of recognised models are introduced and their strengths and weaknesses considered, along with other curriculum ideas which might be thought to have value for the gifted and talented. Typical amongst these might be CASE (Cognitive Accelerated Science Education, Shayer and Adey 1981), philosophy for children, critical thinking, etc. From this range the practitioner-researcher will choose a repertoire of approaches which are thought to be appropriate to his/her needs, taking into account context and clientele. Approaches are chosen to respond to weaknesses in provision which have been identified through the systematic audit process. For example, in a very traditional school introducing ideas on philosophy may be one way to encourage more flexible thinking about methods of classroom delivery. Equally, in schools in England, where teachers are required to show learning outcomes for each lesson, a focus on Bloom's (1985) taxonomy may help in planning more effectively for higher levels of thinking.

Stage 4: Intervening to improve

This stage involves the teacher or teachers devising a careful intervention plan which records action to be taken, timescale and data collection methods. Consideration will also be given at this point to methods of judging success. Usually such an intervention will occur over a fixed period of time so that at the end a judgment can be reached as to whether the intervention has been successful and should be permanently implemented.

Stage 5: Reflecting and beginning the next cycle

Here the teacher or teacher team reflects on progress and outcomes and decides on the next steps. Depending on the nature of the intervention the next steps may involve implementation of the approach on a permanent basis, adoption of the approach across the whole school or section of the school, or a second cycle of the process to revisit the issue and try another approach.

SAMPLE INTERVENTION TOPICS

- Using questioning to extend the able Year 10 students.
- Raising the profile of the needs of underachieving able pupils.
- Developing enrichment strategies in a school for pupils aged four to nine years.
- Specialist guidance for non-specialist teachers.
- Planning lessons using an enquiry-based approach.
- Developing a consistency of approach to gifted pupils throughout the school.
- Developing a whole-school approach to questioning as a method of creating challenge.
- Improving children's ability to explain and pose questions.
- Developing inter-school transfer arrangements to support able pupils.
- Implementing and evaluating an acceleration programme.
- Developing strategies for maths teaching for ages seven to nine years.
- Raising teacher expectations through the introduction of an assessment procedure focusing on outcomes for able pupils.
- Mentoring as a way of supporting exceptionally able pupils.
- Writing strategies for able thinkers who find writing tedious.

OPTIMUM CONDITIONS FOR STRUCTURED TINKERING

Structured tinkering seems to work best where the teacher is part of a learning community. Individual teachers benefit from being supported through this process either by other teachers or by a formal coach. University lecturers can be an effective coach in this process since they are well practised in objective reflection. This realisation led to the development of course framework to enable teachers to learn how to become structured tinkerers. Structured tinkering is not dependent on course involvement and successful projects have operated outside of this (Bristol LEA 2001) but such a course does help to support teachers in their early attempts to investigate their practice. Groups working in this way may be configured in different ways (see Tables 10.1, 10.2 and 10.3).

In Table 10.1 there is a shared focus, with teachers investigating exactly the same issue or different dimensions of the same issue.

In Table 10.2 teachers have a shared general theme but are looking at how it functions at different times in a child's life as well as in different circumstances.

Table 10.1 A shared focus

All members of the group investigating the same issue e.g. maths in the early years	All the teachers in a single school
"	Selection of teachers from a large school
"	Selection of teachers from a group of schools
"	Individuals from a variety of schools

Table 10.2 A shared general theme

All members of the group have some common interest but also differences e.g. a theme of underachievement but teachers teaching pupils aged 5 years to 16 years	All the teachers in a single school
"	Selection of teachers from a large school
"	Selection of teachers from a group of schools
"	Individuals from a variety of schools

Table 10.3 A common field of study

All members working under the general heading of improving gifted education	All the teachers in a single school
"	Selection of teachers from a large school
"	Selection of teachers from a group of schools
"	Individuals from a variety of schools

SOME REFLECTIONS ON STRUCTURED TINKERING

The main problem related to using teachers as designers is that it requires teachers to reflect upon what is happening in their classroom. Of course all good teachers do this already to some degree, otherwise they would be unable to assess the progress of individual pupils, but the type of reflection needed in order to become a curriculum designer is of a higher level and at the pinnacle of teaching skill.

Teachers must develop the ability to teach and observe simultaneously and to catalogue the information they are receiving through observation. A reasonable question to ask relates to whether this model for improving curriculum design for the able/gifted is realistic in terms of teacher time and teacher ability. As a teacher I cannot help but think that thoughtful, confident, creative teachers are what we need for all our children and encouraging this type of approach to teaching helps to attract thoughtful individuals and to develop skills in reflection and critical analysis which improve the learning opportunities for all children.

Evidence collected by external evaluators of the structured tinkering approach (Ofsted internal report on M level course at Oxford Brookes University 1998) confirms its effectiveness, highlighting the progress made by teachers in understanding the complex needs of gifted pupils in their classes and also their success in identifying and implementing change strategies. The structured tinkering approach is now well established, with cohorts of teachers working regularly either on accredited courses or as part of research learning communities to develop effective provision in their schools.

Fink (Ontario, keynote talk to Sandwell schools 2002) suggests that in judging the success of educational change we should focus not on whether a school is complying with an agreed policy, but rather whether the change achieved is long lasting and has a real impact on pupils' learning. Structured tinkering is creative, flexible, imaginative and builds capacity in the teaching profession. Whilst it lacks the neat, tidy linearity of many of the more conventional models for educating gifted children it instead offers an alternative which is routed in the teacher's existing skills and practice and it enables the gifted to be educated within the ordinary school.

References

Bloom, B. (ed.) (1985). *Developing Talent in Young People*. New York: Basic Books.
Bristol LEA (2001) *Flying High in Bristol*. Bristol: Bristol LEA.
Denton, C. and Postlethwaite K. (1985) *Able Children – Identifying Them in the Classroom*. Windsor, Berks: NFER/Nelson.
DfES (2001) *Schools Achieving Success*. London: HMSO.
Eyre, D. (1997) *Able Children in Ordinary Schools*. London: David Fulton.
Eyre, D. *et al.* (2002) *Effective Teachers of Able Pupils in the Primary Schools*. Oxford: National Primary Trust.
Fink, D. (2001) *Sustaining change: Keeping moving schools moving*. Unpublished paper presented to the Sandwell Local Authority, Birmingham, England.
Fink, D. (2002) Keynote speech to Sandwell schools. Ontario, Canada.
Freeman, J. (1998) *Educating the Very Able: Current International Research*. London: HMSO.
Gallagher, J. J. (1985) *Teaching the Gifted Child*. Boston: Allyn & Bacon.
Gardner, H. (1983) *Frames of Mind: The Theory of Multiple Intelligences*. New York: Basic Books.
Gardner, H. (1999) *Intelligence Reframed: Multiple Intelligences for the 21st century*. New York: Basic Books.
Gardner, H. (2000) 'The giftedness matrix: A developmental perspective'. In R. C. Friedman and B. M. Shore (eds) *Talents Unfolding: Cognition and Development*. Washington, DC: American Psychological Association.
Hickey (1998) In Maker, C. J. and Nielson, A. B. (1995) *Teaching Models in Education of the Gifted*. Texas: Pro-ed.

HMI (1992) *Education Observed: The Education of Very Able Children in Maintained Schools.* London: HMSO.

House of Commons Education Select Committee (1999) 'Highly able children'. Third Report of the Education and Employment Committee. London: HMSO.

Maker, C. J. and Nielson, A. B. (1995) *Teaching Models in Education of the Gifted.* Texas: Pro-ed.

Ofsted (1998) Internal Report on M level course at Oxford Brookes University.

Popper, K. (1944) 'Piecemeal social engineering'. In D. Miller (ed.) (1987) *A Pocket Popper.* Glasgow: Fontana.

Renzulli, J. S. (1977) *The Enrichment Triad Model: A Guide for Developing Defensible Programmes for the Gifted and Talented.* Mansfield Center, CT: Creative Learning Press.

Renzulli, J. S. and Reis, S. M. (1985) *The School-wide Enrichment Model: A Comprehensive Plan for Educational Excellence.* Mansfield Center, CT: Creative Learning Press.

Riding, R. and Rayner, S. (1998) *Cognitive Styles and Learning Strategies.* London: David Fulton.

Robson, C. (1993) *Real World Research: A Resource for Social Scientists and Practitioner Researchers.* Oxford: Blackwells.

Sammons, P., Hillman, J. and Mortimore, P. (1996) *Key Characteristics of Effective Schools.* Ringwood, Hampshire: MBC Distribution Services.

Shayer, M. and Adey, P. (1981) *Towards a Science of Science Teaching.* Oxford: Heinemann.

Sternberg, R. J. (1986) 'A triarchic theory of intelligence'. In R. J. Sternberg and J. E. Davidson (eds) *Conceptions of Giftedness.* Cambridge: Cambridge University Press.

Van Tassel-Baska, J. (1992) *Planning Effective Curriculum for Gifted Learners.* Denver, CO: Love Publishing.

Van Tassel-Baska, J. (1994) *Comprehensive Curriculum for Gifted Learners.* Boston: Allyn & Bacon.

Chapter 11

Double exceptionality

Gifted children with special educational needs – what ordinary schools can do to promote inclusion

Professor Diane Montgomery

Inclusive education is a complex and contentious area and has preoccupied teacher educators for many decades although not necessarily under this title. It arose in responding to 'individual differences' in the 1960s, in the 'selective schools versus comprehensive education' debate in the 1970s, in relation to the issue of 'special needs in ordinary schools' in the 1980s, again in the 1990s in the 'integration versus inclusion' debate and now in relation to differentiation and gifted education.

The EPPI-Centre review (Dyson *et al.* 2002: 7) identified three key perspectives in promoting inclusion:

1   Responding simultaneously to students who differ from each other in important ways, some of which pose particular challenges to the school;
2   Maintaining the presence of students in school but also maximising their participation;
3   A process which can be shaped by school action.

This chapter will seek to address these issues in relation to gifted children with special educational needs (SEN).

Recently Barton (2003) has argued that inclusion is a means to an end, not an end in itself, and Dyson (1999) has talked about 'different inclusions', both of which are important considerations. They both suggest that developing inclusion is very much about change in education. Thus, inclusion becomes political as it is moving the schools' agenda in one direction whereas government policies, such as the standards agenda, are working towards another (Benjamin 2002). Anything concerned with change in education is about transformation for there are, in us, deep structural barriers to change which can include the social basis of the dominant cultural definitions of 'success', failure' and 'ability'. Making changes related to these is essentially political and this is what is involved in developing inclusive education (Barton 2003, Whitty 2002).

Inclusion may also help to avoid 'the selection and differentiation of pupils leading to the reproduction of inequalities; a form of teaching and learning which is competitive and hierarchical; and the embrace of instrumentalism which harnesses education to the economic goals of society' (Quicke 1999: 3). It is just such processes of selection and differentiation with which both gifted education and the realm of special educational needs have been associated. The integration of pupils with SEN came to be seen as a process which frequently isolated pupils in their classrooms and effectively segregated them from the main provision when it was 'delivered' by differentiated inputs or outputs strategies. In integration pupils were being helped to adapt to the schools' demands.

For inclusion to succeed it is the teaching methods and the school itself which are adapted to suit the pupils' needs. These needs centre round full participation in all class and school activities. In the process of becoming more inclusive it may be necessary to remove barriers to learning, including the learning barriers set up by teachers' own learning histories and teacher education itself.

Finally, the concept of 'special need' is also under scrutiny, for the labelling process can lead to exclusions within classrooms for the learning disabled and the gifted. It can even lead to exclusions from schools for those with challenging behaviour. Thus the notion of 'removing barriers to learning' (DfES 2004) has become part of the definition of need.

EXTERNAL AND INTERNAL BARRIERS TO LEARNING IN GIFTED EDUCATION

It may seem strange to some people that gifted and talented children experience barriers to learning. How indeed can they be gifted if they fail to learn? An examination of the adult population however shows that many achieve eminence or high status in industry, commerce and the professions without ever having demonstrated their giftedness and talents as pupils in schools. It is only after school or on return to education that they begin to reveal their true abilities. A recent survey of 300 executive industrialists by the CBI (2004) found that 40 per cent had been underachievers at school. Hughes and Dawson (1995) interviewing adult dyslexics found that in school they had been too bright for the slowest groups and could not cope with the written work of the top groups. These adults described how their feelings of frustration were vented through misbehaviour. They said they would have felt better if someone had at least recognised and understood their difficulties. Streaming and tiered assessments do not address such problems and dyslexia is only one of many barriers to learning to be uncovered in schools.

In a sense we can suggest that it is often school itself which prevents many children from revealing their abilities. This may be because there is no place in school for them to develop their particular type of talent. In addition the local environments and subcultures of some schools are intolerant of differences between students. The result is that a pupil who is perceived as different may attract bullying, bright children are accused of being 'boffs' or 'professors' and derided, while others may be tormented because they are said to be gay, black, girlie, Asian, Chinese, fat, wearing spectacles, unfeminine, uncool and so on ad infinitum.

Some of this scapegoating may be due to human nature, the response to overcrowding or attitudes fostered by the media, but all of it is linked with the nature of the regimes in schools. Where there is a rigid attitude from those in authority, a heavy pressure to maintain standards, frequent testing and a coercive ethos we have an environment in which scapegoating and low-level bullying takes place and even seems to be encouraged (Galloway and Goodwin 1987). It can make life very sad, even unbearable, for those who are its victims.

Unhappiness, however created, can cause some children to be withdrawn in school, occupied with their own thoughts and fears and not open to new learning. They 'act in' their problems. Others may do the reverse and 'act out' or become difficult to manage at school, at home or both and become set on a career in disruption and exclusion. Bright children may at first seem to fit in well to rigid classroom regimes but then the novelty will wear off and their resultant behaviour becomes a nuisance. Any such change in behaviour should be a cause for concern and explored.

Many gifted children learn, early on, to underperform so as not to be picked on by peers or praised by the teacher. Very quickly they may adopt the daydreaming position, quietly gazing at the teacher as though listening intently, but their minds are elsewhere. Such habits build over time and are difficult to eradicate.

One of the complaints of bright children in classrooms is the endless repetitions they have to endure and they develop the habit of switching off or switching out in order not to go berserk with boredom. Young children less indoctrinated into the school ethos may simply refuse to participate in class activities and insist on sitting in the reading corner all day studying books or working on number games. Those who survive in classrooms often do so because they have the propensity for fitting in and adapting to the school norms but are never motivated to make an effort to do more than 'just enough'. They slip through the system and enjoy life in their own ways. Occasionally a particular topic and learning approach will stimulate them to do their very best, and teacher and peers are amazed at the achievement level attained. As it is not maintained the achievement is ignored as just 'a flash in the pan'.

These barriers to learning are social and educational, created by the school ethos and the teaching methods. They cause a wide range of pupils, including the more able, to underfunction, but in addition to these external barriers to learning there may be internal ones which pupils bring to school.

Giftedness and talent (high ability) are more widespread than is generally believed but IQ tests and teacher assessments frequently fail to identify them, especially in underfunctioning groups. This can be because the high ability can compensate in many different ways for particular disabilities so that the pupil, for example in tests, appears to function at an average level and thus is overlooked for gifted education provision.

When remedial provision is considered, the difficulties of highly able students often do not seem severe enough because their needs are masked. It is thus typical that 'doubly exceptional' children, those with both high ability and special educational needs, are not taught at a level commensurate with their intellectual needs. In some cases attention is directed only to the special need. The result is that many of these doubly exceptional children underfunction as the expectations of their teachers are set too low and the curriculum provision is intellectually inadequate.

Although a significant number of highly able pupils are never identified as gifted or learning disabled, suitable curriculum provision directed to their intellectual needs in ordinary classrooms can enable us to find and help them (along with their less able peers) to become higher achievers and overcome their learning disabilities. This can occur in a process called curriculum based identification (CBI) (Shore 1991). It can help to have a checklist (see Table 11.1) such as that below to aid identification but it will not pick up the 'cruisers'; CBI is necessary for this.

As can be seen from the checklist in Table 11.1, the main underlying theme is a lack of interest in and an inability to produce written work of a suitable quality to match the perceived potential of the child or the demands of the curriculum. This may have secondary consequences such as inattention, avoidance, low motivation and self-esteem, negativism and behavioural problems. It may help to think of these groups of able/gifted learning disabled as having different patterns of difficulties.

Table 11.1 Profile of typical able underachievers in school

- Large gap between oral and written work
- Failure to complete school work
- Lack of interest in school work
- Poor execution of work
- Persistent dissatisfaction with achievements
- Avoidance of trying new activities
- Does not function well in groups
- Lacks concentration
- Poor attitudes to school
- Dislikes drill and memorisation
- Difficulties with peers
- Low self-image
- Sets unrealistic goals

Compiled from Whitmore (1982), Silverman (1989), Butler-Por (1987), Wallace (2000)

Group 1: a *discrepant* double exceptionality (usually identifiable)

- those who have been identified by discrepancies between high scores on ability tests and low achievement in school subjects or standard assessment tasks (SATs);
- those who show discrepant scores on IQ tests between verbal and performance items or within scales but may be performing in class at an average level;
- those who show an uneven pattern of high and low achievements across school subjects with only average ability test scores;
- those whose only high achievements seem to be in out-of-school or non-school activities.

Group 2: a *deficit* double exceptionality (usually the disability masks the abilities)

- those who have a specific learning difficulty (dyslexic-type difficulties) in the presence of depressed ability test scores;
- those with spelling or handwriting difficulties;
- those with gross motor coordination problems, or visuomotor impairment.

Group 3: a *deceptive* double exceptionality (usually not identified)

- ability measures seem to fall within the average but not the gifted range;
- pupils with social and behavioural difficulties;
- daydreamers, uninterested in school, 'lazy' pupils, 'cruisers';
- pupils from linguistically disadvantaged backgrounds and second-language learners.

The common thread running through all three groups is that the majority of these gifted and talented students may be satisfactory or even very good orally but are poor at writing down ideas or almost anything else at more than an average or below average level. The underlying reasons for these difficulties cannot be explored in detail here but the chapter references will enable these to be followed up.

PATTERNS OF SPECIAL EDUCATIONAL NEEDS (SEN) WHICH IMPACT ON SCHOOL LEARNING IN GIFTED AND NON-GIFTED POPULATIONS

1   Specific learning difficulties (SpLD) such as
    a)   verbal learning difficulties – dyslexia (reading and spelling difficulties), dysorthographia (spelling difficulties without reading difficulties), and mild dysphasia (language difficulties)

b) nonverbal learning difficulties such as dysgraphia (handwriting difficulties), dyspraxia (developmental coordination difficulties), attention deficit hyperactivity disorder (ADHD) and attention deficit disorder (ADD).

2 Physical sensory and medical difficulties (PSM). These include the hearing and visually impaired, and those with physical and/or medical conditions such as cerebral palsy, extra small or large stature, limblessness, spina bifida, multiple sclerosis and so on.

3 Social, emotional and behavioural difficulties (SEBD), e.g. isolates, elective mutism, depression, school phobia and truancy, attention seeking, disruption, bullying, wandering, vandalism, lying, theft, arson and violence.

4 Special populations – autistic spectrum disorders (ASD), autism and Asperger's syndrome; Down's syndrome (DS); central communicative disorders (CCD) – developmental dysphasia both receptive and expressive.

Students with PSM and special populations are in very small numbers, and their needs are addressed elsewhere (Montgomery 2003). In brief, when those with PSM have their special need catered for (e.g. in visual difficulties the provision of large vision aids, increased structured auditory information and feedback) then their needs are much the same as other gifted children.

Students with Asperger's syndrome and autism have distinct patterns of difficulties and behavioural rituals which affect their social and communication skills as well as their perception and thinking. The more intelligent they are the better they learn to manage their difficulties, especially by adolescence. However, they need specific and direct training in procedures and social protocols. Even so, they tend to be isolates and appear somewhat eccentric. School achievement can be good where the topics command their interest and require a large amount of factual or technical learning.

Children with Down's syndrome seem to have abilities and talent in a different pattern from the rest of the population but also include high achievers who can run their own lives and gain academic success in school subjects. We still have much to learn about how to teach these children to develop their talents to the full.

It is thus the groups of students with SpLD and SEBD who make up the majority of cases of gifted underachievers in mainstream schools. It is these two groups plus the 'cruisers' who are the focus of attention here.

SEBD are not always related to problems vulnerable students bring with them to school but can be created by schooling itself. Schlichte-Hiersemenzel (2000) recorded the plight of many gifted German pupils who had become behaviourally and emotionally disturbed because of their unchallenging mainstream education. Sisk (2000, 2003) described similar results of 'ill-fitting environments' for USA students and McCluskey et al. (2003) recorded the same for Canadian students. In the UK we have many case examples but no systematic research into the plight of such students. We know that 10 per cent of pupils in pupil referral units

(PRUs) and centres for SEBD fall into the more able range (Cole *et al.* 1998) and that many gifted entrepreneurs failed in school. Some failed because of dyslexic difficulties but others, who were 'school averse', responded by becoming difficult to manage and were excluded or 'resigned' from school early. Their talents and abilities went unnoticed.

With SpLD there are also the internal barriers to learning to be considered. Most dyslexic but highly able students eventually learn to read adequately but their spelling and writing remains poor. Many more have no difficulties with reading, often reading fluently before entry or quickly on entry to school but have severe difficulties in spelling. Yet others have no dyslexic or dysortho-graphic difficulties but have mild handwriting coordination difficulties which affect spelling and writing. A quick handwriting speed and spelling test can iden-tify these students so that special help can be given (Montgomery 2003).

THE ISSUE OF PROVISION IN GIFTED EDUCATION

In gifted education world wide two traditions have grown up. The most pervasive is the North American model, the problem-based approach, in which it is con-sidered that the mainstream education is unsuitable for the gifted and that this is a problem for which they need some form of special provision: a defectology type of model.

The current approach in England has been to adopt this model (DfEE 1999) and so we read of master classes, summer schools and the selection of the 'top 5 to 10 per cent' for some form of 'special' provision. This of course raises a range of not only general issues – equality and equity, democracy and elitism, eugenics, and nature versus nurture – but also more specific issues such as social engineer-ing, inclusion, identification, assessment, curriculum and pedagogy.

However, a second tradition has been advocated since the 1970s. This has promoted the education of gifted children in mixed ability settings by upskilling their teachers. It has been promoted by various experts in the field and by the National Association for Able Children in Education (NACE). The training offered by these sources has operated for more than two decades as an 'under-ground' movement. But it has enabled interested teachers to make good curriculum provision in mainstream education to meet the needs of the most able and through this they have promoted the learning of all the pupils (HMI 1992).

In this second model the terms 'gifted' and 'talented' tend not to be used but are replaced by terms such as 'the more able' and 'the highly able'. Instead of 'gifts' there is talk of 'potential abilities', for many gifted individuals do not show their giftedness in school. Early researchers such as Hollingworth (1942) and Pickard (1976) had shown that with good quality teaching most highly able children (up to IQ levels of 150) could be well catered for in mainstream educa-tion. This represents a level of IQ above three standard deviations and has an incidence of one in every thousand. The problem, thus, is to define 'good quality' provision so that those missed by standard assessments are not deprived of a good education.

We can see the two main types of approach to gifted education reflected in the curriculum provision in schools in that it is either 'structural' or 'integral'. In *structural provision* the school modifies the way it caters for groups by adopting such strategies as grade skipping, acceleration, setting, compacting, special schooling and so on. In *integral situations* the provision is a 'way of life' in which the methods are incorporated into the ordinary school curriculum so that all children can enjoy the enrichment and extension.

To help distinguish integral provision from structural forms of differentiation the term *developmental differentiation* was coined. It refers to:

> the setting of common tasks to which all pupils can contribute their own knowledge and understanding in collaborative activities and so structure their experiences so that all can achieve higher learning outcomes.
>
> (Montgomery 1996)

Developmental differentiation encompasses the constructivist approach to learning. Its second main feature is that it offers 'cognitive challenge' or 'brain engage' opportunities within the ordinary curriculum subjects. This is in contrast to most types of structural provision which offer faster tracking through the standard curriculum or teach topics in primary level, for example, that would normally be met in secondary school or higher education. In order to meet the broadest range of needs of the gifted and talented and also enhance the learning opportunities of all children an audit of a school's provision should reveal seven types or levels of curriculum provision in every school (see Figure 11.1).

There would seem to me to be four forms of provision which can be offered by every teacher to support the education of gifted and talented students, the doubly exceptional, the underachievers and the 'cruisers', and also help children of all abilities in mainstream classrooms. This begins by enhancing the skills of all mainstream teachers so that the everyday provision they offer to students is more cognitively challenging within the normal curriculum. This is beginning to be adopted by a separate arm of the Government's administration (DfES 2002) in the development of the 'Teaching and Learning in Foundation Subjects' initiative at Key Stage 3. It focuses upon the development of thinking skills, open questioning and independent study. However, it needs to be developed as an initiative in all Key Stages and to be extended in scope to encompass a wider range of cognitive abilities and skills which we might call the 'cognitive curriculum'.

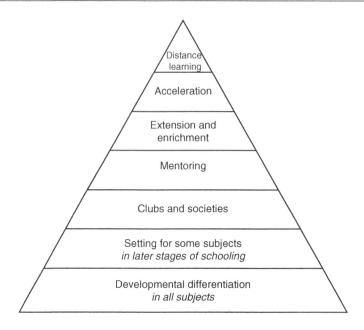

Figure 11.1 The seven types of gifted education provision that should be available in every school

Provision 1: The cognitive curriculum (Montgomery 1996, 1998, 2000a and b)

The cognitive curriculum consists of: developmental positive cognitive intervention (PCI) for every child in every lesson; cognitively challenging questioning – open and problem-posing; deliberate teaching of thinking skills and protocols; reflective teaching and learning; creativity training; cognitive process teaching methods such as cognitive study and research skills, games and simulations, experiential learning, investigative learning and problem solving, collaborative learning, and language experience methods.

What was clear from studies that introduced these techniques into mainstream teaching was that intrinsic motivation was developed and children's time on-task extended as was their enjoyment long after the lessons ended. Disaffected children remained at school for these lessons and gifted students recorded such things as 'This is much better than the usual boring stuff we get'. They all began to spend extended periods of time on- instead of off-task. The quality of their work frequently exceeded all expectations as did that of the most modest of learners and there were sometimes the most surprisingly interesting and creative responses from unsuspected sources. The collaborative nature of the tasks meant that mixed ability groups could easily access the work and all could be included in the same tasks with no diminution of achievements of the highly able (Montgomery 1985 and 1996, Hallam 2002). These methods were all used as part of the developmental differentiation techniques rather than methods of differentiation by inputs which, although now popular again, simply reproduce a stratified system of education (as in selective schooling) within the classroom.

Another aspect of this type of provision is that it allows students to be more participative and allows them to choose from a range of response modes to cater for their different talents (Gardner 1993) not 'intelligences'. Thus their learning experiences are individualised.

Provision 2: The talking curriculum

This is a curriculum which emphasises and embeds talking and reflection about learning before writing and recording in a variety of response modes such as: TPS (Think – Pair – Share), circle time, small group work, group problem-solving, collaborative learning, reciprocal teaching, peer tutoring, Thinkback (Lockhead 2001), role play, games, and drama, debates and 'book clubs' (Godinho and Clements 2002), presentations and 'teach-ins', poster presentations, exhibitions and demonstrations, and organised meetings.

All these are intimately related to the cognitive curriculum and examples are found in the Montgomery references provided earlier. Underachievers and the doubly exceptional with writing difficulties in particular need to talk things through before they are set to writing them down. In fact all young learners need such opportunities for often we do not know what we think until we try to explain it to someone else. Where such children come from disadvantaged cultural and linguistic environments the talking approaches are essential (Lockhead 2001). This helps not only vocabulary learning and comprehension but develops organisational skills in composition and argument. To support the organisational abilities direct teaching of '*scaffolds*' can be especially helpful and is the logical extension of a talking and developmental writing curriculum.

Extending the range of response modes permitted to include concept mapping, pictorial and performance modes, exhibitions, and so on can free up learners to demonstrate more easily what they have learnt and help them develop research skills and function as autonomous learners. It helps them extend their learning skills rather than cement them into a so called 'learning style'.

Provision 3: The developmental writing curriculum (Montgomery 1997a and b, 1998, 2000a, 2003)

A whole-school approach to developing handwriting and spelling skills, the developmental writing curriculum should include scaffolds to support weak organisational skills. A policy on cognitive process strategies for teaching spelling (CPSS) (Montgomery 1997a and b, 1998, 2000b), plus a school policy on an agreed format for teaching fluent joined handwriting in both primary and secondary schools, are essentials. Research has shown that over 50 per cent of pupils had substandard spelling skills and more than 70 per cent were not sufficiently fluent in handwriting (Montgomery 2003) to cope with the demands of their education. Among these pupils were substantial numbers of the most able, and in some respects it was noted that success in many schools was more dependent on writing speed than intellectual prowess.

Writing is still widely used as the main response mode in schools. Developing a school policy towards writing can help teachers develop kinder attitudes to writing difficulties and help them intervene to support and develop writing skills without creating a problem or 'special' need.

Provision 4: A positive approach to behaviour management in classrooms (Montgomery 1989, 1999, 2002)

Positive behaviour management and classroom control have been extensively researched in the observation and feedback to teachers in over 1,200 lessons (Montgomery 1984, 1988, 1999, 2002). During this research four interrelated strategies for improving teaching and reducing behaviour problems were evolved. These were 'Catching the children being good' (CBG); 'Positive cognitive intervention' (PCI) in lessons as outlined in the cognitive curriculum above; 'Management, monitoring and maintenance' (3Ms) as a set of tactics to gain and maintain class control; and the development of a tactical lesson plan (TLP) which showed what the pupils would be learning and doing rather than the teacher. In coaching teachers to use these strategies, teachers in difficulties were helped to become successful, and disaffected and disruptive pupils became calmer and more interested in learning.

These techniques also helped develop a school ethos and classroom climate which fostered a *positive learning environment* so that education became a form of therapy.

TRANSFORMATIVE LEARNING FOR TEACHERS?

Students arrive at college with very clear ideas about what good teaching is. Not surprisingly these 'theories' appear to be very much modelled upon their own experiences of schooling (Zeichner and Tabachnick 1981) and are deeply embedded in the unconscious. Their views of the 'good teacher' are centred on the transmission model (McDiarmid 1990) and hinged on the notion of telling or showing. For many, learning equated with remembering rather than the development of understanding, and this had not changed radically over the decades.

The researchers also found there was a low regard amongst teacher education students for theoretical concerns. This seems to be encouraged by the Teacher Training Agency's (TTA) technician approach to teacher education (Barton 2003). Teacher educators on the other hand are trying to promote a constructivist theory of learning, which advocates that pupils need to play a central role in the construction of their own learning if they are to acquire the knowledge and skills to equip them for lifelong learning.

However, what happens in practice in schools does not match this and the transmission model is prevalent worldwide. In the light of this Raths (2001) suggested that teacher education programmes were largely ineffective in improving the current practice of teaching and Korthagen and Kessels (1999) confirmed that there was a lack of transfer between the theoretical content of pre-service programmes and teachers' practice. Once in teaching their practices were very difficult to change (McNamara 1995). Jones (1996) put this resistance down to the pressures of being a full-time teacher. Added to these pressures we have had the Chief Inspector for Schools in England over a period of years demanding that teachers engage in more direct teaching of the whole class and Ofsted inspections being used to reinforce this, driving teachers towards the transmission model. The National Curriculum with its ten separate subjects, even after it was pruned, has also forced teachers into a preoccupation with transmitting the syllabus knowledge and this is most easily done through 'direct' teaching/transmission methods. Pupils from this system are now entering teaching courses and so are also likely to have these methods deeply embedded in their subconscious.

In fact when we use other methods, incorporating the cognitive and talking curricula described above, with pupils in schools they often do not think that it is 'real' school work, especially when they are having fun.

Recent studies by Kroll (2004) showed the difficulties experienced, even by trained teachers, on a Masters programme in transforming their theories about teaching. Kroll traces the changes in students' ideas over three years from naive perceptions based on their teaching and pre-service education programmes towards embracing a constructivist theory of teaching and learning. Constructivism in learning changes brains (Stones 2001), thus it is not surprising it takes so long and is such an involved process. It explains why technician-style education cannot achieve this or maintain the strength of any new initiative.

SOME CONCLUSIONS ON THE ISSUES OF PROVISION FOR ABLE UNDERACHIEVERS

The research that underpins these brief outlines of what represents good gifted education provision for children with SEN can be seen to have wider implications for the education of all pupils in mainstream schools. As their teachers become more knowledgeable and expert in making the developmental form of gifted provision, so then issues of selection and equity, elitism and social engineering become irrelevant. All pupils can have equal access to the resources and the provision. Where there are supplemental provisions such as those shown in Figure 11.1 then access to these can be arranged on the basis of self-referral, permitting pupils to have the choice and encouraging them to try these different opportunities in, as Freeman (2001) suggests, a 'sports' approach.

In the case of other doubly exceptional students with learning disabilities it is essential to try to identify their high potential so that remedial provision can be geared to their high ability as well as their special need. One of the key problems in remedial provision has been the repetitive and rote-learning techniques needed by some programmes. Too much emphasis on rote learning can be counterproductive in a rote memory-averse young person and more cognitive strategies are recommended.

Good provision for gifted students has, at its core, methods and materials that offer cognitive challenge and seek to develop the intellectual and cognitive skills of the learners in real-world situations and problems. Such provision is not significantly different from that which benefits all learners and the teaching for learning initiatives around the country is likely to show the way forward.

This is in contrast to the selection for a form of grammar school education – acceleration. After the 1944 Education Act this system was a success in developing a meritocracy and giving access to higher education and careers for a large number of the poor. We now we need to improve upon this system and learn from the disadvantages it created in consigning 80 per cent of the population to feel failures, its social divisiveness and its failure to identify large numbers of the most able whilst including many who were not.

The reason the doubly exceptional deserve our special attention is that if we can get their education right it will have benefits throughout the system. To achieve these benefits four interrelated forms of provision have been recommended – developing the cognitive and the talking curricula in all subjects, and establishing a coherent writing curriculum and a positive approach to behaviour management in schools and classrooms. It is through these techniques that emotional literacy and intrinsic motivation can be developed as well as academic success.

General educational provision in mainstream schools should be made inclusive and suitable for all. This means incorporating the cognitive curriculum and the teaching for learning approach into all levels of teaching in schools and also in higher education (Montgomery 1995, 1996, 2004). This does not involve large changes to the school curriculum but small modifications to the way in which it is taught: what Eyre in this volume calls 'structured tinkering'.

What has been written in this book relates to changing teachers' practices. This can only occur if we can change the theories about good teaching for all children. This means teachers must grasp the principles of constructivist learning theory but this will only occur when they are subjected to its practices at their own level (Montgomery 1993, 2004). Short training inputs only reach the converted: transforming the theory and practice of teaching and learning of all teachers requires sustained training programmes of teacher education designed on constructivist principles. A revolution in higher education should suffice.

References

Barton, L. (2003) 'Inclusive education and teacher education. A basis for hope or a discourse of delusion?' Professorial Inaugural Lecture Series, Institute of Education, London.

Benjamin, S. (2002) *The Micro Politics of Inclusive Education*. Buckingham: Open University Press.

Butler-Por, N. (1987) *Underachievers in Schools: Issues and Interventions*. Chichester, W. Sussex: John Wiley.

CBI (2004) Verbal report of a survey of entrepreneurs and underachievement in schools. BBC Radio 4 *Today* Programme.

Cole, T., Visser, J. and Upton, G. (1998) *Effective Schooling for Pupils with Emotional and Behavioural Disorders*. London: David Fulton.

DfEE (1999) *Excellence in Cities*. London: Department for Education and Employment.

DfES (2002) *Teaching and Learning in Foundation Subjects at Key Stage 3*. London: HMSO.

DfES (2004) *Removing Barriers to Achievement: The Government's Strategy for SEN*. London: Department for Education and Skills.

Dyson, A. (1999) 'Inclusion and inclusions: Theories and discourses in inclusive education'. In H. Daniels and P. Garner (eds) *Inclusive Education*. London: Kogan Page.

Dyson, A., Howes, A. and Roberts, B. (2002) 'A systematic review of the effectiveness of school-level action for promoting participation by all students' (EPPI-Centre Review). In *Research Evidence in Education*. London: Institute of Education.

Freeman, J. (2001) *Gifted Children Grown Up*. London: David Fulton.

Galloway, D. and Goodwin, C. (1987) *The Education of Disturbing Children*. London: Longman.

Gardner, H. (1993) *Multiple Intelligences: The Theory in Practice*. New York: Basic Books.

Godinho, S. and Clements, D. (2002) 'Literature discussion with gifted and talented students'. *Educating Able Children*, 6 (2), pp. 11–19.

Hallam, S. (2002) *Ability Grouping in Schools*. London: Institute of Education.

HMI (1992) *The Education of More Able Pupils in Maintained Schools*. London: HMSO.

Hollingworth, L. (1942) *Gifted Children Above 180 IQ Stanford Binet*. New York: World Books.

Hughes, W. and Dawson, R. (1995) 'Memories of school: Adult dyslexics recall their schooldays'. *Support for Learning*, 10 (4), pp. 181–9.

Jones, S. (1996) *Developing a Learning Culture: Empowering People to Deliver Quality, Innovation and Long Term Success*. New York: McGraw Hill.

Korthagen, F. A. J. and Kessels, S. F. A. (1999) 'Linking theory and practice: Changing the pedagogy of teacher education?' *Educational Researcher*, 28 (4), pp. 4–17.

Kroll, L.R. (2004) 'Constructing constructivism: How student teachers construct ideas of development, knowledge, learning and teaching'. *Teachers and Teaching*, 10 (2), pp. 199–218.

Lockhead, J. (2001) *THINKBACK: A User's Guide to Minding the Mind*. London: Lawrence Erlbaum.

McCluskey, K. W., Baker, P. A., Bergsgaard, M. and McCluskey, A. L. A. (2003) 'Interventions with talented at-risk populations with emotional and behavioural difficulties'. In D. Montgomery (ed.) *Gifted and Talented Children with SEN*. London: David Fulton.

McDiarmid, G. W. (1990) 'Challenging prospective teachers' beliefs during early field experience. A quixotic undertaking?' *Journal of Teacher Education*, 42 (3), pp. 12–20.

McNamara, S. (1995) *Changing Behaviour*. London: David Fulton.

Montgomery, D. (1984) *Evaluation and Enhancement of Teaching Performance*. Kingston, London: Learning Difficulties Research Project.

Montgomery, D. (1985) *The Special Needs of Able Pupils in Ordinary Classrooms*. Kingston, London: Learning Difficulties Research Project.

Montgomery, D. (1988) 'Appraisal'. *New Era (in Education)*, 68 (3), pp. 85–90.

Montgomery, D. (1989) *Managing Behaviour Problems*. Sevenoaks, Kent: Hodder and Stoughton.

Montgomery, D. (1993) 'Fostering learner managed learning in teacher education'. In N. Graves (ed.) *Learner Managed Learning* (pp. 59–70). Leeds: Higher Education for Capability/World Education Fellowship.

Montgomery, D. (1995) 'The role of metacognition and metalearning in teacher education'. In G. Gibbs (ed.) *Improving Student Learning* (pp. 227–53). Oxford: Oxford Brookes Centre for Staff Development.

Montgomery, D. (1996) *Educating the Able*. London, Cassell.

Montgomery, D. (1997a) *Spelling: Remedial Strategies*. London: Cassell.

Montgomery, D. (1997b) *Developmental Spelling: A Handbook for Teachers*. Maldon, Essex: Learning Difficulties Research Project.

Montgomery, D. (1998) *Reversing Lower Attainment*. London, David Fulton.

Montgomery, D. (1999) *Positive Appraisal Through Classroom Observation*. London, David Fulton.

Montgomery, D. (ed.) (2000a) *Able Underachievers*. London: Whurr.

Montgomery, D. (2000b) 'Supporting the bright dyslexic in the ordinary classroom'. *Educating Able Children*, 4 (1), pp. 23–32.

Montgomery, D. (2002) *Helping Teachers Improve through Classroom Observation* (2nd edn). London: David Fulton.

Montgomery, D. (ed.) (2003) *Gifted and Talented Children with Special Educational Needs*. London: David Fulton.

Montgomery, D. (2004) *MA in Gifted Education by Distance Learning*. London: Middlesex University.

Pickard, P. M. (1976) *If You Think Your Child is Gifted*. London: Allen and Unwin.

Quicke, J. (1999) *A Curriculum for Life: Schools for a Democratic Learning Society*. Buckingham: Open University Press.

Raths, J. (2001) 'Teachers' beliefs and teaching beliefs'. *Early Childhood Research and Practice*, 3 (1), pp. 14–22.

Schlicte-Hiersemenzel, B. (2000) 'The psychodynamics of psychological and behavioural difficulties of highly able children: Experiences from a psychotherapeutic practice'. In D. Montgomery (ed.) *Able Underachievers* (pp. 52–61). London: Whurr.

Shore, B. M. (1991) 'How do gifted children think differently?' *Journal of the Gifted and Talented*, Education Council for Alberta Teacher's Association, 5 (2), pp. 19–23.

Silverman, L. K. (1989) 'Invisible gifts, invisible handicaps'. *Roeper Review*, 12 (1), pp. 37–42.

Sisk, D. (2000) 'Overcoming underachievement in gifted and talented children'. In D. Montgomery (ed.) *Able Underachievers* (pp. 127–49). London: Whurr.

Sisk, D. (2003) 'Gifted with behaviour disorders: Marching to a different drummer'. In D. Montgomery (ed.) *Gifted and Talented Children with SEN* (pp. 131–54). London: David Fulton.

Stones, E. (2001) 'Mr Chips changes brains'. *The Psychologist*, 13 (2), pp. 78–80.

Wallace, B. (2000) *Teaching the Very Able Child*. London: David Fulton.

Whitmore, J. R. (1982) *Giftedness, Conflict and Underachievement*. Boston: Allyn and Bacon.

Whitty, G. (2002) *Making Sense of Education Policy*. London: Sage.

Zeichner, K. M. and Tabachnick, B. R. (1981) 'Are the effects of university teacher education "washed out' by school experience?' *Journal of Teacher Education*, 32 (3), pp. 7–11.

Chapter 12

A curriculum of opportunity

Developing potential into performance[1]

Belle Wallace

There is no universally agreed definition of the pupils who generally would be assessed as 'more able'. Descriptions include genius, gifted, exceptionally able, very bright, high flyer, very able and more able. However, in general terms, approximately 20 per cent of the school population may be considered 'more able', while the top 2 per cent could be considered 'exceptionally able'.

The identification of more able and talented pupils is linked to the particular context, and in every school there will be a group of pupils who require extending, regardless of how they compare with more able and talented pupils in other schools. It is comparatively easy to identify the extremes in any cohort of pupils, but defining a cut-off point to separate out a group of more able and talented pupils from others is problematic and often unhelpful. Labelling pupils as 'gifted' or 'exceptional' does not take into account the vitally influential factors of opportunity, growth, support, personality and maturity. Also, pupils given such a label may feel under huge pressure to fulfil school and parental expectations.

THE DEVELOPMENT OF MORE ABLE AND TALENTED PUPILS

Figure 12.1 shows the interrelating qualities and attributes which underpin high achievement and which schools need to develop to enable more able and talented pupils to reach their full potential, and to function effectively as highly performing adults.

Adult achievement of high-level performance requires a significant cluster of attributes from each segment of the High Performance Constellation as outlined in Figure 12.1.

- *Abilities*. All human beings possess varying degrees of potential across the full range of human abilities. However, each human being has a differentiated profile across these abilities. It is important, therefore, to provide all learners with opportunities to *discover* their strengths, and then to *develop* these strengths while receiving support to strengthen abilities that may be weaker.

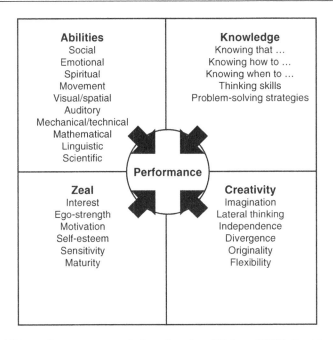

Figure 12.1 High performance constellation. Based on Wallace (2000) *Teaching the Very Able Child: Developing a Policy and Adopting Strategies for Provision.* London: David Fulton (A Nace/Fulton Publication).

- *Zeal.* High-level performance certainly requires zeal or passion, together with ego-strength and the self-confidence to persevere. Highly successful adults have had to work with tenacity and perseverance: to keep practising, to keep searching, to devote long hours to research. They have had a positive perception of the self and an awareness of the goals they wanted to reach. Schools, therefore, need to ensure that learners' self-motivation and self-confidence are strong and goal-directed.
- *Creativity.* Exceptional performance is characterised by high-level creativity. This requires the courage to think and do things differently from the norm; to ask unusual questions; to disagree with 'conventional' thinking; and often to walk a lonely path in search of new solutions and ideas. Learners in schools need to have opportunities and encouragement to find new ways of thinking and doing; to have challenges that demand genuine exploration into new ideas.
- *Knowledge.* All people, both young learners and adult learners, work from a base of knowledge and skills, but the knowledge and skills need to be applied in thinking and solving problems. Intelligence is the capacity to see and solve problems that can be traditionally academic, immediately practical, or philosophically abstract – problems ranging from hypothetical or simulation scenarios to situations drawn from everyday life.

IDENTIFYING MORE ABLE AND TALENTED PUPILS

A wide range of qualities, characteristics and processes contribute to high potential and achievement, hence identification necessarily involves a range of strategies and procedures. Moreover, the assessment of pupils is a dynamic process that is continuous and flexible – the identification process should not be a 'once and for all' diagnosis. Importantly, precocious early development does not guarantee advanced adult performance: many pupils will only develop as they gain confidence and greater maturity. A school policy of inclusion should, therefore, continuously provide all learners with equal opportunities to discover their potential; differentiation of learning tasks then becomes the equitable corollary to ongoing diagnosis of learning needs.

Teacher assessment of pupil potential

To identify more able and talented pupils, teachers may use information from a wide range of sources, e.g. teacher checklists to structure observations of pupil dialogue or performance; group tests; self/peer/parent questionnaires. Such evidence must then be used to ensure that pupils' learning needs are met. To accomplish this, teachers need to:

- promote active involvement of pupils in their learning
- be fully aware of the profound influence assessment has on motivation
- develop modes of effective feedback to pupils
- adjust their teaching to take account of the results of assessment
- teach the skills that pupils need to assess themselves and understand how to improve.

Teacher assessment in the early years

It is self-evident that potential develops into high-level achievement over time with adequate nurturing and the provision of appropriate learning opportunities. However, there are a number of indicators of early potential, such as: accelerating through early milestones; speaking early and developing an advanced vocabulary with understanding; learning easily with little repetition; or showing particular abilities in, for example, musical, physical or artistic activities. But it is essential to remember that many children are late developers, and/or need the opportunities provided by an enriching early years' environment in order to discover what they can do.

Teacher assessment in the primary and secondary years

The checklist for primary and secondary years in Table 12.1 outlines a range of qualities often shown by more able and talented pupils: no pupil would portray

Table 12.1   Checklist for identifying primary and secondary children who manifest high-level ability

More able and talented children may:

- Be confident and competent
- Express own feelings
- Attribute ideas to others
- Be self-effacing
- Reflect on own performance

- Possess extensive general knowledge, often know more than the teacher, and find the usual reference books superficial
- Show good insight into cause–effect relationships
- Easily grasp underlying principles, and need the minimum of explanation
- Quickly make generalisations, and are able to extract the relevant points from complexity

---

- Have exceptional curiosity and constantly want to know why – are inventive and original when interested
- Ask searching questions which tend to be unlike other children's questions
- Often see the unusual rather than the conventional relationships – are able to pose problems and solve them ingeniously
- Display intellectual playfulness, fantasise and imagine, and are quick to see connections and to manipulate ideas

---

- Give inventive responses to open-ended questions
- Have a keen sense of humour in the unusual, and are quick to appreciate nuances and hidden meanings
- Appreciate verbal puns, cartoons, jokes, and often enjoy bizarre humour, satire and irony

---

- Criticise constructively even if sometimes argumentatively
- Be unwilling to accept authoritarian pronouncements without critical examination, and want to debate and find reasons to justify the why and wherefore

---

- Have mental speeds faster than physical capabilities so are often reluctant to write at length
- Prefer to talk rather than write, and often talk at speed with fluency and expression
- Be reluctant to practise skills already mastered, finding such practice futile

Table 12.1 continued

- Read rapidly and are able to retain what is read, and to recall detail
- Listen only to part of the explanation and appear to lack concentration or even interest, but always know what is going on
- Jump stages in learning, and are often frustrated by having to fill in the stages missed
- Leap from concrete examples to abstract rules and general principles
- Have quick absorption and recall of information, seem to need no revision, and are impatient with repetition

---

- Be keen and alert observers, note detail and are quick to see similarities and differences
- See greater significance in a story or film and continue the story
- See problems quickly and take the initiative
- Have advanced understanding and use of language, but are sometimes hesitant as the correct word is searched for and then used

---

- Become absorbed for long periods when interested, and be impatient with interference or abrupt change
- Be persistent in seeking task completion when motivated and often set very high personal standards – are perfectionists
- Be more than usually interested in 'adult' problems such as important issues in current affairs (local and world), evolution, justice, the universe, etc.
- Be concerned to adapt and improve institutions, objects, systems, and can be particularly critical of school, for example

---

- Be philosophical about everyday problems and common sense issues
- Be perceptive in discussion about people's motives, needs and frailties
- Daydream and seem lost in another world
- Show sensitivity and react strongly to things causing distress or injustice
- Empathise with others, and often take a leadership role; are very understanding and sympathetic

---

Taken from Belle Wallace (2000) *Teaching the Very Able Child: Developing a Policy and Adopting Strategies for Provision.* London: David Fulton (A NACE Fulton Publication). With permission all the qualities but each pupil could portray a significant cluster of traits. The important factor underpinning the use of such a checklist is that teachers and parents need to provide the opportunities which allow pupils to demonstrate the behaviour.

Identifying able but underachieving pupils

However, it is not sufficient to recognise only those pupils who are manifesting positive learning behaviour and high school achievement. Many pupils develop the chronic syndrome of underachievement. For example:

*   Many pupils learn to coast through the school system doing the minimum required – just enough to get by. This pattern of response leads to long-term underachievement and these children need recognition and challenge to work to their full potential. Underachieving but potentially able pupils often fill pages with neat, tidy work and may decorate their books as a time-filling task, or do the work set for homework during the lesson. Although they hold back from being the centre of attention and seldom put up their hands, they know the answer when asked directly.
*   Underachieving pupils may also appear to be daydreaming and although they don't often ask questions themselves, they are often consulted by other children who need help. Such pupils get on quietly without supervision but do only as much as is needed to get by, sometimes spinning out a task so that they finish just as the lesson ends!
*   Despite absence, underachieving but potentially able pupils catch up quickly on key concepts missed and in a one-to-one conversation show a surprising awareness of issues and a wide general knowledge. Although on the fringe of the most popular peer group these pupils are generally accepted by others, often being elected as chairperson or scribe in group work.

Identifying able but disaffected pupils

There is, however, another subset of underachievers: these are the pupils who aggressively show behaviour that masks achievement. They are often the most problematic pupils to deal with since their negative school behaviour requires immediate attention, negating any possible recognition of underlying potential for high performance. Some examples include:

Able pupils, who, for a variety of reasons, become disillusioned with their schooling and develop long-term behaviour patterns that are negative and often disruptive. This behaviour masks the potential ability and the longer the behaviour continues, the more difficult it becomes to moderate and change.

Able but disaffected pupils who are often anti-school and very critical of its values, making scathing remarks about teachers and lacking enthusiasm for most school subjects. They are not interested in seeking teachers' approval and their work may be poor and incomplete. Despite irregular attendance these pupils are often able to keep pace with others but they watch the time and are anxious to finish the school day.

Many of these pupils are bored, lethargic and lack motivation. They are easily distracted and often at the root of mischief and practical jokes, using their abrasive humour and ironic perception of other people's weaknesses. They also distract and manipulate others and can be moody and bad tempered.

Outwardly self-sufficient, such pupils often seek older friends, finding it difficult to form relationships with peers and teachers. They may be impatient, critical, rude and insolent, apparently easily frustrated and lacking in kindness to others. They can, however be very astute in argument and self-justification with good survival skills'.

(Wallace 2000)

Equal opportunities issues in the identification process

When identifying more able and talented pupils within a policy of inclusion, schools need to ensure that opportunities are provided for *all* pupils to enable them to fulfil their potential. Schools should give due regard to all groups of pupils including:

- pupils with disabilities
- pupils who use a home language that is different from school
- pupils from minority ethnic and religious groups or different cultures
- looked-after children', young carers and pupils from families under stress.

There is currently much debate about boys and underachievement. Boys, in comparison to girls, are generally later in the development of fine motor skills. It is not uncommon for girls to produce neat pages of work while boys have a tendency to be reluctant recorders. Teachers need to be alert to the impact of their expectations on pupil performance and aim to provide a broad, balanced and enriched curriculum for all pupils.

Assessment of potential across the full range of human abilities

So far the discussion has centred on identifying the indications of potential with regard to general ability'. However, if schools are to embrace the concept of an inclusive curriculum of opportunity for *all* pupils, then they need to address the challenge of identifying pupils' potential across the full range of ten human abilities: social, emotional, spiritual, visual/spatial, auditory/sonal, physical/somatic, mechanical/technical, linguistic, mathematical and scientific. All human beings have potential across all the abilities, but each individual has a unique profile of strengths and weaknesses (Wallace *et al.* 2004).

Table 12.2 provides a checklist outlining the essential characteristics that signify potential within each of the human abilities. Obviously, while one ability may be dominant, human potential is manifested through different activities which combine and interrelate across more than one domain. For example, the base of being truly human resides in the range of strengths across an individual's social, emotional and spiritual abilities. A dancer also possesses ability in visual/spatial, auditory/sonal and physical/somatic domains. An engineer possesses strengths in visual/spatial, physical/somatic, mechanical/technical, linguistic, mathematical and scientific domains.

Table 12.2 Checklist outlining the essential characteristics that signify potential within each of the human abilities

Characteristics	Activities for observation
1 Linguistic potential	
Uses advanced vocabulary and structures accurately and creatively	Summarising a story extracting key points
Can use complex structures to sequence and explain ideas	Devising word games
Shows understanding in dual language	Telling a story with fluency and expression
Empathises with characters and issues Identifies differences in purposes and styles	Performing drama and role play Recalling an event with detail
2 Mathematical potential	
Remembers and generalises mathematical rules	Multi-level pattern and shape puzzles
Solves multiple-step problems	Multiple-criteria matching and sorting puzzles
Uses unusual sequences	Open-ended, multiple-step problems
Sees relationships and connections among numbers, symbols and/or shapes	Games of logic
Investigates patterns and sequences	Games of strategy
Can work forwards and backwards through a sequence	
Makes mathematical comparisons	

Characteristics	Activities for observation
3 Visual/spatial potential	
Solves hands-on problems easily	Construction/design activities
Spots visual similarities and differences	Observation activities
Experiments with techniques and methods	Drawing, painting, texture and tactile activities
Constructs or draws with unusual detail and perspective	Multi-level 3-D, tangram and jigsaw puzzles
Uses shapes, textures, tones creatively	
Experiments with 2-D and 3-D ideas	
4 Somatic/physical potential	
Has accurate sense of space, speed, direction and shape	Games requiring large-motor or fine-motor movement
Links movements and sequences fluently	Obstacle courses
Has wide repertoire of skills and movements	Dance, drama and mime activities
Has good control of gross and fine movement	Multi-sequence movements
Responds to flavours and textures accurately	Taste and texture puzzles
Mimes with accuracy and expression	
Expresses feelings, moods, ideas expressively	
5 Auditory potential	
Responds to melody, rhythm and beat	Dance and drama activities
Interprets sounds and tones accurately	Song and band activities
Learns melodies easily	Movement and rhythm games
Recognises moods and qualities of sounds	Musical games
Recognises voices and body music as expressive instruments	Listening activities
6 Social potential	
Shows empathy with others	Games involving other people
Understands rules and values	Role-play activities
Sees cause and effect of happenings	Playground behaviour
Involves or considers others in decision-making	Dance, drama and mime activities
Considers others when expressing own feelings	Small group work
Leads and/or follows as appropriate	Discussions of issues and behaviour

Characteristics	Activities for observation
7 Emotional potential	
Identifies and describes own feelings	Discussions about behaviour of characters in stories
Identifies causes and effects of own feelings	Games
Expresses and releases negative emotions	Dance, drama, and mime activities
Sees the effects of expressing emotions in certain ways	Playground behaviour
	Discussions about highly emotional topics
8 Spiritual potential	
Understands symbolism	Cooperative activities
Concerned about 'fair play'	Discussions of social behaviour
Settles arguments (also social)	Drama and role-play activities
Is a peacemaker	Playing or working in groups
Asks questions about human values	Discussions of moral dilemmas
Shows openness to all points of view on religious questions	
Wonders about universal questions	
9 Scientific potential	
Likes experimenting with plants, animals, chemicals or environments	Collecting and grouping things
Notices fine details in natural phenomena	Investigation activities
Sees connections, collects data, uses evidence	Sequence activities
Builds and makes models of scientific information or ideas	Building and making models
Spots inconsistencies	
10 Mechanical/technical potential	
Uses tools and techniques with accuracy	Lego and Multifix activities
Manipulates techniques creatively	Designing, making and drawing activities
Enjoys building and making devices	Making and manipulating moving structures
Manipulates shapes, rotation, angles	
Fixes machines or devices	

Note: These characteristics are in line with Key Stage 2 National Curriculum Frameworks.
Taken from Wallace *et al.* (2004) *Thinking and Problem-Solving: An Inclusive Approach.* London: David Fulton (A NACE/Fulton Publication). With permission

Using standardised tests as indicators of high potential

Informed and aware teacher observation can be intuitive, dynamic and empowering for pupils. However, the use of standardised group tests can provide useful additional information about pupils' performance across a range of basic skills needed for school and examination success, for example, reading, spelling and mathematics. But such tests must be used with caution as they cannot predict the ultimate level of achievement of any pupil, and certain skills and attributes can only be observed in group work, for example, active listening, oral reasoning and tenacity in pursuing arguments. Care must also be taken to ensure that any test selected is understood for its specific purpose, in that it provides additional, relevant information and is part of a whole school assessment policy. Table 12.3 shows the advantages and disadvantages of using standardised group tests as tools for identifying high-level potential and achievement.

Finally, individual diagnostic assessment may be carried out by an educational psychologist when a school needs further guidance with regard to the child who presents a conflicting array of learning behaviours.

Table 12.3 Advantages and disadvantages of standardised group tests

Advantages	Disadvantages
Tests can confirm a pupil's competence over a range of basic skills needed for learning.	Most paper and pencil tests measure a limited range of skills/abilities (i.e. not problem-solving, higher-order skills).
A high score on a non-verbal test with a low score on a verbal test can be an indication of high-level reasoning but low academic performance.	Standardised tests require convergent thinking and give no opportunities for divergent or creative thinking.
Tests can enable pupils' performance across a range of skills to be compared.	Tests cannot measure abilities across the range of Multiple Intelligences.
Some tests can support a teacher's assessment of a child who has high levels of logical reasoning.	A standardised group test only gives an indication of current performance and cannot indicate a pupil's potential to learn under optimum conditions.
A high score for reading with a high score for comprehension usually correlates with high general ability.	Pupils with poor reading skills are disadvantaged by such tests.
Group tests can be used to provide data for target setting and for monitoring school standards. They can provide common information on transfer between schools.	Some pupils are nervous in a formal test situation. Some may be unfamiliar with the test items while others may have received 'coaching'.

Self and peer identification

It is important to help learners to identify their interests and capabilities for themselves while maintaining a school ethos which celebrates and develops strengths and supports individual needs. Schools can help pupils to identify their own needs and those of their peers by providing an intensive programme of enjoyable and challenging activities which allow pupils to:

- reflect on activities across the full range of human abilities, noting ways in which they best process information and show their learning
- identify their own and their peers' strengths and aptitudes, for example, in role plays such as surviving on a desert island, or running a school of the future
- develop their emotional intelligence by engaging in debates which explore important moral and ethical issues that relate to their own lives, and to be actively involved in projects which seek to serve community, national and global needs.

Examples of activities that allow pupils to recognise and acknowledge one another's strengths are given below.

Exercise A   Organising our community

Imagine that your class is stranded on an island with no links to the outside world. You do not know when you will be rescued. There is plenty of fruit, fish, fresh water and vegetation. Discuss how you would organise everyone in your class so that each person is using their ability in the best way. Everyone must have a useful job and a chance to earn the respect of the whole community. Here are some questions to start you off, but you can add any job that you think is important. You can also think of the special talents the pupils in your class have, and think of a job especially for them.

- Who would be fair in organising the food?
- Who would be good at building shelters for us to live in?
- Who would be best at settling arguments?
- Who would be good at organising games?
- Who would be good at providing entertainment?
- Who would be good at getting us all to work together?

Exercise B Organising our own school

Imagine that you are given the chance to organise lessons for your class but there are no teachers: you have to teach yourselves. Remember that you must learn the skills you need to earn your own living and the skills you need to enjoy your leisure. But don't think only of yourself. Think also of the jobs that are needed for you to live a safe, healthy and happy life. Which lessons will you organise and who will teach them? Here are some ideas to start you off, but you can add any lessons you think are important. You can also think of the special talents some of your classmates have and organise lessons when they teach you their special skills.

Who would teach these subjects?

- Music
- Art
- Computer science
- Food technology
- Dance
- Maths
- RE
- Athletics
- Writing
- Speaking
- Building technology
- Geography
- Reading
- Sport
- Drama
- History

Involving parents

Parents and carers have a vital role to play in the education of their children. Sometimes they need help and guidance from the school in order to deal with problems. At other times they can provide support and expertise for the school. The quality and ease of communication between home and school has a direct bearing on the well-being of all learners from early years through to adolescence.

MAKING PROVISION FOR MORE ABLE PUPILS WITHIN A POLICY OF INCLUSION

There is no one formula for organising a large state or public school so that all pupils can engage in appropriately challenging learning opportunities that personalise their individual learning needs. This section summarises the main points in the debate about various organisational strategies which may be used by primary and secondary schools. But whichever form of organisation is developed, it needs to be flexible so that adjustments can be made in the light of specific pupils' needs.

Mixed ability classes or groups

Children certainly need opportunities to learn how to work together so that they learn to appreciate each other's strengths and support each other's needs. More able and talented pupils can contribute ideas to stimulate and inspire debate and discussion, but they can also learn that other children have valuable ideas to contribute. However, where schools are celebrating the collective multiple abilities of pupils, each pupil can find a moment of personal recognition which makes it easier to accept and live with individual differences. Living in a democracy demands that we understand and function in a mixed ability society. However, working with mixed ability classes is most professionally demanding since the teacher needs to recognise and plan for individual strengths and weaknesses. If learning activities are not carefully differentiated the more able pupils may coast, feel frustrated and repeat work they have already mastered. Mixed ability grouping needs expert planning for appropriate challenges across a wide spectrum of ability, and essential use of group and individual activities.

Setting

Setting pupils, although a method of grouping pupils more narrowly on certain criteria, still needs carefully planned differentiation since within any one set of pupils there will be a diverse range of abilities. More able and talented pupils need the challenge of working with others of similar interests and abilities: setting pupils for some subjects does make it easier for the teacher to develop a faster pace, or to work in greater depth and breadth with opportunities for reflection and independent thought. However, sets tend to remain fixed and it is difficult to retain the flexibility that enables learners to move between groups when they demonstrate progress.

Working with an older group for some subjects: flexible grouping

Some more able and talented pupils are so advanced in a particular subject (often mathematics) that they need the intellectual challenge of older pupils for some of the time. A school ethos which celebrates all pupils' abilities can accommodate this level of flexibility without making such an arrangement seem 'unusual'. However, younger pupils need the emotional maturity to cope in an older group, and the older pupils need the maturity to accept this arrangement. Moreover, the planning within the school needs to accept and accommodate the need for such flexibility.

Acceleration

Sometimes moving a pupil permanently to an older year group can alleviate the problems of slow pace and frustration experienced by many more able and talented pupils. However, this needs to be accomplished at an early stage so that the pupil can form friendship groups. The pupil needs to be physically, emotionally and socially well developed and must remain with the same peer group during the move from primary to secondary school. It must also be emphasised that acceleration by one year does not completely meet the intellectual needs of highly able pupils who are often able to work at levels several years above their chronological peers.

Fast tracking (compacting or target setting)

Fast tracking describes a strategy whereby pupils can move faster through the basic programmes of study in order to move into more advanced individual or small group work. There are benefits to this practice if a pupil uses acquired skills to work in greater depth and breadth on real problem-solving activities. Often a mentor (who may be an expert from outside school) can provide tutoring and support. However, there is little merit in fast tracking if the pupil skates superficially through narrow content for the sole purpose of taking a GCSE (General Certificate of Secondary Education) examination early. The purpose of fast tracking is to alleviate the repetition of content and skills already mastered, thus creating time for intensive project work in depth and breadth.

ENRICHING, EXTENDING AND DIFFERENTIATING LEARNING FOR ALL PUPILS

The importance of careful, flexible planning and appropriate differentiation has already been stressed. This section suggests the underlying rationale and strategies for the planning of appropriate differentiation. It is important to stress at the outset that all pupils need to acquire the skills of learning how to learn: the skills of enquiry and research, the skills of logical and creative thinking and problem-solving along with the skills of self-monitoring and self-assessment. Differentiation does not mean that only able learners should acquire these enabling life-skills, but does mean that able learners can acquire these skills more quickly and can apply them in more complex depth and breadth of content.

In addition, differentiation applies holistically across the whole content of the curriculum. It is not sufficient to rely on, for example, a 'challenge box' in the classroom (e.g. puzzles, problems and extended reading) for pupils who complete work early. If differentiation is appropriate and meaningful, pupils should be fully engaged until the series of lessons or the extended project ends!

We will now consider a range of strategies which can apply to all pupils across a range of levels and content complexities, but the fundamental strategies will enable teachers to respond to the needs of more able and talented pupils by:

- helping pupils to develop and make effective use of cross-curricular strengths
- further enriching and extending the curriculum, accommodating the full range of multiple abilities
- planning challenging questions which develop higher-order learning skills
- systematically training problem-solving and thinking skills.

Higher-order learning skills based on Bloom's taxonomy

Bloom's (1956) taxonomy of educational objectives still provides a useful framework for planning thinking and learning tasks. It is important to stress, however, that the taxonomy should not be used as a hierarchy, but as a flexible framework for planning. *All pupils* can undertake activities developed using the framework, but the learning skills for more able pupils need to be developed using increasingly complex content.

The following text presents an analysis of activities based on Bloom's original taxonomy and is taken from Wallace (2000).

The taxonomy is made up of the following:

1   *Remembering*   Pupils need to know and recall various types of knowledge' as a basis for action. No-one can think in a vacuum: there is a core of relevant experiential and factual knowledge and theories that pupils need in order to engage in a thinking activity. To do this efficiently they need to acquire and use a range of research skills and basic subject skills such as procedures in maths and science and technical skills in literacy, art and ICT (Information and Communication Technology). Given practice at asking the right questions pupils will learn the criteria for good questioning and be able to select relevant facts. Importantly, pupils need to learn how to present ideas using a diverse range of efficient recording and communication skills. To support their learning they need demonstration and examples, practice and opportunities to share with others. Remembering is involved in activities which ask: *What happened when — Make a list — Write an account — Make a summary —*

2   *Comprehension*   Pupils need activities that demonstrate understanding. The lower order comprehension tasks include: paraphrasing, explaining and selecting relevant information to answer a question. However, more able and talented pupils need to use *higher-order* comprehension skills. They need to learn how to interpret knowledge by presenting a new perspective, comparing and contrasting data and viewpoints, re-ordering information and examining consequences. Higher-order comprehension is shown through activities such as:
Write a summary of the main points — Explain why that happened — Discuss this from the point of view of— What are the similarities between — Explain the

*differences between — What would have happened if —?How would this affect
—? Why did — react in this way —? What were the results of this—?*

3   *Application*   The acquisition and understanding of knowledge is inert, and
only becomes active knowledge when pupils use the knowledge to solve a
problem. Pupils need opportunities to manipulate or construct something
using their new knowledge, to convert the knowledge into a different format, apply it to a similar situation, build a model, illustrate it and apply it to
an example. Applying knowledge involves the following activities:
*How would you use this to —? How does this rule apply —? How can you use
what you have learned to solve this —? Does the same principle apply in this —?
What else do you know that would apply —? Is this the same kind of —?
Construct a diagram to show — Conduct an experiment to prove — Paint a picture to show —*

4   *Analysis*   Pupils need to understand overall relationships and patterns.
Pupils need to fit the pieces of the 'jigsaw' into a whole: they need to identify
connections, patterns, sequences and themes. They need to see the big picture' and to be aware of how the bits' they are learning are contributing to a
coherent plan of the 'whole'. While this applies to all pupils, able pupils particularly can appreciate the big picture': they can cope with complex
scenarios and intricate themes. Analysis can be shown through activities
such as:
*In what ways are they the same —? different —? better —? worse? What was the
overall plan——? How do the elements combine —? Discuss why the causes had
inevitable consequences — What is the general rule? — Explore the possible future
consequences —*

5   *Synthesis*   Pupils need to create something new with the knowledge and
skills they learn. Knowledge lies in a stagnant pool unless it is used for thinking and action. If all learning is merely the acquisition of other people's
knowledge, then nothing new is created. Able pupils using any of the multiple abilities will become the creators of the future. Pupils need to design,
invent, imagine, change and improve. Synthesis is shown in activities that
ask:
*Do you agree with —? How would you change —? What would happen if —? Is
there another way —? Is there another conclusion? — In how many ways can you
——?*

6   *Evaluation*   Pupils need to make decisions and judgments. Impulsive decisions and actions which cannot be justified usually result from bias,
prejudice and woolly thinking. All pupils can be taught how to balance decisions against reason and evidence, more able pupils will become the leaders

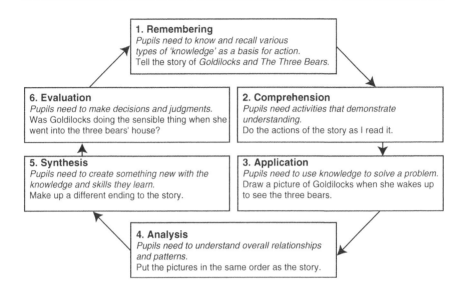

Figure 12.2 Using Bloom's taxonomy in an early primary context

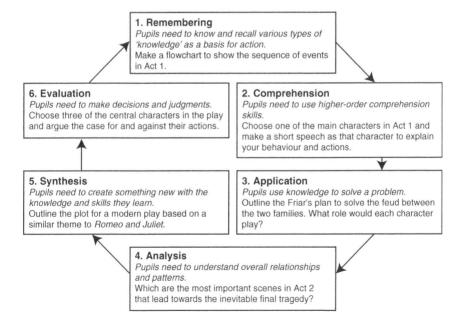

Figure 12.3 How Bloom's taxonomy can be applied to *Romeo and Juliet* to develop higher-order learning skills for older pupils

and decision-makers on behalf of future generations of people. Evaluation can be developed by asking pupils:

How do you know —? On what grounds can you justify —? What is the evidence —? Why would you make that decision—? What are the arguments for and against —? Why do you believe —? Did — have a valid case —? Draw a conclusion giving reasons —

The range of higher-order learning skills can be used by all pupils at any age, although the content for able pupils should always embody material of greater complexity. Obviously as learners become more mature the content used as the basis for higher-order thinking becomes more age-appropriate. In addition, the thinking questions can be answered at levels of varying complexity.

The examples on the following page show how the taxonomy outlined above can be used a) in an early primary context, and b) in a secondary context.

Figure 12.2 illustrates how tasks based on *Goldilocks and the Three Bears* can develop higher-order learning skills for young pupils.

Figure 12.3 illustrates how tasks based on *Romeo and Juliet* can develop higher-order learning skills for older pupils.

Problem-solving and thinking skills based on the TASC framework: Thinking Actively in a Social Context

All pupils can become more efficient problem-solvers with training and practice, but they need models, examples, and regular and sustained experience of working in a problem-solving way across the curriculum. As we have already stressed, the complexity of the problem presented to or negotiated with the pupils varies according to the age, experience and ability of the pupils. The following analysis is taken from Wallace (2001).

While there are a number of programmes which aim to teach problem-solving and thinking skills, the basic requisites that should be clearly evident in any thinking-skills programme are set out in the TASC framework (Figure 12.4).

- *Gather and Organise: What do I know about this?* Pupils need to gather and organise what they already know at the beginning of a new topic or series of linked lessons; only then can teachers and pupils identify what is already known and understood. This is the critical point from which differentiation of lesson planning begins. Such differentiation is essential if repetition of knowledge and skills already mastered is to be avoided.
- *Identify: What is the task? Evaluate: How well did I do?* Identifying the meaning and requirements of the learning activity, together with the criteria for evaluation, is an essential process before any learning activity is begun. These stages of thinking can be used to model questioning techniques such as (Identify) What questions should I ask about the task? Do I fully understand what I must do? What do I need to find out? How will I judge the

Figure 12.4 The TASC problem-solving framework: Thinking Actively in a Social Context. Taken from Wallace (2001) *Teaching Thinking Skills across the Primary Curriculum: A practical approach for all abilities.* London: David Fulton (A Nace/Fulton Publication). With permission

success of the task?; (Evaluate) How well did I do the task? What must I do to improve? How can I work more efficiently?

The criteria for the successful (and high quality) completion of any activity need to be established at the start. All pupils need examples of competent work to analyse the success criteria; more able and talented pupils need examples of excellence which they can analyse to identify traits to replicate in their own work. In evaluating their work they can then learn to measure the degree of their success against known criteria.

- *Learn from Experience: What have I learned?* Learning is crystallised when pupils reflect on the 'what' and 'how' of their learning. All pupils need to see how they are changing and progressing. This process of metacognition lies at the very root of learning how to learn. At the end of every topic of work, learners need to analyse what new knowledge, skills and concepts they have acquired and how else this newly acquired learning can be used across the curriculum and in life outside the classroom. In an inclusive classroom, problems can be set in varying degrees of complexity for individual or small-group work.

An example of the process can be seen in Figure 12.5. The children at Key Stage 2 decided to organise their end-of-term disco and they used the TASC wheel to guide their planning.

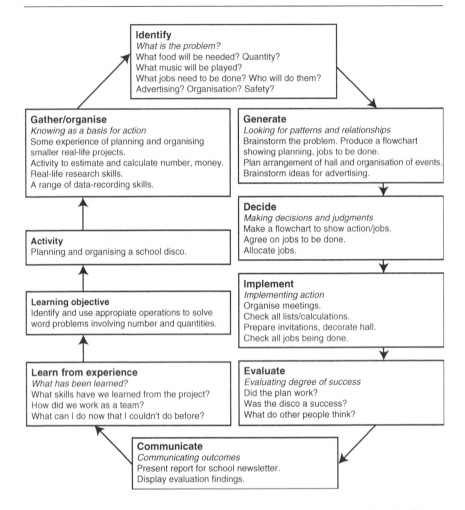

Figure 12.5 The TASC problem-solving framework: planning and evaluating the school disco. Taken from Wallace (2001) *Teaching Thinking Skills across the Primary Curriculum: A practical approach for all abilities.* London: David Fulton (A Nace/Fulton Publication). With permission

Note: In using the TASC Wheel for lesson planning, the learning objectives are clearly defined and, in this instance, the task is specified although the ways of accomplishing the task are open for debate and decision-making. The most effective provision for more able and talented pupils is teaching which uses a range of strategies to differentiate learning. Enrichment and extension opportunities can be developed through cross-curricular skills and multiple intelligences. Pupils also need opportunities to develop higher-order learning skills, problem-solving and thinking skills in order to become creative and independent thinkers.

OPPORTUNITIES BEYOND THE CLASSROOM

Schools increasingly provide a range of opportunities for out-of-school learning for their pupils. However, these activities are often planned as part of a school's provision for more able and talented pupils whereas, the writer argues, all pupils would benefit from enriching out-of-hours learning experiences. The differences in the activities that are provided need to lie in the degree of extension challenge presented to the pupils. They are, however, not a substitute for the enrichment and extension which should take place in the classroom. A more able learner is not just 'able' at the end of a school day or on a Saturday morning.

Opportunities beyond the classroom may allow more able and talented pupils to specialise in certain areas and to work with a wider range of peers and adults in different environments. Such activities can provide a rich supplement to mainstream schooling. For example:

- Saturday morning classes
- sharing expertise between schools and colleges
- using local business and industry
- using local experts and professional people
- mentoring.

DEVELOPING EFFECTIVE WHOLE-SCHOOL POLICY INTO PRACTICE

The key processes which support high achievement have been discussed and the importance of a safe and supportive environment has been stressed. When all pupils feel valued and a wide range of achievement is celebrated there will be no stigma attached to high achievement in any domain of human ability. Effective pastoral systems should ensure support for the personal, social and emotional needs of all pupils, including the more able, who are often ignored when there are seemingly more urgent behavioural problems that need to be dealt with.

Any school policy, if it is to support consistency and effective practice, needs to be developed with the whole school staff but this can be a time-consuming task. Schools may develop a distinctive policy for more able and talented pupils, or may refer to the needs of these pupils in their learning and teaching, assessment and curriculum policies, all of which make a significant contribution to effective whole-school practice.

A policy for more able and talented pupils should include reference to:

- why a policy for more able and talented pupils is needed
- the school's definition of more able and talented pupils
- strategies used to identify more able and talented pupils with a clear rationale for their use

- how the school provides for these pupils including pupil groupings, differentiation strategies, planning for multiple abilities, and developing higher-order learning skills, problem-solving and thinking skills
- assessment of more able and talented pupils (including feedback to pupils/pupil self-assessment, peer assessment)
- how personal, social, emotional needs are addressed
- staff roles and responsibilities regarding more able and talented pupils
- resources for extension activities
- the involvement of parents
- the monitoring of teaching and learning of more able and talented pupils: observations, work sampling, planning, discussions with pupils' parents, etc.
- an action plan for implementing the policy
- plans for monitoring and evaluation of policy
- staff development
- transition issues
- links with outside agencies/out-of-school-hours learning.

Leadership and management

The headteacher and senior management team (in small schools, the whole school team) have a key role to play in raising the profile of more able and talented pupils in the school. Their needs should be considered as an integral part of all whole-school and subject policies and development plans.

The coordination of practice and provision for more able and talented pupils will be strengthened by having a nominated member of staff with overall responsibility for more able pupils across the ten multiple abilities. However, the coordinator will require support from senior managers to effectively meet their responsibilities, which may include:

- leading on the implementation of whole-school policy
- liaising with subject colleagues to raise awareness of the needs of more able pupils and plan enrichment and extension
- identifying more able pupils and sharing information with colleagues
- developing own expertise and leading/arranging professional development
- linking with partner schools to ensure effective transition of more able pupils
- liaising with parents, outside agencies, the LEA
- overseeing resources
- monitoring and reporting regularly to headteacher, senior management, parents and governors.

The governing body, together with senior managers, need to consider the effectiveness of the school's policy and practice for more able and talented pupils. This will include areas such as staff development and the involvement of parents/carers. The school should report to the governors on a regular basis and this may be helped by nominating one governor to oversee policy and provision for more able and talented pupils.

The role of the LEA

It is important that the LEA takes a leadership role in supporting schools in the development of good practice and raises awareness of the fact that meeting the needs of more able pupils leads to higher standards for all. The LEA may provide opportunities for schools to cooperate as cluster groups in providing for more able and talented pupils. The LEA also needs to establish a policy with schools and take responsibility for organising appropriate in-service opportunities so that schools can share effective practice and further develop their knowledge and expertise. Training opportunities should also be provided for senior managers, governors as well as coordinators and class teachers.

CONCLUSION

There is no one formula that any school should adopt to develop provision for more able pupils. Any strategies which are developed will emanate from the strengths of the staff, the needs of the pupils and the opportunities which arise from the community activities and personnel involved.

In a school climate which celebrates individual differences across the range of multiple abilities the school ethos will promote and support a policy of inclusion alongside a policy of individual differentiation. The key processes which allow for individual development should be built into lesson planning, and should systematically build in appropriate challenge for all pupils.

A system of education which caters for the diversity of pupils' needs is founded on the belief that pupils first need inclusive and enriching opportunities to discover their strengths and interests. Once identified, those strengths and interests can be nurtured and supported, and potential developed into performance.

Note

1   The essence of this article was used as the base for developing a National Policy for Wales (2003).

References

Bloom, B. S. (1956) *Taxonomy of Educational Objectives: The Classification of Educational Goals*. New York: David McKay.

Wallace, B. (2000) *Teaching the Very Able Child: Developing a Policy and Adopting Strategies for Provision*. London: David Fulton (A NACE/Fulton Publication).

Wallace, B. (2001) *Teaching Thinking Skills Across the Primary Curriculum: A practical approach for all abilities*. London: David Fulton (A NACE/Fulton Publication).

Wallace, B., Maker, C. June, Cave, D. and Chandler, S. (2004) *Thinking and Problem-Solving: An Inclusive Approach*. London: David Fulton (A NACE/Fulton publication).

Supportive and extended reading

The Assessment Reform Group (1999) *Assessment for Learning: Beyond the Black Box*. Cambridge, UK: University of Cambridge School of Education.

The Assessment Reform Group (2002) *Testing, Motivation and Learning*. Cambridge, UK: University of Cambridge School of Education.

Clark, B. (1992) *Growing up Gifted: Developing the Potential of Children at Home and at School*. New York: Macmillan.

Clarke, C. and Callow, R. (2002) (2nd edn) *Educating the Gifted and Talented: Resource Issues and Processes for Teachers*. London: David Fulton (A NACE/Fulton Publication).

Eyre, D. and McClure, L. (2001) (eds) *Curriculum Provision for the Gifted and Talented in the Primary School*. London: David Fulton (A NACE/Fulton Publication).

Goleman, D. (1999) *Working with Emotional Intelligence*. London: Bloomsbury.

Hymer, B. and Michel, D. (2002) *Gifted and Talented Learners: Creating a Policy for Inclusion*. London: David Fulton (A NACE/Fulton Publication).

Leyden, S. (2002) (3rd edn) *Supporting the Child of Exceptional Ability at Home and at School*. London: David Fulton (A NACE/Fulton Publication).

Porter, L. (1999) *Gifted Young Children: A Guide for Teachers and Parents*. Buckingham: Open University Press.

Renzulli, J. S. (2002) 'A Reflective conversation with Joe Renzulli'. In Ron Knobel and Michael Shaugnessy (eds) *Gifted Education International*, 16 (2), pp. 118–127.

Sternberg, R. J. (2000) 'The concept of intelligence'. In Sternberg, R. S. (ed.) *Handbook of Intelligence*. Cambridge, UK: Cambridge University Press.

Wallace, B. (2002) *Teaching Thinking Skills Across the Early Years: A Practical Approach for Children aged 4–7*. London: David Fulton (A NACE/Fulton Publication).

Wallace, B. (2002) *Teaching Thinking Skills Across the Middle Years: A Practical Approach for Children aged 9–14*. London: David Fulton (A NACE/Fulton Publication).

Wallace, B. (2003) *Using History to Develop Thinking Skills at Key Stage 2*. London: David Fulton (A NACE/Fulton Publication).

Index

Lightning Source UK Ltd.
Milton Keynes UK
UKOW06f1807250615

254130UK00004B/167/P